FRAGILE FUTURES
The Uncertain Economics of Disasters, Pandemics, and Climate Change

This book revisits a distinction introduced in 1921 by economists Frank Knight and John Maynard Keynes: that between statistically predictable future events ("risks") and statistically unpredictable, uncertain events ("uncertainties"). Governments have generally ignored the latter, perceiving phenomena such as pandemics, natural disasters, and climate change as uncontrollable Acts of God. As a result, there has been little if any preparation for future catastrophes.

Our modern society is more interconnected and more globalized than ever. Dealing with uncertain future events requires a stronger and more globally coordinated government response. This book suggests a larger, more global government role in dealing with these disasters and keeping economic inequalities low. Major institutional changes, such as regulating the private sector for the common good and dealing with special harms, risks and crises, especially those concerning climate change and pandemics, are necessary in order to achieve any semblance of future progress for humankind.

Dr. Vito Tanzi has been Professor and Economic Chair at the American University, Director for twenty years of the Fiscal Affairs Department at the IMF, and Undersecretary for Economy and Finance in the Italian Government. He is Honorary President of the International Institute of Public Finance in Munich, Germany.

Fragile Futures

The Uncertain Economics of Disasters, Pandemics, and Climate Change

VITO TANZI
Independent Scholar

CAMBRIDGE
UNIVERSITY PRESS

CAMBRIDGE
UNIVERSITY PRESS

University Printing House, Cambridge CB2 8BS, United Kingdom

One Liberty Plaza, 20th Floor, New York, NY 10006, USA

477 Williamstown Road, Port Melbourne, VIC 3207, Australia

314–321, 3rd Floor, Plot 3, Splendor Forum, Jasola District Centre, New Delhi – 110025, India

103 Penang Road, #05-06/07, Visioncrest Commercial, Singapore 238467

Cambridge University Press is part of the University of Cambridge.

It furthers the University's mission by disseminating knowledge in the pursuit of education, learning, and research at the highest international levels of excellence.

www.cambridge.org
Information on this title: www.cambridge.org/9781009100120
DOI: 10.1017/9781009109246

© Vito Tanzi 2022

First published 2022

Printed in the United Kingdom by TJ Books Limited, Padstow Cornwall

A catalogue record for this publication is available from the British Library.

ISBN 978-1-009-10012-0 Hardback

CONTENTS

ACKNOWLEDGMENTS

This book was mostly written during the period of isolation imposed by the current pandemic. That isolation reduced the personal contacts that often have an impact on one's writing. As a consequence, there are very few individuals whom I need to thank.

First of all, I must thank my very long-time and dear friend, Dr. George Iden, whom I have known since the days when we were young students at Harvard. He read an earlier version of the book and provided useful comments. The second person I would like to thank is my son, Alex Tanzi, Senior Editor at Bloomberg News. He alerted me to reports dealing with climate change and global warming that I might have missed and which discussed relevant issues. The third person to thank is my wife, Maria, a statistician by training, who, for many months, managed everything in the house and who, at times, must have felt that she was living with a zombie, because I was totally absorbed by the writing and did not participate in most house chores, even those that should have been my responsibility. She always assisted me with her usual grace and full dedication. She was also helpful with computer problems that often mystified me.

Comments received from two anonymous readers were very useful in making me revisit some issues.

Perhaps I should also mention the value of Wikipedia in providing some difficult-to-get information on long-past disasters.

Legum Servi Sumus ut Liberi Esse Possimus
(We are servants of the laws in order to be free)

Marcus Tullius Cicero, 106–43 BC

Part I

Uncertain Future Events and Reactions to Them

1 INTRODUCTION

Taxation, regulations, and public spending have traditionally been the main instruments available to governments to promote collective and/or national goals. And governments have been the main institutions through which the citizens of countries can pursue, or hope to pursue, collective, national goals. Of course, it is not easy to determine precisely what the collective needs, or the national goals, are at any given time in any given country, nor how much taxation is necessary to finance their provision and to promote those objectives. Some governments are clearly better than others at delivering those goals and some goods extend beyond the frontiers of single countries.

The collective needs or the objectives change over time, because of technological and social developments, and so does the capacity of governments to collect taxes and to regulate efficiently. Therefore, the broad government role must change and governments may or may not be able to satisfy citizens' needs.

For democratic countries with market economies, the usual assumption has been that collective needs can be determined democratically, and that their determination will suggest the desirable tax levels and the needed regulatory policies. The democratic process can also determine how the tax and regulatory budget should be allocated among citizens, and how the money, collected through taxes, or occasionally through loans, ought to be spent. When this is done optimally, it can be claimed, as Cicero did two millennia ago, that "we [will be] the servants of the laws in order to be free."

Naturally, there will always be some individuals, or some groups, that will think that the tax level, or the public debt level, whatever they are, are too high; and others who will think that they are too low, and not sufficient to pay for collective needs. Others are likely to think that the tax burden is not allocated fairly among the country's citizens. Still others will think that the money collected is not being spent efficiently, or equitably. The same is true with the regulatory budget, which is criticized by some as being excessive, costly, and too limiting of personal freedom, and by others as not regulating enough. These debates make democracies exciting and, at times, difficult places to live in and easy to criticize. They also make some individuals think nostalgically of times and places where decisions were, or are, made less democratically and more quickly by controlling parties and authoritarian governments. Furthermore, in the normal framework that has characterized public finance decisions, the assumption has remained that the public goods are national and dealing with them requires national policies and not multinational or global collaboration and policies.

Over the last century, views about taxation changed significantly, and, more broadly, so did those about the desirable economic role that the public sector should play in the economy. Broadly speaking, and recognizing the strong opposition that has continued to come from libertarian or conservative groups, the desirable government role was extended over past decades. It came to include, especially:

(a) the need to *redistribute* some income and some wealth, from richer to poorer, deserving citizens, when the distribution generated by the market is not considered fair and has become too unequal (however, it has always been recognized that in market economies there are likely to be efficiency limits to redistributive policies; and the redistributive policies have remained national);

(b) attempts by governments to promote, with their policies, full, or fuller, employment of labor and capital, especially during recessions; and

(c) the promotion of a better allocation of resources to deal with national public goods and with various market failures that exist in most market economies.

The desirable tax level and the use of the tax revenue have normally been considered, by tax experts and by governments, to be those required by countries during *normal* times, and not during times of crisis. Occasionally, especially during wars, or in anticipation of wars, some additional revenue and some new regulations (rationing or price controls) were seen to be needed, and tax levels and some tax rates, as well as some new regulations, were temporarily pushed up or introduced.

In normal, peaceful times, the tax level and tax structure have been assumed to be those consistent with and sufficient to satisfy the normal requirements of citizens and enterprises in efficient markets in a democratic political system. This system is usually one that directs government policies toward the support of the voting citizens, and toward the political objective of remaining in power, by winning the next elections. Taxes, therefore, are expected to be *efficient in their long-run impact*, and *sufficient* to satisfy the *routine and immediate* needs of citizens; and so are regulations. These have been the basic, broad, and guiding principles in public finance in recent times (Tanzi 2020a).

In *normal* times and economic situations, governments are expected to keep tax levels as low as possible, and tax structures as efficient as possible, and to focus public spending and regulations on meeting the *immediate* needs of citizens and the economy. Also, when fiscal rules are created to guide and constrain the government's actions, the rules are expected to operate during normal times, as, for example, with the Growth and Stability Pact of the European Monetary Union. That Pact set the maximum fiscal deficit of the member countries at 3 percent of GDP, and the desired public debt at 60 percent. Member countries were expected to aim for and live by those rules.

Fiscal rules and "fiscal councils," created to monitor and enforce fiscal rules within countries, became popular institutions, especially since the 1980s, both with economists and with some governments. Several governments, as well as the European Monetary Union, adopted the rules, and some countries adopted the councils (Kopits 2004). US "states" had introduced the balanced budget rule many years ago, mostly in the nineteenth century, and the US had occasionally debated the possibility or desirability of introducing a balanced budget rule for federal government.

However, exceptional events, such as wars or the Covid-19 pandemic, can make rules set in the past for normal times, which had seemed realistic when set, totally unrealistic. This presents governments with a dilemma: whether to stick to the agreed rules or do what many citizens would expect governments to do during times of exceptional circumstances – that is, to help them to deal with those circumstances. Pandemics and climate change also raise questions about global needs that cannot be efficiently pursued by independent national actions.

The problem is that the expected behavior of the government, as that behavior was established by public finance theory (see, e.g., Musgrave's influential 1959 book), and the fiscal rules that had become popular, especially since the 1980s, ignored the possibility of *uncertain* or *unexpected* future developments and needs, such as pandemics and major natural disasters. These might require different government behavior, at least during emergencies. The fiscal rules had not taken into consideration these unforeseen and uncertain events when they were created for the expected determination of government behavior. They had also ignored extranational dimensions.

Uncertain developments had attracted little, if any, attention, from either experts or governments, because they were difficult to anticipate and to prepare for. Therefore, when a major, unexpected event happens, the guiding theory, or the fiscal rules, fail to provide guidance on what the government's policy should be. The recent confusion on the role of governments in the ongoing pandemic is an indication of this lack of guidance from the theory. There is clearly a case of what might be considered a *theoretical failure* in how to deal with such events, even when they might have happened before and thus should not have been considered *totally* unexpected. As we shall report in the second part of this book, pandemics and epidemics have happened at various times in the past, as have other major natural disasters, in addition to wars.

Generally, *uncertain, future* events, until they become a reality, have not influenced the current tax and public spending levels of governments, and have had little influence on the regulatory budget. Until these events materialize, and thus cease to be uncertain, they have had no impact on government decisions, nor on those of private agents.

A democratic government that spent a significant amount of money, or imposed stricter regulations, to prepare for what are still considered *distant* and *uncertain* needs, events that might never materialize, or might not materialize for a long time, most likely would pay a political price in popular support, and in the support of voters, in democratic countries with market economies where that support is important. Governments would likely be criticized for wasting money during good, or normal, times.

In markets that are assumed to be competitive, private enterprises will focus on surviving and on making profits for their shareholders. They will minimize the current use of labor and capital inputs in their economic operations. They will keep inventories low to contain costs. Enterprises that allocated significant current resources to deal with future and still uncertain events would risk becoming less competitive in the short run.

An exception might be pharmaceutical companies that search for new drugs, and that expect to benefit from the time-limited monopoly power that they would enjoy from the sales of these new drugs, if they were successful in their research. These companies rely on "venture capital," which is provided by rich investors who take into account the high probability of failure by *single* enterprises, but balance that failure against potentially large gains by successful ones (Tanzi 2018a, 2020b).

In conclusion, neither governments nor most private enterprises are likely to give much thought or to pay much attention to potential, *future* events, events that are still *uncertain*, such as future epidemics, pandemics, and major natural disasters. When, or if, these events become a reality, there will have been little preparation for them, alongside confusion and a lack of clear guidance on what to do, as the current pandemic has shown. Different countries have gone different ways. Governments will be asked to intervene, but they will immediately face the obstacle of the existing fiscal rules, which might constrain some of them, as has been the case for local governments in the USA during the Covid-19 pandemic.

The theories of taxation and market behavior by enterprises – theories that were developed over many decades – were developed for normal situations and not for periods of uncertain, future crises. They were based initially on the Darwinian concept of evolution, which implied slow changes over long periods of time. They were also influenced by the nineteenth-century strong faith in progress, promoted in part by the Industrial Revolution that would prove to be the most radical of all revolutions.

The theories that were developed focused on the achievement of *equilibrium* and *optimality*, as Paul Samuelson had shown in his classic 1947 book. As Bernstein (1996, p. 216) put it: "the classical economists [especially during the nineteenth century] had defined economics as a riskless system that always produced optimal results," not one for unusual conditions. Over the years, many economists kept finding exceptions to that assumed, riskless system in the real world, but the essence of the system did not change in any fundamental way.

It should be stressed that the equilibrium theorized by laissez-faire and by classical and neoclassical economists was always that of the long run. They would have been blind not to observe that, in the short run, some market failures could and did exist, at least in some parts of the market. However, they believed that, over time, the forces of competition would prevail and bring the market back toward equilibrium and efficiency. For them, equilibrium, like evolution, was a dynamic process.

That view has been central to the disagreements between Chicago School economists, who have emphasized the long run, and Keynesian economists, who have focused more on the short run, and especially on the role of business cycles.

Keynesian economists saw disequilibria, due to business cycles, as common development, rather than as exceptions. They saw them as an essential part of a capitalist economy (Rohatinski 2017, pp. 100–101; Vicarelli 1984). The problem is that as unexpected, random crises or events become more likely, the longer the time period considered becomes. An event that is not likely to happen in one year may become much more likely to happen in ten, or even more so in a hundred years. The long run is more likely than the short run to experience what at one moment in time may be considered *unlikely, random* events.

As we shall report in this book, countries are not free from events and occurrences that at times challenge citizens' lives, destroy their properties, and affect normal operations. These events call for special, or exceptional, reactions by communities and governments, and not just by single, uncoordinated, individual reactions. Over the past century or so governments have often been called to intervene and "to do something" in situations when "everything seems to fail" (Moss 2002).

As the ability of governments to raise taxes, improve their administrative capabilities, regulate markets, and spend public money improved, so did the citizens' demands on them to do more (Tanzi 2018b). However, these demands were mostly related to what governments were expected to do to deal with *recognizable* risks, risks faced by many citizens, such as invalidity, illness, old age, and unemployment. Governments' policies were progressively created or modified to deal with some of these risks. In some countries, governments were more ambitious and more efficient than others in dealing with them. However, governments generally continued to ignore needs that might be created by uncertain events, such as the coming of future pandemics or climate change.

The roles that governments have played in dealing with *recognizable risks* faced by citizens have been described, analyzed, and criticized in many books. We shall ignore those roles in this book. However, discussions of the actual or potential role of governments to deal with *exceptional situations*, situations that did occasionally arise in the past and that can be expected to keep arising in the future, have remained almost nonexistent. This is a potential, desirable government role that has been largely ignored by economists and by political scientists, except for discussions, especially since the 1980s, about "global warming" and some other environmental issues.

Since the 1980s, environmental issues have been receiving increasing attention on the part of some economists and others, but still relatively limited action by governments, and there is little agreement among either economists or governments on what should be done. Some economists and some governments, such as the Trump administration and that of Brazil, have continued to ignore these problems and to believe and have faith in the free market and in spontaneous innovations to deal with some of these environmental issues. They would prefer that the government stayed out of these issues. Other governments, such as the Biden Administration, which came into office in January 2021, believe that the government should intervene and play some or major roles in dealing with some of these problems.

The aim of this book is mainly to call attention to the very limited role that governments have played in the past in dealing with exceptional situations, situations that may have involved pandemics and other major disasters. Some of these disasters may have been limited, in space and time, in their impact. They have been strictly *national* in impact. Others may have had a wider geographic range. The latter include some pandemics, including those brought about in 1918–20 by the "Spanish flu" and in 2020–21 by Covid-19. Climate change is clearly an event with very wide geographic range.

At the time of this writing (second half of 2020, early part of 2021), nobody knows how long the current pandemic will be with us, and what final impact it will have on economies and on social arrangements. Except for the example of smallpox, the viruses brought by past pandemics were never totally eradicated. They became endemic if somewhat controlled by medical progress. It is likely that Covid-19 will also become endemic, but better controlled.

In 2020, GDPs fell by as much as 10 percent in some countries and millions of workers lost their jobs. It was the greatest annual fall for economies since the Great Depression. In late 2020 and early 2021 the pandemic is still with us and has been getting worse in several countries. Governments have seemed, and continue to seem, confused about what to do: Should they try to sustain and push aggregate demand, as many have argued they should? Or should they mainly assist "essential workers" and those who have been more exposed to the pandemic, many of whom have lost their incomes, risking going hungry with their families? In particular, the choice between regulating personal behavior and public spending has been subjected to much debate, and to much disagreement, in several countries, especially in the USA.

Major, global pandemics, and problems such as global warming, require collaboration between governments of different countries in order to deal effectively with them. Many natural disasters may still need only national attention, except when they hit very poor countries, as with the earthquake that killed hundreds of thousand people in Haiti in 2010. Some countries may be too poor to deal with these major national disasters without outside help. The rest of the world should feel some obligation to help these countries and play a role in doing so. In other cases, more coordinated international collaboration is needed. Providing vaccines to poor countries during pandemics would be one way of assisting them.

The potential desirable role of national governments in dealing with pandemics and disasters when they come has changed significantly over the long run. Today, many governments would be both more capable and should be more willing to step in during these major crises than they have been in the past. Citizens expect them to do so. However, existing fiscal rules may create political and temporary constraints on some of them, in terms of how much to spend and how much to regulate.

The second part of this book will provide some historic records of major epidemics, pandemics, and natural and other disasters, and of the extent to which governments did play some role in dealing with them. Only the major ones could be mentioned. As one would expect, the government role was very limited in the distant past, for lack of knowledge and administrative and financial resources.

The third part of this book will focus more on the present, and will discuss governments' reactions to the current pandemic, and especially to the growing problems of climate change, which have presented the world with complex problems and somewhat uncertain future consequences. The hope is to make this book accessible to a broad range of interested readers, and not just to professional economists, and to stimulate some thinking on the issues covered. The book provides a lot of information that many potential readers may not have and that they should find useful. They are likely to find the discussion of global warming particularly disturbing and worrisome and some will disagree with its main conclusions.

Chapter 2 will discuss, in a hopefully approachable style, some theoretical issues that may determine the interest and may influence the ability of governments to anticipate crises, and determine their capacity to better prepare for them and to intervene when the crises become a reality. The chapter will focus especially on the distinction that exists between crises that can be predicted with some degree of statistical accuracy and those that are not so predictable. It will stress the role that *uncertainty* plays, especially in democratic countries with market economies. It is not appreciated how the distinction between *risk* and *uncertainty* – a distinction that is often not fully understood or appreciated – often guides or restrains the actions of individuals and governments. It can at times become a fundamental distinction that encourages some behavior that could be considered irrational. Behavioral economics should allocate more attention to it.

An important conclusion of the book will be that, perhaps, in today's economies, there is overinvestment in providing protection against *risky* events, those for which the risk is statistically measurable, and underinvestment in protection against *uncertain* events, events for which the risk cannot be measured statistically. It is argued that countries should make a greater effort to be better prepared for the coming of events that are uncertain, such as pandemics and some major natural disasters, that are likely in the future but remain uncertain as to the specific time and scope. Governments should not be complacent. Some preparation for those events may reduce their impact when and if they come. There may be events that, while statistically unpredictable, are more likely than others. The former may require and deserve more attention than they have received to date. Climate change is among them.

2 RISKY VERSUS UNCERTAIN EVENTS

Normally, *future* major crises, such as those created by pandemics and by big natural catastrophes, are considered rare anomalies in more or less smoothly working economies. They are seen as *random events* that are not expected to occur. Because of that, economists have had difficulties dealing with them and incorporating them in their analyses (Moss 2002, pp. 40–41). Future events, which are difficult to predict with some degree of reliable, statistical probability, often do not change the modus operandi of governments, or of private enterprises or most individuals. They simply continue to assume that such events will not materialize.

This is especially so in countries with established democracies and with market economies. It may be less true in countries that do not have these characteristics, but have more centrally controlled economies and are thus less conditioned by short-run considerations or constraints. In the distant past, the governments that built the Great Wall of China or massive city walls around some European towns were clearly not responding to short-run considerations, but to long-run and uncertain threats. But they were not democracies.

Over the past several centuries, mathematicians and scientists, or often gamblers with mathematical skills, tried to determine mathematical expectations from some games or activities that were repeated many times, such as trips by ships to distant places. The Italian mathematician Girolamo Cardano, the Dutch physicist Christian Huygens, the French mathematician Blaise Pascal, and the Swiss mathematician Daniel Bernoulli applied their mathematical skills, often to card games, to determine expected values and fair playing prices. They progressively introduced notions such as "risk aversion," which depended on the fact that the marginal utility of wealth is likely to fall the more wealth one has, so that a given gain might be valued, by most individuals, less than an equivalent loss;

the importance of diversification in spreading investments to reduce risk; and the concepts of adverse selection and moral hazards that may compromise an insurance market.

Many of these concepts proved important in the development of an insurance industry, an industry that determined the premiums that were charged on the bases of *expected* losses. They were also important in the development of stock exchanges. Both insurance companies and stock exchanges already existed in the eighteenth century. The above markets were based on the belief that expected and fair values of many activities could be determined from available information. They were based on the concept of risk, which is something that with enough observations can be statistically determined. Of course, the greater the number of observations and the larger the sample, the more reliable the estimated values will be.

The possibilities of *uncertain, future* events, including health crises and major catastrophes, generally do not enter into the *routine* policy decisions of democratic governments, or into the current planning and behavior of private enterprises, including insurance companies, in market economies. They are seen as rare or unique events, not repeated events the outcome of which can be predicted.

Keynes (1921b) was one of the first to analyze this difference and difficulty, in one of his books, *A Treatise on Probability*. He had worked on this book for several years before publishing it in 1921, a year that was particularly turbulent, when Russia was undergoing the Leninist revolution, Germany had been experiencing hyperinflation and was facing the problem of how to pay the huge war debt imposed by the winners of World War I, and Italy had started to flirt with fascism. Uncertainty about the future was a major political factor in many countries and in economic developments.

In that book, Keynes showed that statistical relationships, developed on the basis of observed, past events, often turn out not to be useful for making investments, or for some other decisions. He gave examples of forecasts which had been based on such available knowledge and which had been proven wrong. He was talking of uncertainty related to future forecasts of variables such as interest rates, output or prices, as made by different observers, and not about genuine uncertain events. If he had lived in our time, he could have mentioned the forecasts of the US 2016 presidential elections, based on surveys or polls that proved to be wrong, or the investments in the housing market, made before the

2007 subprime crisis, or forecasts by experts on Wall Street about full employment that have frequently been optimistic.

The investments made in the housing market until 2007 had been based largely on the observed behavior of housing prices over past years. The continuing rise of those prices had led many individuals to expect that the price of houses could only go up. Therefore, buying a house, with low equity and with relatively cheap credit, was a clear win-win investment. Some people who had no savings and no job jumped into the housing market. That market became progressively more irrational, attracting more investors. Those who provided mortgages, who should have known better, became careless, especially when they could package, securitize, and sell the packaged mortgages to distant and misinformed pension funds, which thought they were investing in a safe asset. In this way, the original lenders could pass on any existing risk to others. Complexity in contracts had combined with myopia to smooth the road to the crisis (Lewis 2010).

The forecasts proved to be very wrong, even though they had been based on much statistical information and on much greater computer capability that had become available in previous years for many investors. Especially in the years that followed the expansion of the global financial market that had made it a world market, "rocket scientists" and other "quants" (people with strong quantitative skills) had been brought into the financial market to make it more rational and more information-based, and to staff hedge funds and other financial institutions.

In his 1921 book, Keynes had shown an awareness of the distinction that existed between statistically determined estimates of *risk* and statistically unmeasurable *uncertainty*, although his analyses and the examples he had used had only hinted at his full awareness of that distinction. He would be more explicit in *The General Theory* fifteen years later, when he wrote: "It would be foolish, in forming our expectations to attach great weight to matters which are very uncertain." In a footnote he clarified that "by 'very uncertain' I do not mean the same thing as 'very improbable'." He added that "our usual practice being to take the existing situation and to project it into the future, modified only to the extent that we have more or less definite reasons for expecting a change." While "practical men" "always pay the closest attention to the *state of confidence*," "economists have not analyzed it carefully" (Keynes 1936, p. 148).

Keynes was not aware of, and did not cite, the other important book on that topic which was also published in 1921, by Frank Knight. In 1970 there would be another important contribution to the role that uncertainty might play in markets. It was made in an article by George Akerlof, who identified informational uncertainty in some market exchanges, such as the market for used cars. In his view, the uncertainty that existed in that market damaged it and similar markets. His contribution was related to inefficient or biased information in market exchanges, and not on the role that "unexpected events" can play that is the main theme of this book. Interestingly, in 1977, some years after Akerlof's article was published, a book that had "uncertainty" in the title, a book that was considered important enough to inspire a television series, and that had been written by a strong follower of Keynes, J. K. Galbraith, had stressed "vested interests," but not "uncertainty," as guiding individual decisions. Galbraith's book also failed to cite Frank Knight's 1921 book.

The subprime financial crisis of 2007–08 and the "Great Recession" that followed it, as well as the Covid-19 pandemic of 2020–21, which seemed to come out of nowhere, affecting economic activities and employment in a major way, have recently stimulated some relevant writings, such as papers by Pindyck and Wang (2009), and Martin and Pindyck (2019), and the recent book by Kay and King (2020). These recent works discuss some economic aspects of "unanticipated events." However, until the present time, uncertainty had remained a somewhat vague, intuitive concept that had played a relatively minor role in determining, or influencing, economic decisions, by both individuals and governments. Perhaps a significant exception had been a 2007 book by Frydman and Goldberg that had dealt with the role of imperfect knowledge in estimating future exchange rates and other variables.

Some earlier writings had focused on related aspects, such as the *irrational exuberance* of investors and the *misbehavior of markets*, that might not operate in the smooth, regular way assumed by traditional economists, and to a greater extent by economists of the Chicago School (Shiller 2000; Mandelbrot and Hudson 2004; also Greenspan 2007). Mandelbrot had been sharply critical of the "efficient market hypothesis" and of the common assumption that many variables, such as the prices of commodities, and interest rates, are characterized by normal probability distributions that give little weight and pay little attention to tail events (see, especially, Chapter 1 above).

In a book published in 2009, Richard A. Posner had referred to "the difficulty of determining the *riskiness* of the new financial instruments" that had contributed to the financial crisis of 2008. On p. 60, he had referred to Knight's distinction between risk and uncertainty. Posner implied that this distinction had been hidden in claims made by "financial professionals," and at times by "rocket scientists," about new and complex financial instruments that they were generating and promoting. These new financial instruments were pushed to unsophisticated buyers in the financial market by clever professionals, who claimed that the complexity of the instrument (which at times made them difficult to understand even for financial experts) had made them less risky. Greenspan would say that the risk had been spread more widely, thus making it more bearable and, in a sense, "less risky." The financial crisis showed that this was clearly not the case.

Greater modern confidence in the ability of these smart and highly paid "professionals" who claimed to know better had increased the incentives for less sophisticated investors to invest in what were still, essentially, *uncertain and at times highly questionable* investments. Complexity had often become an attractive package, one frequently used to hide the distinction that had continued to exist between *measurable* risky investments and *uncertain* investments (Posner 2009, pp. 109–110). This had led some trusting investors, who should have known better, to ignore that important distinction, as several pension fund managers and others had done in the years before the financial crisis (Lewis 2010). The crisis would lead to the bankruptcy of some large banks, and to the need for large government support for others in order to prevent the collapse of the whole financial system. Some questionable practices would also become common, including the manipulation of LIBOR by insiders.

Perhaps the same reaction to uncertainty influences decisions in the field of technology and in other areas. Boeing, which had been a most trusted plane manufacturer, was fined more than two billion dollars for having "lied" about some safety features of one of its technologically most advanced new planes, which had crashed twice in the space of a few months. Apparently, some of Boeing's engineers had been aware of the possibility that some features of the plane might not function properly and could lead to accidents. It is perhaps difficult to believe that highly trained, well-paid, and presumably responsible individuals would lie about such a serious possibility. It may seem more reasonable to believe that the (distant?) possibility of a mechanical failure that could lead to major disasters must have appeared to them not as a risk, but as a very distant possibility, one so uncertain and not quantifiable that it could be ignored, especially recognizing the financial implications for Boeing of revealing such concerns.

People in charge of inspecting costly infrastructures, such as atomic plants, electric grids, dams, funiculars, and bridges, are often faced with a difficult decision when they find some irregularities. The decision is whether to shut down the activity and face, or generate, high immediate costs, or to minimize the danger in their own mind and just assume and hope that nothing bad will happen, at least until the next inspection. More often they have chosen the second option, which has no costs until something bad happens.

This common kind of irrationality, at times, does lead to disasters, as happened with the collapse of the Morandi Bridge in Genoa (Italy) in August 2018, and the fall of the funicular in Stresa (also Italy) in May 2021. In both cases, inspections had indicated the existence of some irregularities, but the irregularities had been minimized and ignored. This kind of systemic irrationality may be more common than we realize, and it should receive more attention because of its costly consequences.

Interestingly, in the Senate Hearings of February 23, 2021 on the events that took place at the US Capitol on January 6, 2021, the ex-Sergeant at Arms of the US Senate would state that the reason for the lack of preparation by the Capitol Police for the attack on Congress was that police prepare for "probable" and not for "remote to improbable" events. The problem is that the difference between "probable" and "improbable" events can become very small, and the perception of that difference is often influenced by "irrationality."

It may be theorized that there might be a tendency (perhaps an irrational one) in human beings to ignore unpleasant or costly possibilities that are in the future and are so uncertain that they cannot be quantified. Such irrationality may explain the behavior that would seem incomprehensible on the part of the Boeing engineers or the inspectors of infrastructures. The possibility that irrational behavior contributes to attitudes that make us ignore uncertain and unpleasant future events merits attention by behavioral economists and by psychologists who deal with human behavior.

Kahneman's 2011 book makes no reference to the work of Keynes or Knight, or to the distinction between risk and uncertainty. However, he does recognize that "very rare events ... are sometimes ignored all-together" (p. 315), except when "an unlikely event becomes the focus of attention" (p. 316). This might imply that a government that wanted to introduce, say, more stringent regulations, to better protect individuals from earthquakes, or spend money to better protect cities from level 5 hurricanes, should introduce them shortly after such major events happen, when they are still vivid in the public's memory.

Future crises and many other future events are often impossible to predict with any degree of useful precision, as to their *timing*, their *severity*, and, for some events, their *duration*. If these predictions could be made, they would allow governments and private enterprises to consider taking specific actions to better deal with them before they happen and when they became a reality. Whether they would in fact take these actions or not is another question. They could do so by putting aside some *current* resources to be better prepared for those crises, if and when they came. For example, while it may be rational to expect that, *at some point in the future*, major disasters (earthquakes, hurricanes, volcanic eruptions, etc.) are likely to happen, especially in some given regions (California, Florida, Louisiana), the future is a long time, the life expectancy of individuals is limited, and governments and enterprises have limited resources that can be used to achieve short-run and well-identified objectives. There are always some urgent needs claiming the use of scarce, available resources. As a consequence, short-run needs often take precedence over uncertain and future ones.

Generally, the closer in time and the more predictable an event is, the more reaction and preparation can be expected for it. Time is always an important factor in economics, but it often plays more of a role than it should. (See Rohatinski 2017 for some theoretical analysis of the role of time in economics.) The *timing* and the *severity* of epidemics, and of major hurricanes, earthquakes, fires, tsunamis, tornadoes, and other possible natural disasters, including nuclear disasters, cannot be predicted. Without such predictions, efficient preparation for them, or the creation of insurance markets to deal with their unknown costs, do not seem possible and no attempts are made.

Still, uncertainty is also a question of degree. Some events, such as earthquakes in California, or major hurricanes in Louisiana or Florida, though still uncertain as to their timing and scope, are more likely than other events, such as a meteor hitting San Francisco. Therefore some uncertain events should play *some* role in policy decisions and in preparation. The objective should be to build resilience and a better ability to respond to the disasters, for example, by building stronger structures or, in the case of pandemics, stronger health systems. Perhaps there should be a category between clearly risky events and truly uncertain events.

In an important book, first published a century ago, in 1921, the same year as Keynes' book on probability (and based on the author's doctoral dissertation), the economist Frank Knight, who in 1928 would join the University of Chicago and became an influential member of the "Chicago School of Economics," addressed the theoretical question of how a perfect, competitive market, the kind of market that many economists at that time assumed existed, could generate profits for the enterprises that operated in it, when the theory predicted that perfect competition would drive the profits to zero. In his analyses, Knight introduced more *explicitly* than had been done by Keynes, the fundamental distinction between what he called *risk* and what he called *uncertainty*. This insight would become important in some future analyses, but it would not have much impact on policies or actions.

Knight defined risky events as those for which the probability of occurrence can be determined statistically, using available, real-life, observations. The more information we have, and the more reliable that information is, the better can be the statistical estimation of the occurrence of these future events. On the basis of the available observations, and of the predictions that can be derived from them, insurance companies can and do develop markets that allow individuals and enterprises to protect themselves from future, risky events, by paying an insurance premium to the insurance companies for this protection. The premium becomes part of the normal costs of operation of the economic agents. It can, thus, be passed on in the prices of what they sell without disturbing the market. The risk is shifted to the insurance companies that can spread their investments among many risky activities, to keep their costs predictable. The market equilibrium is not affected.

In his 1921 book, John Maynard Keynes had expressed skepticism that it was often possible to deal efficiently with future events, as was done by insurance companies, without adding some extra premium to the statistically determined risk to take into account the unexpected. That extra premium would be difficult to determine, therefore affecting the theoretical market equilibrium. Knight's more precise distinction between risk and uncertainty became more influential than Keynes' in economic thinking because it introduced more explicitly than Keynes had done the distinction between (presumably insurable) risk and (uninsurable) uncertainty. If some events are not predictable, they may raise the question of whether the government should have a role in protection against their possible occurrence.

With the passing of time, the distinction between risk and uncertainty became somewhat less sharp than Knight had made it out to be, reflecting in some way Keynes' skepticism about the accuracy of measuring risk, and because of the various ways in which uncertainty might enter into events and influence intuition and decisions. This development had some consequences for the role that policy could play. For example, in a book which became a bestseller, a professional financial operator with a mathematical background, Nassim S. Taleb (2004), explored in some depth the roles that could be played by risk, luck, uncertainty, and also irrationality – roles that had been treated less deeply in Knight's and Keynes' analyses.

In his book, and in two later books that he published, in 2007 and 2012, Taleb revisited Keynes' (1921b) analysis and argued that, statistically determined risk, based on probability distributions, estimated on the basis of *past* events and *past* knowledge, could give a false sense of security, because it tended to ignore the occurrence of tail events in statistical distributions. More importantly, it ignored unusual information that was not known to have happened in the past. In Taleb's colorful description, probabilities, based on past knowledge, which had assumed that swans are always white, can become wrong when black swans are discovered somewhere, say, in Australia. Or the assumption that the production of atomic energy is safe can change after a major atomic accident has occurred, as in Chernobyl, Ukraine (Plokhy 2018) or Fukushima, Japan. As we shall argue later, climate change might create black swans in some areas.

The discovery of the existence of "black swans," events outside the normally acquired, past knowledge, which have not been expected to occur, can create new and unexpected situations. They can change past perceptions of risk. In some sense, Taleb argued that the distinction between *risk* and *uncertainty* may be somewhat arbitrary, because the statistical estimation of risk is always based only on knowledge that is available at a given time. It ignores the possibility that there may be knowledge that is important but is still unknown. Insurance companies occasionally get into serious financial difficulties when "black swans" appear, or when tail possibilities that had been largely ignored materialize in insured events, as they did in 2008 for AIG, when the firm faced bankruptcy when unexpected events materialized, leading to huge losses. Although Taleb hardly acknowledged the work of Knight, the relationship of his work to Knight's 1921 work was obvious.

Uncertainty was significantly different from *risk* in Knight's analysis, and it was not and could not be based on knowledge available at a given time. It referred to events for which no reliable statistical probability could be determined and quantified, because the needed information simply does not exist. As a consequence, no efficient insurance markets could be created to allow private agents to protect themselves against such occurrences by paying an insurance premium. This created a classic case of missing markets.

Major catastrophes might be tail events in known probability distributions; or they might be events characterized by true uncertainty. In the *General Theory*, published in 1936, Keynes had written that "[i]t would be foolish, in forming our expectations, to attach great weight to matters that are very uncertain" (p. 148). In a footnote on the same page, Keynes had specified that by "very uncertain" he did not mean "very improbable." Therefore, he was not talking of tail events in identifiable probability distributions, but of uncertain events in Knight's definition. In any case, in Keynes' 1921 book the distinction between risk and uncertainty was less sharp than it was for Knight.

Uncertain events are simply beyond statistical prediction, except for the useless prediction that they *may happen at some uncertain, future time.* Therefore, it is not possible to create insurance markets that can charge a fair premium to clients, to deal efficiently with them, in a market economy. Truly uncertain events cannot be part of a perfect market and a perfect market cannot exist when uncertain events are no longer very rare. The abstract existence of such events often creates a classic case of "missing markets" – that is, markets that are needed but cannot be created, because the needed information is simply not available. This "market failure" was given importance by Kenneth Arrow in some of his work in the 1950s, at a time when market failures were attracting a lot of attention on the part of some major economists, including Samuelson, Arrow, Chamberlin, Joan Robinson, Bator and others.

It may be interesting to mention at this point that, recently, an insurance company, Swiss Re, believing that, globally, too many people are not insured (or are underinsured) as they should be in a well-functioning market economy, has attempted to create markets for some of these uninsured "risks" or events. One such a market is based on "the first global risk model to support clients in assessing volcanic risks [that may have economic consequences] and develop suitable insurance products."

Swiss Re reported that one billion people live within 150 kilometers of an active volcano, including cities such as Tokyo, Naples, Catania, Manila, Managua, Quito, and Jakarta. Losses from volcanic eruptions remain largely uninsured, but can be particularly severe for some industries, including tourism. Swiss Re reported that "they [had] helped one of [their] clients in Japan to place an insurance-like product to cover losses from volcanic activity for the hospitality business, [including the risk] of having fewer tourists" (Swiss Re, news release, Zurich, March 23, 2017). Although the probability of losses was based on a lot of past and present information on volcanic activities, the premium was not based on what could be defined as *statistical risk*, but largely on information-supported intuition, on information about the future occurrence of a highly uncertain event, such as volcanic eruption. Therefore, the premium did not reflect and could not reflect an optimal price in a well-working market. It could not make the market more perfect.

Swiss Re was attempting to price uncertainty and not statistical risk, and was recognizing that some uncertain events are more likely to occur than others within a given future time span, and particular areas. This raises the question of whether governments should not do the same and develop programs directed at reducing the consequences of some (more likely but still) uncertain future events. This would replace a desirable market role with a government role (Bevere and Gloor 2020; Bevere and Sharan 2018).

Market failures make markets imperfect, raising questions about the existence, or even the theoretical possibility, of perfect competition, the existence of which had been assumed by laissez-faire economists, and has continued to be defended by economists identified with the Chicago School and the Austrian School of Economics (van Overtveldt 2007). After World War II, market failures had provided justification for larger government spending, higher tax levels, and, following Pigou's work, a larger regulatory role played by governments (Tanzi 2020a). Market failures could and did call for more interventions by governments in the economy, which led to the expansion in public sector activities that took place, especially in the decades that followed World War II, and these would be criticized by several influential, conservative economists, including Friedman, Hayek, Mises, and Buchanan.

Lack of necessary knowledge and other issues raised questions about what role governments could play in relation to major *uncertain* events, and, especially, whether governments would be able to play that role in an efficient and equitable way (Tanzi 2020c). This book discusses the question a bit more closely, recognizing that this is a difficult task and that it is easier to raise questions than to suggest answers to the questions raised.

Because of changes in what the author, elsewhere, has called the "ecology of taxation" (Tanzi 2018b), which occurred after the Industrial Revolution, modern governments now have easier access to more public revenue than did governments in the distant past. They can also hire better-educated and trained individuals. Therefore, in principle, they could develop, and some have developed, several public programs in anticipation of particular risks that are faced by most citizens. These risks include old age, invalidity, illnesses, and unemployment. These risks can be better estimated statistically, within some limited margins of error. However, there is still no preparation for future and uncertain catastrophic events, even when the probability of those events occurring in the not too distant future has increased, as is the case today with epidemics, pandemics, or climate change.

Governments must be better prepared to react to catastrophic events in the best way they can, often without clear guidelines. Some of the guidelines that exist, such as fiscal rules, if rigidly enforced, can become obstacles to needed government interventions during major crises. Just think of the role of balanced budget constraints on the fiscal deficits of subnational government in the USA, or the Stability and Growth Pact rule in the countries that are members of the European Monetary Union. Apart from the uncertainty of events, there is the additional problem that the characteristics of these events, when they occur, may be significantly different than anticipated, requiring different government interventions. This is the main issue that will be analyzed to some extent in later chapters.

Frank Knight concluded that in a perfectly competitive market profits could not exist in the presence of what he defined as insurable *risk*, while uncertainty and its companion, luck, could create conditions that are more favorable to some enterprises than to others, thus allowing them to make profits. The profits would disappear only in truly stationary, perfect markets, in markets characterized by unchanging perfect conditions – that is, in situations without short-run uncertainty and with truly perfectly measured and insurable risks.

For various reasons, these situations are not likely to exist in the real world. If they existed, they would create a stationary world, one with perfect competition, but probably also one without, or with little, growth. The existence of disorder, luck, monopolistic competition, and other such random factors brings imperfections to the market and creates opportunities for some enterprises that are not available for others. These differences can explain the presence of profits in some enterprises, and losses in others, even in markets that are reasonably well working and competitive. As a Nobel Prize winner in medicine argued some years back, it is *imperfections* that create opportunities and conditions for progress in many areas, not perfection (Levi Montalcini 1987). Perfection can exist only in static situations.

In an article published in 1923, Knight, who had been brought up within a strongly religious family, expressed criticism of some *ethical* aspects of the capitalist system, because in his view it tended to reduce most values to monetary measures, a point strongly made more recently by some philosophers and by Pope Francis (Sandel 2012; Pope Francis 2015). However, Knight continued to believe strongly that because it gave much weight to personal liberty, in spite of its ethical shortcomings, the capitalist system was superior to other possible alternatives, especially socialism, that was receiving a lot of attention by economists and by the general public in the early 1920s, after the Russian Revolution.

Socialism was being given a real-life test in Russia, by Lenin, and had been attracting a significant popular following in several European countries, which then had large socialist parties, and even in the USA. An increasing number of intellectuals, including some in American and British universities, had come to see some versions of socialism as both possible and a potentially desirable alternative to the "inequitable" or "unethical" capitalist system that existed in the 1920s and that would lead to the Great Depression in the 1930s.

It may be of historical interest to point out that Knight's critical observations of the ethics of capitalism and his views of socialism were echoed to some extent, and at about the same time, by John Maynard Keynes, who came from a different social background. Keynes also criticized "the metaphysical or general principles upon which ... laissez faire [had] been founded," and expressed some strong criticism of the largely unregulated capitalism that prevailed in the "roaring 1920s" (Keynes 1926). However, he had not been much impressed by what he had seen in Russia during a honeymoon visit there, accompanied by his Russian-born, ballerina wife (Keynes 1930). He had called attention to the "religious" aspect of Russian socialism and to the fanaticism of some of its followers – fanaticism that he considered "contrary to human nature." He predicted that socialism "will surely end in defeat."

In spite of this similarity of views, on both the ethics of capitalism and the nature of socialism, and in spite of their related views on risk and uncertainty, Knight strongly opposed the decision by the University of Chicago to give an honorary degree to Keynes in 1940. He argued that Keynes did not merit it (Bernstein 1996, p. 222). One reason for Knight's opposition may have been his annoyance with the fact that Keynes had given Knight's work only a very marginal, and somewhat critical, mention, in a footnote, in the *General Theory* (Keynes 1936).

Returning to the theoretical ground related to the work of the market, it can be added that as long as different enterprises face different kinds of uncertainties, including those created by unknown, future events, and including those associated with luck, such as stumbling on new important innovations or organizational techniques, different monopolistic power, irrational behavior by some, and other factors, a market economy can and will create differential possibilities of profit for different actors. Douglass North (1990, p. 77) called attention to the importance that Knight had given to the role of organization, and to the successful attempts by some entrepreneurs to reduce some uncertainties. He mentioned that this aspect of Knight's work was related to the later work by Ronald Coase (1960) on why firms exist.

This chapter has discussed some issues that make it difficult for governments and for private enterprises in democratic countries with market economies to make preparation for future uncertain developments or events that cannot be forecasted, as to timing and intensity. Of course, even the possibility of such events, though difficult to measure statistically, should be an additional reason for governments to have efficient administrations, and to reserve some "fiscal space," *just in case* they need to intervene.

Governments should also always make efforts to see whether actions that they are taking, or arrangements that they have allowed, may not in time lead to future difficulties; or at least they should not contribute to them, as seems to have happened in particular cases. Some public spending, as for example that on research related to future pandemics, can be justified on grounds of being better prepared to face future pandemics.

Some of the work of the US National Institute of Health can easily be justified along these lines.

The difficulties that democratic governments and private enterprises in market economies face in dealing with uncertain events might be considered both a market failure and a political failure for these kinds of societies. These difficulties are likely to lead to overspending on what are considered risky future events, and less spending and less preparation than there should be for "uncertain" events. In principle, authoritarian governments with state enterprises may be less affected by these failures because they may be less constrained in their actions by competition or by polls.

In connection with Covid-19, the OECD has assigned a failing grade to countries for their inability to anticipate and prepare for the coming of that pandemic – given past experiences, its coming should not have been such as a total surprise as it appears to have been.

3 TAXONOMY OF DISASTERS

Major disasters that are difficult to forecast and to prepare for come in different forms, shapes, and costs, in both human lives and loss of property. Both of these costs may be immediate and easy to estimate or determine when the events happen; or they may be spread over a long period and be more difficult to estimate.

Some disasters, such as earthquakes, tornadoes, and tsunamis, come suddenly, often with no anticipation or warning. They may last only a few seconds and do little damage. Or they may last a few minutes or longer, and leave major destruction in property and many losses in human life. Some earthquakes may be followed by aftershocks or by tsunamis, which may bring additional damage. Some cyclones may be followed by floods, which may add to the damage. For the countries or communities affected, it may take a long time to recover from such destruction of property and may require much spending. It is more difficult, or often impossible, to recover from losses of human life.

Earthquakes may affect only specific areas or specific countries, as with the San Francisco earthquake of 1906, that of Tokyo in 1923, that of Messina in 1907, or that of Haiti in 2010. Others may cover wide areas that may extend to several countries, such as one that took place in 1348 that was reported to have damaged Naples and Venice and been felt as far away as Greece and Germany; or the more recent one, of December 26, 2004 in the Indian Ocean, near Sumatra, that was felt in many countries and in two continents. Some earthquakes take place under the seas or oceans, and may generate tsunamis that may be very destructive of life and property, as was that near Sumatra in 2004, or that in Japan in 2011.

Some disasters may take more than a few minutes to have their full impact and, given today's knowledge, they may be more predictable, in both the time and the places where they may do damage. This may help save lives, but not property. These disasters include tornadoes, hurricanes and typhoons, tsunamis, and volcanic eruptions. Some of these natural phenomena last longer than earthquakes, generally more than a few minutes, and some may last a few days and be very destructive of specific areas and lives. This is normally the case for major hurricanes and typhoons, which, with some exceptions, damage only specific areas and single countries. Volcanic eruptions may occasionally affect weather patterns and also plane flights, so their impact may extend beyond national borders.

There are some destructive phenomena that are more extended in time and that occasionally affect large areas, at times even whole continents, or even the whole world. Among these damaging phenomena must be included pandemics and famines, and possibly atomic disasters, as well as very rare, major meteor hits and exceptional volcanic eruptions. The effects of these disasters can last years and can affect extensive areas and many peoples. Some of them (such as epidemics, pandemics, and famines) mostly affect human beings directly, rather than their wealth and property.

The fact that the impact of some disasters may last for extended periods will inevitably affect production and income creation, thus reducing standards of living and life expectancy, especially for some groups. It may also create more of an argument for governments to play some adapting or alleviating role. This is currently the case with the Covid-19 pandemic, which has affected some selected groups and countries particularly hard and has required obvious government intervention, with increased pressure for governments to intervene in different ways.

There are some future phenomena that, with much less uncertainty, can be anticipated, within some time periods. This is the case now of global warming, a phenomenon connected with manmade climate change, over which there may still be some uncertainty in the minds of some (or many) individuals as to timing and final full impact, but increasingly less uncertainty about its existence. Any uncertainty that surrounds this phenomenon should not be used as an excuse to ignore it by responsible governments.

Global warming is not likely to create immediate destruction, as would be created, for example, by an atomic war, or by the impact on the planet of a large meteor or a major volcanic eruption. Its impact is likely to come in stages, and each stage might become more damaging than the previous one.

In the same category as global warming belong problems created by: (a) overuse of antibiotics, which is making infections more resistant to available drugs; (b) the use of plastics and pesticides that are contaminating seas, rivers, and land; (c) the general contamination of rivers and oceans; (d) the deforestation of some important areas, such as the Amazon and other rainforests; and (e) issues that may not yet have fully entered the public perception, such as drilling for oil and minerals in pristine areas like Alaska and the Arctic, or the impacts of some new technologies, including artificial intelligence.

Man-generated global warming is a phenomenon that, if it is real and many leading scientists are not wrong, to some extent and at some future time will involve the whole earth. However, some parts of the Earth will be affected more quickly and more seriously than others (Wallace-Wells 2019). In its extreme version – that without any significant changes over the years might be felt in a more distant future, say in over a hundred years – global warming might become *the mother of all negative externalities* by making the Earth largely "uninhabitable" for billions of human beings and for other species.

However, it is, first, a phenomenon that is delayed in time in its full effect; second, that will affect different countries in different ways; and, third, that is influenced, or can be influenced, by the behavior of almost every country on Earth. Some countries (such as the USA, China, and, increasingly, India), partly because of their size, are now contributing to it more than others. Dealing with this phenomenon will require the cooperation of most countries. No country could deal with it alone, and a country that tried to do so, while the rest of the world did nothing, might be penalized, to some extent, for being virtuous, at least over the short run, in strictly economic terms.

The existence of deniers of the global warming phenomenon, including the heads of some important countries and corporations and some "think tanks," along with the fact that there are short-run economic costs on current populations in terms of dealing with it, while the benefits are postponed, and that the costs of dealing with it will not be distributed proportionally, or fairly, among countries, or among the population or industries within countries, puts global warming in a special category of disasters requiring different policies.

The governments of some countries, such as that of India, will make, and have been making, arguments that the phenomenon has been largely created in the past by the now-advanced countries, so they should be the ones that should have to carry much of the burden of dealing with it. For the leaders of countries such as India, and other

poorer countries, dealing with poverty is seen as a more urgent objective than protecting the environment.

Global warming will have various dimensions and different impacts,
and will carry different kinds of risks and costs, at least in the short run,
for different places, among social groups, and for different countries.
This puts this phenomenon, and the potential danger that it creates, in a
different category from other disasters. Later chapters will deal with this
aspect. The cost of effectively dealing with global warming will be spread
across generations, because the current generation would have to pay
the major cost in terms of reductions in their standards of living. The
higher the rate of discount of future costs and benefits, the lower will be
the desire on the part of current governments and generations to deal
with it. Countries where life expectancy is long can be expected to want
to do more about this problem than countries with a low life expectancy.

Because of the different characteristics of the above phenomena, the
question of what governments could do to deal with them, or what they
should have done during past disasters is not an easy one to deal with. In
the first place, a distinction must be made between the governments of
today's advanced countries, which have more knowledge, more able
administrations, more financial resources available, and, because of the
role of existing international institutions, more possibility of cooperation, and those of the governments that existed before the modern age.

Past governments had neither the knowledge nor the administrators
nor the financial resources of today's advanced countries, and no chance
of global cooperation. This difference is especially important in terms of
the extent to which different countries can react, or should have reacted
in the past, to destructive phenomena when they hit them. Also, the
reaction of some countries, such as Japan, to a major earthquake, or to a
major pandemic, is likely to be, and can be expected to be, different from
that of a poor country, such as Haiti.

In today's world there is still not much that a country's government or
a private enterprise can do in *anticipation* of some phenomena that may
come suddenly, without any warning. These are the classic, uncertain
events discussed in Chapter 2. In spite of the uncertainty, the known,
even if statistically unmeasurable, possibilities that these events might
happen, at some time in the future, even though the time is not defined,
naturally should be seen as an extra reason for governments to keep
their fiscal accounts under control; and for private enterprises to keep
some profits in reserve, as precautionary balances to be used, just in case.

This should be a basic, fundamental lesson for countries where such events are more likely.

However, the above is a lesson that does not seem to be given much weight by most countries, or by some economists who have been pushing the current view that public debt has become less of a problem in today's world than it had been assumed to be in the past. Therefore, some believe that the fiscal accounts do not need to be kept under control. Others also support the view that Milton Friedman (1970) pushed fifty years ago, and that many pro-market economists have endorsed since that time (Debenedetti 2021), that enterprises should distribute most of their profits to their shareholders and should not keep some in reserve for the proverbial "rainy days." These issues are discussed more fully in the following chapter.

It would seem reasonable to state that countries should have some office with the task of making some regular assessment of possible future events (hurricanes, earthquakes, tsunamis, pandemics, and others) that might visit a country in a not too distant future, presenting dangers not covered by private insurance companies. Such a "risk assessment" would be a useful input in some preparation. Some classification of the likelihood and severity of the events, similar to those that rank earthquakes and hurricanes, might also be attempted, in spite of the obvious difficulties. This might force countries to focus more than they do on "Acts of God."

Finally, the current pandemic and ongoing climate change point to a major failure of the world's institutional architecture – namely, the lack of a global government, or of an effective global institution, capable of coordinating global reactions to disasters that have global dimensions and that require coordinated global responses. Some public "goods" and public "bads" have become increasingly global and can no longer be addressed by uncoordinated national responses. (See Tanzi 2008, for an early discussion of this idea.)

4 DEMOCRACY, CAPITALISM, AND RANDOM EVENTS

In the past, pandemics and other catastrophes have often been considered "Acts of God," or even "God's Revenge" for the bad behavior of mortals. People had called for *repentance*, or even *flagellation*, not for intervention by governments. Such events could not be predicted and, in part because of this, it would have been difficult to make some preparations in anticipation for their coming, even in the presence of more abundant financial means by governments, which was often not the case.

Wars were in a different category. They could not be considered Acts of God and, to some extent, they were, or could be, anticipated, and some resources could be allocated to prepare for them, or to fight them. Wars required the raising of taxation levels, or some borrowing, to finance increases in military spending, at least for a while, as was the case for England during the Napoleonic Wars. For the first time in its history, England introduced an income tax and sold bonds to service the debt. The USA did the same during the Civil War of 1861–65, and again during the two world wars.

In more recent decades, *business fluctuations*, such as the Great Depression of the 1930s and the Great Recession of 2008–09, attracted the attention of economists and policymakers and created some reasons and expectations for governmental intervention to deal with the recessions (Tanzi 2013). Economic fluctuations have more regularity in them than, say, plagues or natural disasters, especially in terms of timing, even though Keynes himself had attributed economic fluctuations to the action of "animal spirits" – that is, to randomness. In time, there came the expectation that governments could and should adopt some policies to fight recessions when they came, and even to adopt some ex ante policies, in anticipation of their coming. This led, first, to what came to be called Keynesian, counter-cyclical policies being introduced during recessions, and the use of "built-in stabilizers," in anticipation of them. Later, it led to the increasing use of monetary policy aimed at sustaining demand.

The "Keynesian Revolution" not only called on governments to increase spending during recessions, and to finance it with fiscal deficit, to create additional aggregate demand, but also led to calls for some other policies, such as permanently increased public spending, in addition to the use of built-in stabilizers to automatically reduce the severity of recessions when they came. This may have been the first call on governments to deal, *on a permanent basis*, with crises with *economic* impact, some of which arrived with more regularity than other crises (Solimano 2020). In the past, governments had occasionally adopted public work programs during crises, to provide employment and some resources to workers and families who had been left without any resources, but there had been no theoretical backing for such programs.

There were *no* similar calls to prepare countries for other kinds of catastrophes. The randomness of many of them, in time and in severity, made this preparation difficult. The way economies and governments are expected to operate in democratic countries with market economies does not create strong incentives for them during normal times, before the crises come, to adopt policies that might make it easier to deal with potential catastrophes when they occur. This preparation might involve spending more money, for example, on hospitals and hospital beds, on building better protections against floods, on building that might better resist major earthquakes, hurricanes, and so on. Such additional spending would inevitably require higher taxes or higher borrowing, which would encounter taxpayer resistance and would likely have political costs for the governments that introduced it. It would also run into difficulties as regards decisions on how to spend the additional money.

For a democratic government worried about the next election, there would not be much political advantage and there would likely be political costs in doing so. The benefits from the extra spending would come later, and at times much later, when other governments might be in power. Or they might never come. However, the costs in higher taxes, or in stricter regulations, would be felt immediately.

The frequency of political elections in democratic countries that makes the relevant time horizon of most democratic governments relatively short, and that creates political pressures on them to keep tax levels low and to use the revenue to satisfy *immediate* rather than future needs, prevents or discourages *democratic* governments from allocating significant resources to provide better protection against future, random, and uncertain events. A government that invested substantial resources in trying to protect citizens against such uncertain future events would be criticized for wasting taxpayers' money, and would run a higher risk of losing the next elections. Uncertainty would often play against future security (Tanzi 2020b).

At times, regulation may be preferred over public spending to promote better safety codes against some catastrophic events. For example, in countries or regions more subject to earthquakes, such as Japan or California, governments have strengthened building codes. In areas subject to major hurricanes, such as Miami, they have imposed regulations to keep buildings a safer distance from the coastline. However, governments have been criticized, at times, for having strengthened these regulations, which have also increased housing costs. The prevalence of homeless people, today, in California has been attributed by critics, at times (and perhaps unfairly), to these strict regulations.

On the side of the private sector, the forces of competition also tend to promote actions, or behavior, that do not encourage enterprises to attempt to deal better with future, uncertain crises, or even with recessions, that might affect them more directly. Private enterprises, which operate in competitive markets, have strong incentives to keep costs low. They do so by squeezing the real wages of workers, minimizing their workforces, and keeping inventories low, relying on "just in time" systems of delivery.

The top managers (CEOs) of private corporations have an incentive to maximize short-run profits and to distribute the profits to shareholders, or to use them to buy shares in their own corporations. This increases the value of the shares, keeps shareholders happy, and helps justify the CEOs' high compensation packages, which, over the years, have been increasingly tied to share values. It also reduces the taxes that shareholders pay on their capital earnings, because of the non-taxation of *unrealized* capital gains that characterizes most tax systems.

It should be mentioned that authoritarian governments (for example, in China) have more power to impose regulatory restrictions. And state-owned enterprises may have more economic freedom to make preparations for future, uncertain events, or for pandemics, when they come. This is because they are less constrained by competitive or democratic requirements. This seems to have been the case of China during the Covid-19 pandemic. It was freer to impose restrictions on its citizens than was possible in the USA, for example.

Corporations in market economies are also encouraged, by tax systems, to make greater use of debt to finance their investments, or even to buy their own shares, especially when credit is cheap, as it has been recently in the USA. The deductibility of the interest paid on the debt, in the calculation of taxable profits, and the nontaxation of unrealized capital gains, makes the use of debt attractive. When the cost of borrowing is kept low by the policies of the central banks, as it has been in recent years, borrowing by enterprises is further stimulated. This leads to high shares of private debt (and to lower tax revenue; Tanzi 2016a).

These and other actions contribute to conditions that make corporations more profitable, but also more vulnerable to crises, when these occur. If the enterprises are "too big to fail," they can hope that the government or the central banks will come to their rescue, as they did during the Great Recession of 2008–09. Workers are often the ones who bear the major costs of economic crises. They are the ones who lose their jobs, their incomes, and, often, even their health insurance.

Milton Friedman, the champion of free markets, in a famous and influential essay, published in 1970 in the *New York Times Magazine*, argued that "The Social Responsibility of Business Is to Increase its Profits." He stated that enterprises do not have "social" responsibilities. Their sole responsibility is that of generating profits for their owners. That position leads to an obvious question: who has the social responsibilities? It would be logical to assume that if business does not have social responsibilities, the government must fully assume those responsibilities.

The problem has been that market fundamentalists, in the decades after Friedman's essay, absolved the enterprises of their social responsibilities, but, at the same time, made it very difficult for the governments of the USA and some other countries to fill the social gap created by the behavior of private enterprises. These governments even dismantled some of the programs that had satisfied those responsibilities in earlier years.

Tax rates on high incomes were sharply reduced; many individuals lost their defined-income pensions; labor unions were dismantled; many social regulations were removed, and so on. At the same time, the income levels of the managers of enterprises increased sharply in contrast with those of the workers in those enterprises (Tanzi 2018a). The assumption or belief of market fundamentalists that trickledown would spread widely the welfare generated by a more productive capitalist system, and that lower tax rates always lead to more trickledown, was shown to be an illusion. Many would argue, and have argued, and lots of data have supported the conclusion, that the trickledown did not happen, especially in the USA and some other

Anglo-Saxon countries, leaving some desirable social responsibilities not attended to (Tanzi 2020c).

The above discussion moves the focus from what governments and enterprises should have done, but did not do, in anticipation of future, random crises, including pandemics, to what they should do when the crises become a reality, at a time when governments are no longer allowed, by popular calls and other pressures, to ignore their social responsibilities. This question will be addressed in a later chapter, with special reference to the current pandemic. It will be argued that not having a strategy to deal with uncertain events may be considered a serious shortcoming of market economies with democratic governments. It is a shortcoming, or a *failure*, that can become evident mainly in times of crises.

In the following two chapters we return to some descriptions of catastrophic events that were experienced by some of today's countries in recent and in more distant years. The descriptions will also mention whatever information we have available of the role that governments played during those catastrophes.

Part II

Pandemics and Other Disasters

5 PANDEMICS, PLAGUES, AND EPIDEMICS

5.1 Introduction

Human beings have not lived and do not live in Shangri-La, but on an often dangerous Earth, and one that in some ways may have become more dangerous with time. Over recorded history there have been many serious epidemics, pandemics, famines, and other natural disasters that have killed millions of people and destroyed much wealth. More people have died from such disasters than they have from wars. Even during the American Civil War as many combatants died of diseases as from direct combat. In addition, over the long run there have been many natural catastrophes that have killed millions more.

While it is difficult to state categorically whether the frequency of the above disasters has changed over the long run, the historical information that we have indicates that epidemics, pandemics, and famines, which are the main topic of this chapter, became less frequent or perhaps less lethal in recent centuries, claiming fewer lives, except in special circumstances and countries, such as Russia and China. However, to some extent, epidemics, pandemics, and famines have remained present, making life precarious and uncertain, and lowering life expectancy for many peoples and for some periods. However, average life expectancy generally increased over the past two centuries, and especially in the twentieth century, due to higher standards of living and reductions in the impact of infectious diseases.

Undoubtedly, the change in life expectancy in the past century, especially in more advanced countries, was due to: (a) higher standards of living, brought about by the Industrial Revolution and, more recently, by faster growth in countries such as China and India, which had been very poor; (b) progress in medicine, which has produced vaccines against infectious diseases and more effective drugs, such as penicillin and other antibiotics; (c) better hygiene practices; (d) some useful regulations and actions promoted by governments (such as the use of quarantine to isolate infected people); (e) the provision of cleaner water; (f) better disposal of garbage; and (g) better sewer systems.

The above factors have contributed to reducing the frequency and intensity of epidemics and pandemics, and have reduced the severity of famines. However, they have not eliminated them and they have continued to affect humanity. In 2020 there was the unwelcome visit of the Covid-19 virus, which seemed to come out of nowhere; at the time of writing we still have no clear idea as to when that virus will leave us. The World Health Organization has also reported that in 2019 measles surged to the highest level worldwide for the past 23 years. Deaths by measles were estimated at 207,000 in 2019. Lack of vaccination was the main cause. Many people are still dying of malaria and other contagious diseases; and many people still do not have access to vaccination for Covid-19, so many will continue to die from the disease.

5.2 Major Pandemics

In part as a consequence of growing globalization in trade and economic activities in general, and the huge increase in world travel for tourism, especially since the 1980s, some of it to previously isolated territories, including remote jungle areas, it has become easier for some viruses and bacteria that might always have existed in isolated areas to move rapidly from the remote places where they originated, and/or from the animals that had hosted them, to other places, accompanying the fast movements of persons, animals, and goods. Rapid means of transportation, such as air travel and faster boats, have made it possible for some infections to move much faster than in the past. (See Garrett 1994 for an early prediction of coming pandemics, and for the factors that may generate them; also Diamond 1999.) The Covid-19 pandemic should not have been as much of a surprise as it seems to have been.

Another factor has been deforestation and reduction of the areas where animals used to live. Many animals have increasingly moved closer to people, thus facilitating the spread of zoonotic diseases. For example, coyotes and deer have been seen in the Washington, DC area, and one nest of Asian giant hornets, which can kill a person, has been recently found in Washington state. Furthermore, a notice from the Geographic Society, of January 5, 2021, informed readers that some chefs have turned to invasive species, including rodents, to serve what they consider new, "delicious dishes." The notice added that there are some 4,000 invasive species in the USA. Some of them can spread diseases that were not previously known.

Epidemics that can become pandemics, because of increasing contacts among people, can now move quickly. They may have become more frequent since the 1980s and there have been several close calls. As mentioned, many infectious diseases originate in specific areas, often in poor, distant places, and in some animals (bats, monkeys, and others), and they can move to populated areas, at times to much of the world, if the right conditions are present. This happened with Covid-19 and, before that, with HIV.

This is a worrisome development, and one that requires more attention from both medical experts and national governments. It should garner more global attention, especially from the World Health Organization and other medical institutions, such as the US National Institute of Health. Ongoing climatic changes are likely to be contributing to this development, as they seem to have done in the past (Oldstone 1998).

In this chapter, we shall take a brief tour through the past two to three millennia, and describe some of the major epidemics and pandemics that took place for which we have some reliable historical records. It is likely that there were others for which historical information is not available, or is very limited. While this chapter will focus on major past epidemics and pandemics, the following two chapters will focus on other disasters, such as famines, earthquakes, volcanic eruptions, floods, hurricanes, tsunami, and others, including atomic disasters.

As Diamond (1999, pp. 202–203), put it in his bestselling book:

> *The infectious diseases that visit us as epidemics . . . share several characteristics. First, they spread quickly and efficiently from an infected person to nearby healthy people . . . the whole population gets exposed within a short time. Second, they are acute diseases; within a short time you either die or recover . . . Third, the fortunate ones . . . who do recover develop antibodies that leave [them] immune against a recurrence of the disease for a long time . . . Finally, these diseases tend to be restricted to humans . . . Diseases of childhood . . . measles, rubella, mumps, pertussis, and smallpox [met the four criteria].*

However, the current Covid-19 pandemic seems to be challenging some of the above criteria and, so far, has killed more than a half million Americans and more than two million people worldwide, and its end is not yet in sight – assuming that there will be an end. Given current evidence of several mutations of the Covid-19 virus at this time, in the early part of 2021, it is not evident that there will be a clear end to this pandemic.

5.2.1 The Attic Plague, or the Plague of Athens

The great Greek historian, Thucydides, provided us with a first-hand and reliable account of one of the earliest pandemics or plagues for which we have historical records, the Attic plague, a plague that he witnessed. The plague ravaged the Peloponnesus region and especially Athens, killed tens of thousands of people around the year 430 BC, and ended the glorious Pericles years (Sierra Martín 2021).

The prolonged Peloponnesian War, among Greek cities associated with Athens or Sparta, as happens in many wars, was accompanied by widespread destruction, famine, and other miseries, and increased the facility with which infections could spread in overcrowded and very poor regions. Thucydides described the effects of the plague on people. He stated that the plague had come from Egypt and Ethiopia, had spread to Asia Minor and to Greece, and had left doctors baffled, because it had symptoms that they had never seen before. The plague killed the infected within a few days and was very contagious. Because of that, the infected would not receive any assistance even from their closest relatives. It led to many deaths over a few years. There are no reliable estimates of the number of deaths.

There is some controversy as to what kind of illness it was. It had been thought that it might have been the bubonic plague, similar to the one that would hit Europe in 1346. However, the meticulous description of the illness by Thucydides did not mention the buboes of the bubonic plague of 1346. Recent thinking has speculated that it might have been some variant of Ebola.

5.2.2 The Plague of Antoninus

Another great pandemic, for which there is a reliable record, was the long one that hit Rome and its territories in the year AD 166. It lasted in some forms until the year 190 AD. It was called the plague of Antoninus, or of Galen. It had been brought to Rome by Roman soldiers returning from Seleucia, an antique city in Asia Minor. It may have been smallpox, although this is not certain. It killed an estimated five to ten million people, or around 10 percent of the population of the Roman Empire.

There were several other epidemics over the following centuries, within the vast Roman Empire, until the year AD 542 that brought the Justinian Flea, another truly major pandemic.

5.2.3 The Justinian Flea

The AD 541–542 pandemic, the plague of Justinian, came to be called the "Justinian Flea" because it was believed to be carried by fleas, at a time when the emperor of the Roman Empire, Justinian, resided in Constantinople (now Istanbul). This plague was reported to have come from Egypt. It affected much of Europe and west Asia. The pandemic lasted for more than a half century, and persisted in some forms for as long as a thousand years.

Initially, the disease spread widely within the vast Roman Empire and infected much of Europe. An eyewitness account of the plague was provided by Procopius, a historian who reported from Constantinople, then the eastern capital of the Roman Empire. He reported that, at its peak, the pandemic caused as many as 5,000 deaths a day in Constantinople alone. That pandemic, which may have been the bubonic plague, has been assumed to have contributed to the decline of the powerful Roman Empire (Rosen 2007; also Diamond 1999, p. 206). It was estimated to have killed thirty to fifty million people, or about half of the population. The connection of this plague to climatic change is discussed later.

5.2.4 The Black Death, or the Bubonic Plague

The worst (historically reported) pandemic was the Black Death, or bubonic plague, which hit much of Europe, Asia, and North Africa, mainly in 1346–53. In milder and sporadic forms it lasted well beyond that time. The Black Death was reported to have come from Asia, perhaps Mongolia. It killed an estimated 75 to 200 million, perhaps as much as 40 percent of the total population at that time.

The plague had followed the slow movements of caravans (which moved few miles a day) along the famed Silk Road and other land trading routes, and the movement of wind-propelled, merchant ships, mainly Genoese and Venetian ships, to Italian ports from the eastern part of the Mediterranean Sea. It had originally landed in a town in the Crimean Peninsula, Kaffa, a town that had been populated mostly by Italians from Genoa and Venice, before making its way to Italy, in the fall of 1346. A lawyer from Genoa, Gabriel de Mussis, left a good account of what had happened in Kaffa.

At that time there was fighting between the Italians from Genoa, who occupied the city, and Tatars and Saracens, who had put the city under siege for some time. Some of the attackers carried the disease. At some point, using powerful war catapults, the attackers threw some infected, dead bodies over the city walls, thus infecting the Genoese and Venetian inhabitants inside the city. Genoese ships then brought the disease to Italy, perhaps originally through the port of Messina, Sicily. From Messina, the disease slowly made its way into the Italian peninsula from where it spread north, a few miles a day, first through Italy and then into much of the rest of Europe, including the British Isles, during the following five years.

According to Lane (1973, p. 19), "The Plague had two forms ... One was the pulmonary disease characterized by the symptoms of extreme pneumonia," and transmitted directly from person to person; the other was the "bubonic form characterized by the swelling, called buboes, which turned black and gave it the name Black Death." The pneumonia could be transferred directly from person to person, but the bubonic form was transmitted by the bites of fleas that carried the disease from black rats to humans. The rats were often carried by ships or accompanied caravans that moved along the Silk Road. The limited speeds at which caravans and sailing ships could travel determined the speed at which the illness could spread. It would take up to five years to spread throughout Europe.

It is reported that the disease killed 40,000 people in Genoa, 100,000 in Venice and in Florence, 70,000 in Siena, 60,000 in Naples, and large portions (at times more than half) of the citizens of many other Italian cities. Somewhere between a third and half of the Italian population and a third of the European population is reported to have perished in those years, in addition to the many millions who perished in Asia. In Europe, the occupants of many monasteries and convents (at that time very numerous) were totally wiped out by this pandemic, as would happen to the occupants of many nursing homes during the Covid-19 pandemic.

The Black Plague, which, over the next five years, slowly spread from Italy to much of Europe, convinced many Christians that the end of the world had come, and that God had sent the Plague to punish mortals for their sins (Tuchman 1978, chapter 5; and especially Kelly 2005). Many religious processions were organized and some believers went into the streets and flagellated themselves to appeal for God's forgiveness. Another explanation for the Plague at that time was that Jews had poisoned the wells. Such "fake news" led to pogroms in some European cities. In Hamburg, they led to the killing of many individuals of Jewish background.

The great Italian poet, Boccaccio (2003), who lived through the Plague, later wrote his literary masterpiece, *The Decameron*, about those years. He and a few other individuals had taken refuge in a villa in the countryside around Florence to escape from the contagion. They had spent part of the time relating stories that they knew. He reported on the effects of the Plague in Tuscany, a region that was among the most affected. He mentioned the extinction of entire families, which, at times, left empty the magnificent palaces that they had occupied, and left much property without anybody to inherit it, because there were no survivors left in some families.

There are various historical accounts of this plague and of the consequences and misery that it brought to the populations of Europe (see especially, Kelly 2005). These accounts underline the inability of governments of those times to do much, or anything, about the effects of the Plague. They also relate the impact that the Plague had on social relations, even on relations among close family members. For fear of contamination, dead bodies were at times left on roads because nobody dared to bury them, and at times they became food for wolves that lived in the neighboring woods. As a witness, Agnolo of Pisa, put it: "Because of fear of contamination, fathers abandoned their children, wives their husbands, and brothers their brothers. Fear became stronger than blood ties." In later plagues, some governments forced condemned criminals to bury the dead. In a sense, these criminals became the "essential workers" for those days.

Ships were often turned away from Italian ports when they arrived carrying people with signs of the illness. "On March 20, 1348, the Venetian Republic imposed the first-ever public policy on quarantine for incoming ships," "although no one was really sure what the plague was, where it came from, or how it was transmitted." "The authorities could have taken the attitude that there was no way to see or stop [the bad air that was believed to bring the plague]." "... instead they enacted a series of laws and procedures to put a sort of curtain between its trading partners and colonies and whatever cloud of invisible contagion was bearing down" (Small 2021, p. 101; see also Porter 1999).

Through this intervention, and for the first time, a government introduced the view that governments had some responsibilities in dealing with health issues. The sick people were required to spend forty days ("quaranta" in Italian) on one of the islands around Venice. The word "quarantine" came from this Venetian rule. (It might also be mentioned that as early in 1284 Venice had introduced child labor laws for the first time; Small 2021, p. 12.) Venice would become an innovator in "Inventing the World" and pointing to a government role, as the title of Small's book suggests.

5.2.5 Economic and Climatic Conditions that May Have Led to the Justinian Flea and the Black Plague

Some comments should be made about some of the conditions that may have facilitated the Justinian Flea, the spreading of the Black Plague, and the Little Ice Age that affected later centuries.

In the first few centuries after Christ, weather conditions had been good. The Romans could expand their empire, helped by the easier movement of their armies, made possible by the road network that they created; their powerful armies could easily cross the Alps and reach the various provinces of the vast empire. Food production had remained good. Weather conditions had changed around the time of the Justinian Flea. Some recent thinking has associated the changes in weather conditions to the eruption, in 536 AD, of the Ilopango Volcano, in what is today El Salvador. That enormous eruption was estimated to have killed hundreds of thousands of people, and it had put an enormous amount of ash in the high atmosphere. The ash had blocked the sun and created a volcanic winter; it changed weather conditions for many years, making it much colder and reducing food production, especially in the north of Europe and in Germany. Food scarcity had forced many German tribes to migrate south, crossing the Alps and eventually contributing to the fall of the Roman Empire that had already been weakened by other difficulties. The next several centuries, until the end of the millennium, would bring the deep and poorer Middle Age and a fall in the population.

After the year 1000, the Italian population, which had fallen to about five million, would more than double in the next two centuries when the weather had much improved. Several Italian cities had become among the largest in the world at that time. One reason for the population growth was the unusually warm and good weather that had prevailed in the first two centuries of the new millennium. That warm weather had made it possible to introduce new techniques in agriculture, which had allowed the production of more food to sustain the growing population (Cipolla 1994).

In the middle of the third century of the second millennium, weather conditions had again dramatically deteriorated and famines had affected areas such as London. The second half of the thirteenth and the fourteenth century had seen unusually cold and rainy weather that had sharply reduced the amount of food produced and led to a worsening of the distribution of income, by raising the rents received by those who owned the land and reducing wages (and food) for workers. The weather deterioration, especially after 1257, had much reduced the food available for the many, poor workers and had promoted a rigid version of the Malthusian theory, that food availability was the main constraint on population growth (Malthus 1890).

Food scarcity had affected the health of many and had been increasing the number of deaths, even before the coming of the Black Plague. Several wars in those years had contributed to more destruction and more misery. Recent research has connected the deterioration in weather conditions after 1257 to volcanic activities in faraway Indonesia in that year. Specifically, on Lombok Island, Mount Samalas had exploded, putting an incredible amount of volcanic pumice ash in the atmosphere and leaving an enormous caldera behind. The 1257 eruption (or, better, explosion) had been a truly biblical one in geological terms, perhaps the biggest in historical times. Mount Etna in Sicily had also become more active in those years. The volcanic eruption had spread much ash in the high atmosphere, blocking the warming effect of the sun for many years and leading to much colder weather.

In the sixteenth century there would be additional major volcanic activities, especially in Vanuatu and Iceland, that would affect the world climate in the following centuries and lead to horrendous floods in various parts of Europe. In the seventeenth and eighteenth centuries, Europe would experience a Little Ice Age that would contribute to epidemics and famines. The volcanic eruption of Mount Tambora, Indonesia, in April 1815, would lead to another year without sun, followed by many very cold, future years.

To add more misery, in 1340, there had also been a major banking crisis in Italy, when Edward II, who had invaded France, had failed to pay debts that he had contracted with Italian bankers. Finally, in 1343, there had been a major earthquake, which had been felt in Italy, Germany, and Greece, and that had caused much damage and many deaths. It may have caused a tsunami that damaged Naples. All these factors had combined in those years to create ideal conditions for a major plague. They had also convinced many that the end of the world was coming.

There are in the world some 1,500 active volcanoes and many inactive ones that can erupt any time. These volcanoes remain major existential threats for humans and for modern life. But these are dangers against which there is no protection. They remain the ultimate "Acts of God."

It is never clear when a pandemic ends. Some of them never end, but go underground when the deaths that they cause fall to what can be considered normal levels for the times. Only rarely do diseases completely disappear. It is likely that the pandemic caused by Covid-19 will never completely disappear. Hopefully it well be kept under control by periodic vaccination. But it will inevitably make some parts of the world less welcoming than others.

5.2.6 Syphilis

A century or so after the Black Plague, another infectious illness also visited Italy and became widespread in other parts of Europe. It was a sexually transmitted illness, syphilis, which at the time went under the name of "French disease," or "Neapolitan disease." In Italy it had been spread originally by the French army that had been occupying parts of Italy. Some believed that it had been brought to Naples from Spain, and to Spain from the New World, after the Columbus trips there (Guicciardini 1964, pp. 278–279).

The spread of syphilis led to the closing of communal baths in various parts of Europe that had provided the sole way of cleaning themselves for many people, at a time when no one had indoor plumbing. This lack of personal hygiene led to the spread of other diseases, because there were no alternative ways for many to keep themselves clean (Petrucelli 1987, p. 388). Until the discovery of the penicillin in the 1930s there would be no cure for syphilis. There are no estimates of how many people may have been killed by this illness.

Another sexually transmitted disease, HIV, 500 years later, would infect and kill millions of people worldwide. Its origin would also be debated, presumably having originated in African primates. There was no idea as to how it was transmitted to humans. For some years it would have a major impact on the population of some African countries especially, killing many young people. Some estimates indicate that up to 44 million people may have been killed by this disease worldwide before drugs were developed that allowed infected individuals to live with it (Chotiner 2021). It was a major pandemic also with its own moral implications for some, because of its more common impact on homosexuals.

5.2.7 The Longer-Run Effects of the Black, or Bubonic, Plague

Pandemics always leave significant and long-lasting changes on the world that they visit. The European Black Plague of 1346–53 may have generated some important, negative and positive, externalities, in the decades that followed it. An important economic consequence of this horrible pandemic was that by having killed so many people, at a time when the Malthusian control of the population (imposed by the limited food that could be produced and consumed) may have been in force, it had drastically reduced the number of mouths to feed and restricted population growth. For the next century, the Plague changed, in a favorable direction, the ratio of arable land to people to feed, reducing poverty and increasing real wages. This was clearly a positive externality. There were also some negative ones.

Greenblatt (2011, p. 113) has written that "[t]he labor shortage [in Italy] after the Black Plague of 1348 had greatly increased the market for slaves ... The traffic [for slaves] was allowed, provided that they were infidels and not Christians." At that time the slaves came mostly from East Europe and from Asia Minor, not from Africa. The origin of the word "slave" probably comes from "slavo," in Italian meaning a person of Slavic (East European) background.

The increase in food supply per capita, and in real wages, since laborers were fewer, relaxed the Malthusian constraint that had existed until then and significantly improved the distribution of wealth and income (Alfani 2021). According to some historians, the sharp reduction in mouths to feed, which increased the food available and raised the standard of living, made it possible in the coming years for more people to dedicate themselves to less essential or to artistic activities, thus leading to the civilizing phenomenon that was to become the Renaissance (which followed by a few decades the end of the Plague). It brought the beginning of a new and more modern world (see, especially, Cantor 2001; Greenblatt 2011; Fletcher 2020).

Another positive externality that may be worth mentioning is that by leaving a lot of empty buildings in important medieval cities, such as Siena and San Gimignano, the physical structure of these cities was left unchanged for future years, so that we can admire their medieval character and their original beauty. Some of these cities are now included in the list of World Heritage Sites compiled by UNESCO.

A conclusion that can be drawn from the Black, or Bubonic, Plague is that major pandemics almost always change both personal relations and economic arrangements, at times for the good, at other times for the bad. At this moment, in the first half of 2021, we have no clear idea of how the ongoing Covid-19 pandemic will change the social and economic arrangements that existed before it. It is a safe bet that it will change them. Many jobs and many economic activities are likely to disappear, or become less common, while others will emerge.

Probably there will be less travel, at least for some years, and many enterprises or activities will no longer exist, including some airlines and many restaurants. For sure, the well-to-do will come out of the pandemic in better conditions than the rest. And governments will emerge with huge debts. We do not know how long this virus will remain among us, continuing to do damage. The longer it stays, the more different the world will be after the pandemic ends. Its impact on globalization, especially, may be significant, at least for a while. People may need vaccine passports to travel. If it follows what we have experienced with the flu, it will modify and remain with us in some form.

As a final point, it may be mentioned that in recent years there have been some disagreements among experts as to the precise medical character of the Black Plague. Some so-called "deniers" have argued that the Black Death was not a plague pandemic, but some other kind of disease (Kelly 2005, Afterword). Whatever the precise medical origin, the pandemic of 1346–52 was most likely the most damaging in known history.

There were more plagues, which were more limited in space than the Black Plague. At times, they were also very destructive of human life. We report on only some of them in the following section, but there were far more than those reported.

5.3 Other Major Epidemics

During the fifteenth, sixteenth, seventeenth, and eighteenth centuries, Italy, Germany, France, the UK, Holland, Russia, and several other countries continued to be affected by occasional epidemics, which at times were called plagues, or became plagues. They may have been the result of different kinds of infections. Some of these, especially in the sixteenth century, continued to make their way first through Italy, which at that time was still the richest, most advanced, and most globalized country in Europe, and the one most directly linked to Asia and Africa, from where epidemics often came, especially through Venice. In 1575–76, there was a major epidemic in Italy, and Venice lost about 70,000 of its citizens.

In 1629–31 there was another major epidemic in Italy (Crauwshaw 2012), especially in the north. Called "The Pest," it was reported to have killed more than a million people. In 1630, in Milan alone, 186,000 citizens were reported to have perished. Like the Black Plague of 1346–52, which inspired Boccaccio to write *The Decameron*, the 1629–31 "Pest" inspired another great Italian writer, Alessandro Manzoni, some years later, to write a novel considered to be the greatest ever written in the Italian language, *I Promessi Sposi* (The Betrothed). *I Promessi Sposi* became the authoritative reference for the Italian language, a reference that had been missing until that time, because of the continued use by most Italians of many dialects and the absence of an official national language.

The 1629–31 epidemics also brought a lot of what today we call "fake news" and "conspiracy theories." Some of these theories blamed certain individuals (often strangers), or particular groups, for intentionally spreading the Pest. Once again, divine intervention from the saints was invoked to stop the epidemic. Large religious gatherings and processions were organized and these probably contributed to the spreading of the disease. Political gatherings, in addition to some religious ones, organized during the Covid-19 pandemic in the USA in 2020, had the same consequence. In 2020, however, the participants lacked the excuse provided by ignorance that had existed in 1629.

"Pest houses" were established by city authorities to house infected people. Trenches were used to dispose of the many dead bodies. And, as happened in 2020 with some hospitals, the "pest houses" were soon overwhelmed by too many patients and became complicit in the spreading of the diseases. As had happened during the Great Plague of 1346–52, there were limited hands to dispose of the many dead bodies, or to take care of the infected. Many children died because of starvation after they became orphans and there was nobody to feed them. However, governments had begun to attempt to play some role.

There were several other major epidemics or plagues during the Little Ice Age of the seventeenth and eighteenth centuries. They continued to kill thousands of people in several countries and cities (Snowden 2019). In 1656, for example, Genoa lost 65,000 of its population to a plague. In 1665, London, which had been visited frequently by plagues since the time of the Great Plague of 1346–52, lost about 69,000 people. Russia, Hungary, and Turkey also lost thousands of their citizens. In 1670, Vienna lost well over 70,000 people. It was likely that the Plague, or the Pest, had taken hold in Europe and kept reappearing from time to time, in different places, when the conditions for it became right.

Various wars and the unusually cold weather trend in the seventeenth and eighteenth centuries, which reduced the amount of food available, contributed to recreating the Malthusian conditions that had existed in the thirteenth and early part of the fourteenth century. Fletcher (2020, p. 89) has described that period as the "Little Ice Age when European temperatures seem to have been generally low. On sea voyages between Spain and Italy poor weather could stretch the voyages to the point where food supplies ran out."

There is some recent evidence, from the relatively new field of biometrics, that relates the average height of humans to the long-run trends in their diet and standards of living; during the seventeenth and eighteenth centuries, the average height of individuals in those European countries for which data are available suffered significant reductions. The soldiers who fought for Napoleon were unusually short by today's standards. The average height of males, for whom there is better information, and also life expectancy, started rising when the positive effects of the Industrial Revolution on standards of living started to be felt, and when more food became available because of more productive use of land, in part due to the "enclosure movement," which brought new agricultural techniques (Deaton 2013), and perhaps better weather conditions.

In 1832 there was a great cholera pandemic in Paris that in a few months killed 20,000 of the city's population of 650,000. As was often the case, the poorer areas of the city that had less hygienic conditions were the most affected. The pandemic provoked antigovernment reactions. Some recent research by the IMF has shown links between epidemics and social unrest (Barrett et al. 2021).

5.4 Plagues and Epidemics in the New World

To the above, mostly European, account of epidemics and plagues must be added those that were brought by European invaders to North and South America, in the years after Columbus' voyages. Available information indicates that at the time when Columbus visited (or "discovered") the New World, the population may have been as large as that of Europe, an estimated 100 million. There were at least two powerful empires in the New World at that time. The first was the empire of the Incas in Peru, which extended along much of the Pacific part of South America; and the second was the empire of the Aztecs, in much of Mexico and Central America.

There were also several important indigenous communities and tribal groups in various parts of North America, including the Pueblo, who left us Mesa Verde and other wonders, and also in some other parts of South America. The Pueblo had occupied the Colorado Plateau for some 2,000 years. While these empires and communities did not have horses or the wheel, they were by no means backward. In several ways, some of them were quite advanced in particular areas, as can be seen from the pyramids that they built, in Mexico and the Yucatan Peninsula, and the fortresses in Peru, along with agricultural techniques that they had followed to produce food, techniques to store food such as potatoes, and the marvelous ceramics and gold works that they left behind.

It has always been difficult to provide a satisfactory explanation of how small bands of Spanish adventurers, those led by Pizarro that conquered the powerful Inca Empire in South America, and those led by Cortés that conquered the equally powerful Aztec Empire in Central America, in the early sixteenth century were able to defeat their powerful opponents and conquer the existing empires. (See Prescott, 1980; Diaz del Castillo 1956; Stirling 2005 for various accounts of these conquests.)

Important factors in the battles had been guns and horses, which the Spaniards had and their opponents did not. Both of these had been unknown to the indigenous warriors. So the view of bearded men, covered in shining armor, sitting on horses, and firing guns that made the sound of thunder, must have been extraordinary and terrifying sights for the Inca and the Aztec warriors. However, the real invisible weapons that the Spanish adventurers had, without even being aware of having, were viruses and germs that were new to the inhabitants of the New World. The natives had no immunity against them and soon started to be infected by measles, malaria, whooping cough, influenza, and, especially, smallpox, and even syphilis, and dying in large numbers.

As an author put it in a bestselling book: "much of the original population of Latin America had been defeated by arms, or disease, or both. . . . In Central Mexico, the Indian population in 1520, the year after Henan Cortes arrived in his galleons, was eleven million; by 1650 that number had plummeted to one million" (Gwynne 2010, p. 54). Similar results were obtained in North America in later years. Only 10 million indigenous people now live in the Americas, compared to the 100 million when Columbus landed. Guns and diseases had played the dominant role in this massive reduction – diseases far more than guns.

The consequence of the contamination was that within a relatively short time the indigenous populations experienced terrible plagues that decimated them. Available information indicates that 90 to 95 percent of indigenous populations may have perished from these diseases, new to them, and within relatively short periods. In Mexico, in 1519–20, five to eight million may have been killed by a smallpox epidemic. Smallpox had been known in the Old World since the time of the pharaohs in Egypt. It was a very contagious disease that continued to kill many nonimmunized millions well into the twentieth century, until it was considered defeated. In 1796, Edward Jenner, an Englishman, had pioneered vaccination against smallpox, but many in the world continued not to be vaccinated and to die from it. It killed up to 60 percent of those infected, especially children.

In 1545–48, the cocoliztli epidemic was reported to have killed 5 to 15 million in the New World. The impression that most Westerners have, and that many continue to have, is that Columbus and those who followed him had found a largely empty continent, one ready to be occupied, civilized, colonized, and converted to Christianity. In the year after Columbus' first voyage, a papal declaration had stated that the people of the New World were to be converted to Christianity, or they could be made slaves. A non-Christian was, by definition, not a human being. Traces of this thinking still persist. In the USA, the "land of the free," where "all men are born equal," slavery was allowed, and so it was in England. In the dialect of the town in Italy where the author of this book was born, the noun for a person is still a "Christian." A Christian at the door means a person at the door. Thus if you are not a Christian, you are not a person. History leaves many traces in languages.

In North America, the part of the Americas that was explored and occupied in later years, initially mostly by North Europeans, with the exception of California, Texas, and some other southern lands where the Spaniards had arrived first, and then by the French, there had not been empires as powerful as those that had existed in Peru and Central America. But even on the east coast of North America there had been many indigenous tribes and communities, some nomadic, and not living off agricultural activities, and some more settled. They were also decimated by Western guns and by imported diseases in later years. "[T]he cholera plagues of 1816 and 1849 … had ravaged western tribes and had destroyed fully half of all Comanche" (Gwynne 2010, p. 6).

By contrast, during the Haitian Revolution against the French in 1803, Toussaint Louverture and his revolutionary followers were able to defeat the Napoleonic forces in part because of the help that they received from the epidemic of yellow fever, from which they had immunity, while the French forces did not (Snowden 2019). Yellow fever epidemics killed many people over the years.

Over the century since the Europeans discovered the American continent, the proportion of native populations who so perished in North America may have been as large as that in the rest of the Americas. The "Indians" who survived in the "Indian Wars" would in time be forced to live in "reservations."

5.5 Changes in the Nineteenth and Twentieth Centuries

The nineteenth century started to bring a different and generally healthier environment for some of the people in countries of western and southern Europe who had access to new developments that included the use of vaccination for some of the infectious illnesses that had killed most people. Life expectancies started rising rapidly and many became freer of *major* plagues and famines, with exceptions (Deaton 2013, pp. 6–7; Snowden 2019).

Vaccination against some infectious diseases, pasteurization of milk, new drugs, more availability of clean, drinkable water, and an increase in indoor plumbing were all developments that helped against some of the major killers. The chronic diseases that have now become common, often associated with older age, were still problems of the future. However, epidemics that occasionally became pandemics continued for diseases such as cholera, typhus, smallpox, polio, shingles, yellow fever, and some others. There would then be the great influenza pandemic of 1918–20, often referred to as the Spanish flu, which killed many millions worldwide, and there would be later pandemics that have continued to the present day.

In the late nineteenth century, the governments of some of the more advanced countries started to acquire more administrative capacity to act, and, in some cases, more financial resources to do so, even though, especially in the second half of the nineteenth century, the laissez-faire ideology that prevailed at times prevented governments from acting more forcefully during some major disasters (Tanzi 2018a). This was especially the case during the Irish famine of the 1840s, a sad and dramatic episode that will be described in a later chapter, and also for some famines in India. Plagues and famines continued to visit some countries, especially in Eastern Europe and Turkey, and continued to cause many casualties. A major exception, in Western Europe, was a serious plague that hit Marseille and several other French cities in Provence in 1720–21. That plague killed large proportions of the populations of those cities.

During the nineteenth and the early twentieth century, the incidence of major epidemics was reduced through the positive effects of the Industrial Revolution, which had started to raise the average standards of living of many families in some countries, leading to better hygienic conditions, partly connected with better government regulations, significant progress in medicine, better climatic conditions, and better and more efficient use of land (through the "enclosure movement" and better agricultural techniques).

Some epidemics, which, for some countries, were due to relatively new contagious illnesses, such as smallpox and cholera, continued to visit particular areas or cities occasionally. In 1918–22, an epidemic of typhus would kill more than two million people in Russia, a country undergoing a particularly difficult period in those years because of the Bolshevik revolution. That epidemic would accompany the "great influenza." Naples also experienced years when cholera became endemic (Snowden 2002).

A major and striking world pandemic was the "great influenza" of 1918–20, beginning toward the end of World War I (Davis 2018). It lasted for about two years and came to be called the Spanish flu, even though it did not originate in Spain, after it was reported that the king of Spain had been infected. By any standard it was a major pandemic. It would kill at least 40 million people worldwide, and close to 700,000 people in the USA. Initially, it had been spread by the soldiers fighting in the war. Soon it spread to the whole world, including the Arctic regions and other distant places (Kolata 2005). Although there remains some uncertainty about its origin, and about its specific medical nature, a current view, endorsed by leading American physician-scientist and immunologist Anthony Fauci, is that it had an avian origin. It was one of the cases that would become more frequent with the passing of the years, in which an illness would cross from the animal world to that of humans, as is supposed to have been the case with HIV, Ebola, and Covid-19. The reverse may also have happened.

Especially during its early phase, the Spanish flu pandemic was minimized as being just a traditional cold and the flu. In the USA, in the early months, there was concern that attention to it would distract from the war effort, toward the end of World War I. A major war celebration was not cancelled in Philadelphia, in late 1918, leading to many contagions and deaths in that city. The pandemic lasted a couple of years and President Wilson was probably infected during the Peace Conference in Paris, at the end of the war.

Due to the decision reached by the winners of World War I to punish Germany for the human and other costs of the war, the outcome of the Paris conference may have led indirectly to disastrous consequences in the following years. Keynes, who had attended the conference, had predicted the impact that the conditions imposed on Germany would have on the country (Keynes 1921a). Those consequences would include fascism in Italy, a country that felt cheated by some of the results of the conference, and Hitler later coming into power in Germany.

An article in the *Harvard Gazette* (Powell 2020), supported by recent research, has suggested that the Spanish flu was in part a consequence of climatic changes. It seems that in the years before and during World War I, the weather in Europe had again become significantly colder, and that change had increased the casualties during the war, and had made soldiers more exposed to infections. (Various detailed accounts of the Spanish flu, or the great influenza, are available, including Kolata 2005 and Barry 2004.)

The above may suggest that the climatic changes observed, especially since the 1980s (this time, significant increases in the average temperature of the Earth and especially higher temperatures in some areas), are likely to bring potentially unpleasant, surprises on the health front, as well as on other fronts in the years to come (including the already noted spread of some tropical diseases, and the introduction of previously unknown ones). Some of these tropical diseases and the insects that carry them have been moving toward the Northern Hemisphere, at a worrisome pace.

The period after World War II saw milder versions of flu pandemics, such as the Asian flu and the Hong Kong flu, and some other variations in more recent years. The recent pandemic, caused by Covid-19, may be a further expansion of this trend. Pandemics almost never completely disappear, but they fade away in part, assuming milder forms.

The HIV pandemic, which in the 1980s and later years killed millions of people worldwide, was supposed to have been imported from Africa. It was one example of transfer of diseases from animals to humans (as Covid-19 probably was). The large increase in tourism to previously isolated places in the rainforests of the Congo, the Amazon, and areas in Borneo, Papua New Guinea, and other places has increased contacts between humans and rare animal species, which are also occasionally eaten. Additionally, in some areas, such as the Congo, there are illegal and hard-to-control markets for rare animals destined for various parts of the developed world. Some of these animals may carry previously unknown viruses and bacteria, against which humans have no or little immunity. HIV and Ebola both passed from animals to humans. Whether the medical industry will be able to create protection against these diseases, and do it quickly enough, remains an unanswered question. The war between humans and microbes is likely to continue in the future, without permanent winners.

Some other strange diseases, some associated with eating beef, appeared some years ago in France and Britain. These were known as "prion diseases," of which "mad cow disease" was one example. It might have started with a cannibal feast in New Guinea (Rhodes 1997). All those who ate beef or used some other products, such as bone meal, were potentially at risk. For a few years, "mad cow disease" terrorized populations and worried medical experts. The impact of humans on the environment and of the environment on humans is often not intentional or well-understood.

It should be added that the invasion of modern agriculture and other economic activities, including mining in previously pristine rainforests, in the Congo, the Amazon and other forests, has been forcing the migration and spread of some animal species out of their previously isolated areas and into more populated areas. This is contributing to the spread of many rare viruses and bacteria, out of those areas into wider, more populated zones. All the above developments may bring back an age when epidemics and pandemics become more frequent, and potentially more deadly, forcing the medical profession to produce vaccines and other remedies against them in record time. The fast production of vaccines and their speedy uses may create other uncertainty related to their effectiveness and safety, as has been happening with some of the vaccines created against the Covid-19 pandemic. Governments should assist medical research with good funding for relevant research, but they should also assist in the distribution of vaccines worldwide (Honigsbaum 2020; Kenny 2021).

6 FAMINES

6.1 Introduction

Famines have been frequent in history and some major ones have continued to occur until recent decades. A nice definition of famines has been provided by Wikipedia:

> *A famine is a widespread scarcity of food caused by several factors, including wars, inflation, crop failures, population imbalance, or government policies. [It] is usually accompanied, or followed, by malnutrition, starvation, epidemic, and increased mortality.*

A famine is now officially recognized as such by the United Nations when "at least 20 percent of the households in an area face extreme food shortage ... Acute malnutrition in children exceeds 30 percent ... and the death rate exceeds two people per 10,000 per day". Of course, in the distant past there was no UN to keep score of famines.

There have been too many famines in the past centuries to be able to give a satisfactory account of them. Some affected small groups, others large ones. They were often connected with the behavior of food prices and with the incomes of buyers (Hackett Fischer 1996). Many were connected with short-term or longer-term changes in the climate, but other factors also played important roles. This chapter focuses on a few important and recent ones and discusses some of the factors that had contributed to them. The casualties that major famines can generate are extraordinary. Famines are clearly among the major calamities that human beings can experience.

To a greater extent than other calamities, famines can be prevented by different and more active government roles. This is a form of disaster where government failure is often most evident, both in their prevention and in dealing with them when they happen. Many major famines had their origin in the actions of governments, especially, but not only, the failures experienced by China and Russia in the twentieth century that generated biblical numbers of casualties.

Many famines happened in the distant past, when the administrative and financial resources of governments and their capacity to act were very limited. Some have taken place in more recent times. Some were created, or aggravated, by government policies, such as the famines in Russia in the 1920s, and in China in the 1950–60 period. Some were made worse by government actions, such as those in India and in Ireland. Some famines were connected with military actions, such as the Nazi siege of Leningrad (now St Petersburg) during World War II. Some were connected with weather conditions, or with plant diseases, such as in the 1840s Irish famines. Often, more than one factor contributed to them, and the weather often played a role.

When these disasters occurred in the distant past, few had expected governments to be able to do much to assist the affected populations. This is less the case in today's world. Now governments are expected to intervene, when *all else fails*, especially in peacetime and when the famine has not been created by those very governments. Only some diehard libertarians might oppose any government-imposed restrictions or actions, as some have been doing against wearing masks and maintaining distance during the recent Covid-19 pandemic. Many references to studies that have dealt with famines can be found in Hackett Fischer 1996 (p. 451). Also, Wikipedia has a very good description of some famines and references to relevant studies.

During periods when many families depended on subsistence farming, and did not sell or buy much food from others, their standard of living depended significantly on the size and fertility of the land available to them, and on short-term weather conditions. When population growth reduced the amount of land that families had available and the amount of food that families could produce, difficulties could develop, especially when, in particular years or periods, weather conditions changed and the food that could be produced decreased from what may already have been a Malthusian equilibrium level, with too little food for too many mouths to feed. In those times, famines became inevitable, and many individuals died of starvation.

In some cases, landownership came to be controlled by a few, and those who worked on land were either slaves, serfs, renters who paid a fixed amount to the landowners to work the land or shared in the crops produced, or daily workers who were paid very low wages. When the prices of the main crops produced fell, or the output was reduced by bad weather, the consequences for many of those who worked on the land could become dire, or even tragic. Modern agricultural arrangements, in which the crops produced are traded, have introduced some flexibility, but the dangers for those who depend on agriculture are still there. Also trade depends on transportation systems. If the surplus of food in one area cannot be transported in time to the areas where there is a famine, the problem cannot be solved. In the past, transportation systems were often very deficient, so you might have surplus in some areas and great scarcity in others.

At times, very high inflation, as in Germany after World War I, may reduce dramatically the incomes that some families have available, reducing their ability to buy food, especially when the price of food has gone up by more than incomes. This happened in the 1920s in Germany. At other times, as during wars, food becomes scarce when many of those who normally worked the land were sent to fight the wars. Food rationing may be introduced. Great depressions, like the one of the 1930s, may generate high unemployment, loss of income for many workers, and low prices for agricultural products. In spite of the low prices, many families may not have enough income to buy food.

There are also situations where the difficulties are manmade, besides those created by wars. In the examples of famines that we describe below, we shall try to identify the main factors and what the governments did, or could have done, to better cope with them.

6.2 Famines in the USA

It may seem strange to think that in the USA, a country with a huge extension of good land and a low population, there could have existed periods when parts of its population experienced great scarcity of food, or even famine. We shall identify four such periods. To some extent they met, or approached, the conditions that are characterized as famines.

6.2.1 Famines Among Early American Immigrants

There is considerable historical evidence that some of the early immigrants to America, mostly coming from the British Isles in the seventeenth century, at times, faced conditions that approached famines, before the newcomers could establish an agricultural and permanent basis for providing them with a sustainable standard of living. At the beginning, they had to depend on hunting and fishing activities for their food, and many of them had not been well-prepared for these activities.

Along the coastal areas of the North Atlantic, the early immigrants at times experienced extreme food scarcity, which may have led, in some extreme cases, to episodes of cannibalism. It is not known how many of these immigrants experienced such famines and how many died from them. At that time there was no established government in those territories, so there was no government role to speak of.

6.2.2 Famines Among Native American Tribes

During the second half of the nineteenth century, some of the new-comers to the continent, many of European background, started moving west and began to occupy territories that had been used by indigenous people, such as the Comanche, the Pueblo, the Hopi, and the Cherokee. Some, but not all, of these tribes had had a nomadic existence and had survived largely by the killing of bison, which in those years roamed in the millions over the vast grassland of the savanna that had been the Great Plains of what in time would be the southwest of the USA. The bison had provided the indigenous tribes with much of their food, and also with skins that they used for covering themselves and for building their tents. As long as the bison were available in abundance, the nomadic "Indian" tribes could sustain their traditional existence.

In the second half of the nineteenth century, especially after the Civil War ended, there were wars between the US federal government, which assumed it had rights over those lands, and some of the "Indian tribes" that had been living in those lands and felt dispossessed. There were also wars with Mexico. The abundance of bison that had existed was rapidly reduced by hunters who, using powerful new rifles, could kill many of them in a short time, mainly for their skins, which had high commercial value.

Within a few years, most of the bison were killed, leaving the "Indian tribes" without their traditional sources of food. Some of the "Indians" were confined, or forced, into "reservations," which were largely jails without walls. Some "Indians" experienced lack of food and even starvation. These problems were added to the illnesses that the natives were experiencing by being exposed to viruses brought by the invaders, against which they did not have immunity.

The history of American "Indians" in what is now the United States is a tragic and still little-known chapter in the settlement of the New World by mostly Europeans that followed the Columbus trips. Given the unusual circumstances that prevailed, it is not meaningful to speculate on what a government could have done to protect the "Indians" from the famines they experienced. It is rather a lesson of what can happen when there is no functioning government in societies in which the concept of community is still missing. The "Indians" who were forced into reservations were often cheated in the agreements or in the promises they had received from those who had invaded their lands (Ehle 1988). It should be added that tribes in Patagonia in South America suffered a similar fate.

6.2.3 Famines During the American Civil War

The Civil War of 1861–65 was undoubtedly the saddest and most tragic episode in the history of the United States. The war between the Southern American States (the Confederacy) and the Northern American States (the Union) killed more than 600,000 Americans, did a lot of damage to the economy, and created permanent animosity between the North and South of the United States of America. Some of the effects of the war have survived until now.

During the Civil War, a significant percentage of the population died of diseases or deprivation, due to lack of food. The "scorched earth" military actions followed by General Sheridan and some others, and the mobilization of many men in the army quickly led to a reduction of the food supply available. That lack of sufficient food was experienced by many civilians, but it was felt especially by prisoners of war, who, in the many thousands, were kept in prison camps and fed with food rations that were far from sufficient to sustain them in good health, or even in life. Many prisoners died of diseases connected with food scarcity or with food of poor quality. In a broad sense, these prisoners, and many civilians, experienced episodes that could be defined as famines.

Once again, given the circumstances, it would not make sense to ask what the government, or the two governments, could have done to prevent the famines. The famines were the direct consequence of the war.

6.2.4 The "Dust Bowl" and the Great Depression of the 1930s

The next episode of famine in the USA is connected with what some consider the greatest manmade environmental disaster in American history. It shows what neglect of environmental considerations can do to an area. It should be a warning about the long-run consequences of ongoing "climate change" and other environmental issues. The "dust bowl" that hit the Great Plains of the United States in the 1930s was the result of the combination of various bad decisions and some unanticipated natural developments.

The first bad decision was the making available to settlers, using the Homestead Act of Congress of 1862, without payment, the land on which Indian tribes had operated and had depended in the past for their living, after the Indians had been killed or forced into reservations. Many families of settlers moved west to the Great Plains, from areas in the east, to occupy their large new farms. They obtained lots and built houses on them. These had been arid lands, covered by permanent grass (the savanna), which in earlier years had fed the millions of bison which had freely roamed the areas and had provided most of the food and shelter on which the native tribes had depended. The permanent grass cover had helped the lands retain some humidity in the soil, and had provided food to the bison.

The second bad decision had been the planting of wheat, by the new farmers, in those arid grasslands. Over the long run, those lands could not support the wheat production, which requires different soil and more rain. However, the high price of wheat, especially, in the 1920s, had made the planting of wheat look like a winner for the new farmers, and had increased that use for large extensions of land.

After a few good years, when production, prices, and profits had been high, and the land had been seemingly productive, the situation started to change. First, the lands started to become less productive. Second, after the stock market crash of October 1929, the price of wheat collapsed. Third, the weather changed, bringing a decade with much less rain and much stronger winds. It was a combination of factors that often brings unpredicted "perfect storms." Soon the lands started developing characteristics typical of deserts. The strong winds were able to lift a lot of loose ground from the soil that had become brittle. This led to progressively more ominous and damaging sandstorms, which moved around and lifted tons of dust. At time, days were transformed into nights by the high winds.

People started getting ill with pneumonia, generated by the dust, which was everywhere. Everything became brown and food and incomes became much scarcer. Many farmers lost their few cattle. Then they sold their tractors to make ends meet and many had their farms repossessed by the banks that held the mortgages. The 1930s was a very bad period for most of them, and especially for their children, who suffered the most. Many schools closed and, for lack of food, children lost on average 10 percent of their weight.

In this tragedy, which the government had been partly, but unknowingly, responsible for creating, the government eventually played an important positive role through some of the policies of the New Deal, introduced by President F. D. Roosevelt. Many former farmers found temporary jobs in some of the work programs introduced by the New Deal. Many migrated to California, and to less arid places where they could start a new life. Eventually, World War II came and the Depression ended, and weather conditions became less hostile. The weather became less dry and less windy, and new methods of agricultural production were introduced that could better utilize the little rain available to that large area.

The discovery, more recently, of a major deposit of underground water, a huge aquifer, under parts of the Great Plains has allowed farmers in the area to substitute some of the water from the rain with the more reliable underground water source, thus returning to the growing of some of the crops, and the raising of cattle, that require more water. However, aquifers are not infinite. In time, they will get depleted. This may lead to another crisis for the area. The timing of that future crisis is uncertain and, as we saw in an earlier chapter, uncertainty and future dangers do not attract much attention on the part of presumably rational individuals, enterprises, and government officials, which are generally focused on the present and on immediate and less uncertain events. In any case, this was a crisis with profound messages for what people can do to the environment. It may have been clearly the first government-made environmental crisis.

6.3 The 1845–1849 Great Irish Famine

One of the best-documented and most dramatic famines of the past couple of centuries was the Irish famine in the 1840s. The causes of the famine were various and complex, and its consequences were broad and felt by several countries. There are many historical accounts of the famine. Before the Great Irish Famine of the 1840s there had been another major famine in Ireland, in 1730–40, which had killed an estimated 300,000 people, and another "subsistence crisis" in 1782–84 (Kelly 1992).

We shall mention some of the factors that led to the Great Irish Famine, and which made it particularly dramatic and damaging for the Irish population. Millions of people would die, or would be affected in various ways, by that famine. At the time when the famine came, Ireland was part of the Kingdom of Great Britain. It was largely an English colony. It was very poor and overpopulated, with a majority of Catholics, who were discriminated against by a controlling Protestant minority. The Catholic families generally had many children.

Ireland did not have valuable natural resources that would attract the then evolving Industrial Revolution that was taking place in other parts of Britain. It also had a climate that did not allow the production of many crops that could sustain the high and growing population. Its land was not particularly fertile and much of Ireland's best land had been diverted, by the often British owners, to the raising of cows, which provided the beef much in demand in England. The poor Irish had been pushed into lands of lower fertility that could hardly supply them with adequate incomes for their typically large families.

For historical reasons, much of the land in Ireland was then owned by Anglo-Irish individuals who generally lived in London and rarely visited their properties. It was an arrangement typical of the *latifundios* of some Latin American countries. In these *latifundios*, ownership is highly concentrated in the hands of individuals who are mostly interested in extracting rents, as absentee landlords, from their properties; they do not live on their property and are not much interested in managing the land themselves. The landlords rented their land to intermediaries, who paid the owners fixed annual rents and were free to use the rented lands in any way they could.

Normally they found it profitable to parcel the rented land into smaller plots that were then sublet to those who actually cultivated the land. They were poor peasants who used the small lots to produce a crop, generally potato, that could grow on these marginal lands, and could directly feed their numerous families. These peasants used old techniques and inefficient methods in the use of these lands. At times, the poor peasants parceled the already small lots into still smaller ones, distributed among various members of their large families. The native Irish population had become largely dependent on the potato for most of their daily food. About a third of the potato crop produced was diverted to the feeding of the cows.

The potato was the crop that made it possible for poor peasants to feed their large families on such small pieces of marginal land. The potato was not an indigenous European crop. It had not existed in Europe in the distant past, but had originated in the High Andes of South America, in

Peru, where it had been grown by the Incas, who had also depended on it. The potato had been imported to Europe, and to Ireland, some years after Columbus had "discovered" the new continent. The potato, *Solanum tuberosum*, would grow well in some European areas, "with moist, cool weather and with relatively long days and warm nights, and would enjoy a deep friable soil" (Hobhouse 2005, p. 251). The potato was one of the two great gifts that the Incas had given to the world, and especially to Europe after Columbus' trips. The other gift had been corn. By 1625, the "potato had become a staple of many Irish families," while in other European countries it had remained a "garden crop or cattle food" (ibid.). Lacking wheat or corn to make bread, the potato had become the main food staple for large Irish families, who often ate little else.

The great reliance on a single crop, potatoes, made many Irish families exposed to the risk of that crop's failure. The failure could come from adverse weather conditions or from other factors. It was, of course, an uncertain risk, and as such it might never come. The reliance on one crop created a situation similar to that in financial decisions of "putting too many eggs in one basket." As a British historian put it: "The Irish problem … was the problem of a [very low] standard of living. Most people in Ireland lived near the starvation level, and depended for their food upon one staple crop, the potato. The potato crop was precarious; if it failed on a large scale, the greater part of the population would starve." Woodward (1962, p. 352) added: "About a third of the [Irish] population lived almost entirely on potato." It was easy to predict what could happen if there were a failure in the potato crop. But the timing of that event was so uncertain that it was not likely to change anything before the failure actually happened.

The Irish famine was provoked by an unpredictable event, a plague that affected the growth of potatoes. In the fall of 1845 there was a major crop failure which accelerated in 1846, creating a situation of intense famine for millions of Irish families, when they could no longer rely on their traditional food staple, and they did not have money to buy other, more expensive foods, such as grain or beef that were still available. Soon, the situation became desperate, and difficult to ignore by the British government, which was faced with the question of what to do about the starving Irish.

There were conflicting pressures on that government. Some, mostly Protestant individuals, argued that the potato famine had been sent by God to punish the Catholic Irish for their crimes and sins, including heavy drinking and being Catholic. Some took the social Darwinian view that the government should let the famine take its natural course, so as to solve, once for all, and in a Malthusian way, the Irish problem of overpopulation. Some argued that the laissez-faire ideology, which then prevailed, prevented the government from intervening, for fear that such an intervention would permanently reduce the personal incentives of the assisted Irish, and would make those who received government assistance become permanently dependent on government generosity. That laissez-faire ideology allowed Ireland to continue exporting corn that it had carried on producing while many people were dying of starvation. There were also some who argued that the government could not ignore the problem of individuals literally dying of starvation, and that it had to do something.

There was some initial, limited action taken by the British government to help the starving Irish. This included some purchase of maize and cornmeal from America, that, because of bad weather, arrived in Ireland only at the beginning of 1846 and was sold at a very low price to those who had money to buy it. Additionally, the Corn Laws, which had kept the price of imported corn high by impeding imports, were repealed. Some public work programs were introduced and by the end of 1846 they were employing half a million Irishmen. Those public work projects were badly administered and were subject to much criticism. "Soup kitchens" were set up for those who could not afford to buy any food, regardless of the low prices.

While these government measures helped to some limited extent, they were far from sufficient (or efficient) to deal with the size of the problem. The laissez-faire ideology that had guided the British government, at that time, kept the measures taken more modest than they needed to be, and the lack of an efficient administration further reduced their effectiveness. There continued to be comments that the Irish would get used to receiving government help, and that that would damage their incentives to work and to take initiative in the long run. There were also comments that it would be good to let the crisis solve itself, as a form of survival of the fittest. The net outcome was the death of an estimated million Irish and the migration of a large share of the Irish population. Within a few years, Ireland would lose more than 20 percent of its total population.

Of those who emigrated, some went to England, mainly to Liverpool; some who could pay the fare, which was very high in relation to low Irish incomes, went to Canada or Australia. Many went to New York and Boston, where they established important Irish communities. Some historians have reported that, because of the bad health conditions of many of those who boarded the ships, and because of the atrocious conditions in the ships during the voyages, a large share of those who tried to emigrate died during the often long trips to new destinations. The United States would, in time, have many Americans with an Irish background. A century later, an American of Irish background, Jack Kennedy, would become the first Catholic president of the United States, and sixty years later, another American of Irish descent, Joe Biden, would become the second Catholic president.

6.4 Famines in Russia, China, and Other Places

In Russia and in China, in the twentieth century, economically naive political experiments, such as the expropriation of land from those who had owned and cultivated it, and the creation of collective farms, run by inexperienced bureaucrats, in which individual incentives had been completely destroyed and arbitrary production targets had been imposed on the farms, led to some situations where food production largely collapsed, creating major famines and leading to millions of deaths. In these cases, the main cause of famines was easier to identify. It was bad government decisions that created the famines. In this section, we shall briefly describe some of these major famines, starting with the one that hit Russia in the 1920s and later.

6.4.1 Russian Famines, 1921–1922, 1932–1934, and 1946

Lenin's Soviet government, which assumed power in Russia after the 1917 revolution, started the process of replacing the existing, limited market economy that had existed in Russia before the Revolution, with central directives: "[y]ears of war, conscription and food requisitioning had devastated agriculture, particularly in the most fertile regions. On top of this, the Volga region had experienced drought in 1920 and 1921 ... The result was famine ... probably about 5 million people died" in that experiment (Hosking 1992, p. 120).

As a result of the sharp increase in state procurement and the sharp fall in grain harvest, in 1931 "a famine took hold which was even more serious than in 1921–22" (Hosking 1992, p. 167). In 1932–33, the Volga and the Ukrainian and northern Kazakh regions were estimated to have lost about six million people to the famine. Hosking reports that "When Kravchenko entered a village in Dnepropetrovsk oblast, he was surprised by the deathly silence. He was told that 'All the dogs [had] been eaten'. 'We have eaten everything we could lay our hands on – cats, dogs, field mice, birds'" (ibid.). Estimates of those who died in this famine are as high as eight million. In parts of Ukraine, "every third citizen ... died of hunger. In ... Volodarka Taion, the death toll was higher – 466 of every 1000 residents did not live to see the year 1934. The mortality rate was especially high among children and the elderly" (Plokhy 2018, pp. 40–41).

The siege of Leningrad by the German army, from the end of August 1941 until January 1944, was one of the most horrendous episodes of World War II. It created another extreme episode of famine in Russia. As Hosking (1992, p. 280), put it:

> cut off from overland communication with the rest of the country, [Leningrad] was in a truly desperate situation ... [T]he siege had not been anticipated, and nothing had been done to lay in supplies for it ... The only supply line lay across thirty miles of Lake Ladoga, to the east of the city ... [H]eavy lorries across the ice [of the frozen lake in winter] could bring in some supplies. In December 1941, 53,000 people died in Leningrad ... Bread ration was 400 grams a day [for manual workers] with dependents getting half that ... People sat at home, without electricity or heat, in the dark in the interminable days of winter burning books and furniture to stay warm in minus 40 degrees temperature] and gradually starved.

The siege was estimated to have killed more than a million people, from the cold and lack of food. To fully appreciate what the inhabitants of Leningrad went through during the siege, and for almost three years, compare their experience with that of families during the current pandemic, when some have been encouraged to be "locked down." In this pandemic there have been loud complaints about the sacrifice of being locked in, in apartments or houses that by and large have continued to have heat, light, television, internet, and, generally, sufficient food.

In 1946, the food situation in the USSR once again became precarious, because high procurement from farmers, to feed the army and other privileged groups, had left very little food for the rest of the population. Cases of cannibalism were reported from the villages, while the press kept the famine secret (Hosking 1992, p. 299). That famine was estimated to have killed up to one and a half million people. In 1952, the grain harvest per acre in the Soviet Union was still lower than it had been in 1913.

6.4.2 Famines in China, India, and Other Places in the Twentieth Century

Over its long history, China has experienced more famines and lost more people to them than any other country. The famine of 1958–61 alone may have killed as many as thirty million people, that being the mid-point in a wide range of estimates from fifteen to forty-three million. That famine, the worst anywhere in the twentieth century, was a consequence of a government policy and not of a natural event. It was the result of the "Great Leap Forward," Mao Zedong's misguided policy aimed at industrializing China, within a short time.

Peasants were forced to abandon their private farms and join "collective farms," while also producing steel in small, antiquated foundries. At times, they would melt the tools they had previously used to produce food, in order to produce the steel to satisfy arbitrarily set production quotas. As had happened in Russia, the personal incentives of individuals working in poorly run, collective farms were destroyed and food production collapsed. Production targets were often faked to hide the extent of the failures. The result was that the Great Leap Forward resulted in a famine of biblical proportions.

In previous years, China had experienced other horrendous famines, often generated by weather changes, In 1907, some twenty-five million people may have died in a famine. In 1976–79, another famine in northern China killed up to thirteen million people. And in famines in 1928–30 and 1942–43, another five to six million may have died. The link that may develop between the weather changes brought by global warming and food production should clearly be a cause for concern in future years, in view of past experiences.

In 1975, an extreme revolutionary left-wing government took control of Cambodia. It was led by a fanatic leader, Pol Pot, who had extreme economic and social views on how to transform Cambodian society and its economy in a short time. The Pol Pot government attempted an even more extreme economic experiment than the one that had been promoted by Mao Zedong in China during the Cultural Revolution that some historians have called a descent into madness (MacFarquhar and Schoenhals 2006). Within a few years, the Pot Pol policies would lead to the death of about a quarter of the entire Cambodian population. Some were murdered because of their former backgrounds, and others died of starvation when food production collapsed. In a visit to today's Cambodia, one can see some public displays of skulls of many of the murdered victims. They are reminders to visitors of that horrible period. Other famines were also experienced by North Vietnam and North Korea.

Over the years, India has been another major country subjected to periodic famines that have resulted in millions of victims. Some occurred during the period when India was a British colony. Accounts of some of these famines are reported in Sen 1981 and 1999. In India, famines have been often the direct consequence of the unpredictability of monsoon rains that largely determine agricultural output in India. When the monsoons fail, famines often follow. The inability, or unwillingness, on the part of the authorities to intervene when large famines have occurred, has been cited as an important contributor to the number of individuals who have died. The view is that often the government should have intervened and could have made a difference.

A large proportion of the Indian population lives close to the minimum subsistence level necessary for staying alive, and this has made it possible for a lack of rain to lead to major famines and millions of deaths. This occurred in the Bengal famine of 1769–73 that killed an estimated ten million Indians; and in the Chalisa famine of 1783–84 and the Doji Bara famine of 1789–93, which between them may have killed eleven million people. In the Indian "Great Famine" of 1876–78 and the Indian famine of 1899–1900, millions of Indians died of hunger and hunger-related illnesses. In the twentieth century, the "Bengal Famine" of 1943, during World War II, is reported to have killed more than two million people.

Various authors, especially Amartya Sen, the Indian-born Nobel prizewinner in economics, have blamed both irregular rainfall and the policies followed by colonial administrators, the British, since 1857, for the consequences of some of the major famines in India. British policies converted many local farms into plantations owned by foreigners, who directed significant parts of their agricultural production toward export crops. At the same time, the fast growth of the Indian population kept the standard of living of many families very close to the minimum needed for survival. When famines occurred, only government assistance could have helped many families to survive. But that government role was not part of the prevailing, laissez-faire paradigm. We find in India a repeat of the Irish experience of 1846.

The assistance that the government might have provided to the starving citizens was often missing, also and partly because of a lack of financial resources, and partly because of ideology, such as laissez-faire concerns that government assistance would reduce the incentives to work of the local populations in the long run. These concerns have led to many political crimes in many countries over the years. Cash transfers to those who had lost the agricultural income would have allowed them to buy some food that was still available, or that would have become available if the means to buy it had been there. Some food could have been brought in from places where it was still available.

We thus find again, in India as we did in Ireland, that the combination of some unpredictable event, such as missing rainfall, or a potato blight, combined with unsatisfactory government policies, can lead to major tragedies. When everything else fails, government has to play the maximum role that it is capable of playing, because it remains the ultimate risk manager. It must not be immobilized by questionable economic theories or short-run limited tax revenue. Its role must involve transfers from those who have to those who need. And this may be based on temporary policies, so as to minimize long-run effects on personal incentives.

Famines are often partly a matter of a poor distribution of income. Economic theories that prevent income redistribution can do a lot of damage, as can some extreme theories promoted by the left that push for absolute equality. Changes in the amount of rainfall, orientation of much production toward exports, and a lack of needed governmental intervention were the main factors that led to many deaths in India. Extreme leftist experiments were the factors that led to famines in China and Russia.

After World War II, agricultural developments brought about by the so-called Green Revolution that introduced new varieties of wheat and rice that were more resistant to weather changes and to attacks by pests, combined with new methods of producing crops, increased the quantity and the safety of food production, and prevented other famines. It also increased the population. The Green Revolution may bring other problems in the future. An American agronomist, Norman Borloug, has been given some of the credit for the Green Revolution.

6.5 Concluding Comments

Food (together with drinking water) is a most essential requirement for living creatures, including human beings. It was for that reason that Malthus believed that the size of the population would be conditioned by the amount of food available, and for a long time it probably was. In England, where Malthus lived, there was no lack of water, but food production was scarce. The larger the amount of food available, the greater the population might be. The Malthusian theory probably worked for much of history until a couple of centuries ago. In the long run and for larger areas, climatic changes were probably the most important factors in determining how much food was available to the people who lived in those areas.

In more recent centuries, lack of food has no longer been such as a constraint on the growth of the world population, except in limited times and places. New crops, new production techniques, new arable land, and more access to sources of water, including underground sources and those provided by dams, relaxed the Malthusian constrain *for the world as a whole*, by increasing the total amount of food produced, especially in the years of the so-called Green Revolution in agriculture. This allowed the population to grow and to reach the recent seven billion level. However, food constraint has continued to exist in some parts of the world and, at times, has led and is still leading to occasional famines.

In principle, those famines could have been alleviated by transfers of food from other parts of the world, where food was still available and even abundant. For this food transfer to take place, governments or international institutions would have needed to play a role. The free market by itself will not do this. At times, governments did play such a role. At other times they did not, or did not do it at a sufficient level to make a difference. An optimistic scenario is that food supply will continue to increase at a sufficient pace in the future to allow the world population to continue growing to the expected ten billion in future years. It is also hoped that the redistributive role of governments within countries and of international institutions across countries will continue and intensify.

A question that must be raised in a book such as this is whether, for the world as a whole, the Malthusian theory has truly become permanently irrelevant, as some optimists assume that it has. They believe that innovation will always be sufficient to generate the needed supply of food, whatever the population growth. Therefore, it should be assumed that the Earth will continue to produce enough food regardless of the population growth and environmental developments, such as climate change, that may cause droughts in several countries.

Should we forget Malthus? Or should we also consider an alternative and less optimistic scenario, even though it concerns a possibility that is in the future and is clearly uncertain? What reasons could make us contemplate that other less optimistic possibility, recognizing that it is an uncertain one, but not an impossible one? The UN has been warning about this possibility, especially for some parts of Africa and also for Southeast Asia. There are various reasons why this alternative scenario should not be completely dismissed. It is clearly connected with long-term developments, including climate change. It is a *black swan* type of event that may become a reality one day, as an increasing number of experts have been predicting.

The reason is that some of the developments of recent years that have increased food supply may also have increased that less optimistic possibility. The world may have made a Faustian deal by bringing the much larger food supply of past decades at possibly high future costs. But, of course, the future remains unpredictable and the pessimistic future may never come. However, consider the following developments.

First, water, an essential element for agriculture, is likely to become a growing constraint on future food production, because some of the glaciers on mountains that feed important rivers are melting. The creation of new dams on rivers, including the Nile, has diverted the reduced flow of water in rivers, reducing their flows in some areas, and even creating potential military conflicts between some countries, such as, for example, Egypt and Ethiopia. Global warming has been reducing the size of glaciers that feed some important rivers. In time, that will result in a reduction of the water that flows in those rivers, reducing the water for agricultural production that had depended on that water. Also the regular amount of rain in some areas is being reduced by droughts, reducing the production of grain and rice, which are very important for feeding billions of the world population.

Second, the use of some artificial fertilizers and pesticides is causing soil contamination in many areas. It has been reported that as much as 40 percent of the agricultural land of the world is now already somewhat degraded by that use.

Third, the use of underground water (aquifers) to irrigate fields in recent years in some areas is fast reducing the available supply of that water. Water tables have been falling in several areas, including Australia, the south of Italy, and other places. In several areas, water overuse is resulting in the accumulation of salt in the soil and in the aquifers themselves. This is clearly a resource that is not infinite and its use requires careful monitoring.

Fourth, some land has been used to produce biofuels, thus reducing the production of grain and other crops for feeding humans.

Fifth, the rapid desertification of some areas is removing some land from productive uses.

Sixth, world population continues to increase at a rapid pace in some regions and to need more food, especially more food that individuals with higher incomes consume more, including beef, lamb, and fish. The production of this meat requires more land than other food, or more fish is demanded. It is estimated that two to three billion more people may be added to the world population over the next decades. They will need much more food and water and more land for housing, roads, and so on. If average income levels keep rising, they will require more meat and fish.

Finally, the amount of fish that the seas provide has been falling because of overfishing, contamination of the oceans, increases in sea temperature, and other factors. The expected rising of sea levels due to global warming will steal more land from other uses, including from agricultural uses.

All the above and other developments, including some connected with "climate change," point to an uncertain but worrisome future. As is the case with most uncertain events, that future might never come, and, because of that, there will be a human, and perhaps even rational, tendency to just ignore it. However, the possibility that it might occur, even though the timing cannot be predicted, should focus some attention on the possibility. The reason is simply the severity of the consequences that would follow if that scenario did in fact materialize. Clearly it is governments and, increasingly, international organizations and agreements, that need to pay more attention to that possibility. This is clearly an area that individuals in free markets, by themselves, will not be able to deal with. Those who want to leave the solution of this problem to the unregulated free market are simply deluding themselves.

7   NATURAL DISASTERS

7.1 Introduction

Unfortunately for humans, while it may appear beautiful and welcoming, especially when seen from space, Mother Earth is not always a peaceful and safe place to live. At times it can become a threatening and dangerous place. This happens when, for a variety of reasons, natural disasters happen. Natural disasters are events generated by more or less spontaneous actions of the Earth. They may result in immediate loss of human life and property, and also set in motion other changes, such as climatic ones. These events may be caused by earthquakes, volcanic eruptions, tsunamis, hurricanes, typhoons, tornadoes, major floods, forest fires, and other similar events, including epidemics and pandemics. Most of them may occur without the contribution of humans.

Major disasters can also be caused, occasionally, by human actions, including forest fires, and atomic and industrial accidents. These may also be provoked by natural events. In this chapter we provide some information on major disasters, especially on some past ones that resulted in major loss of life and property. Disasters are experiences so frequent for humans that only a few of them can be mentioned. The increase in world population in the past couple of centuries and the growing population density in many geographical areas have increased the exposure of humans to disasters and to the higher costs of natural disasters. They have increased both the probability and the cost, affecting humans in a major way. We shall report on some recent disasters, assigning them to a few general categories.

7.2 Earthquakes, Tsunamis, and Volcanic Eruptions

7.2.1 Earthquakes

Earthquakes are a consequence of the movement below the Earth's surface of tectonic plates, along geological faults that exist in the plates

(Winchester 2005). These movements can release enormous energy that makes the ground surface shake, at times violently. This shaking may cause the collapse of manmade structures, especially of buildings, and may also cause landslides and other damage. Seismographs can now measure the intensity of earthquakes. The measure commonly used is the Richter scale, which classifies earthquakes as micro, moderate, strong, major, and great, and assigns a number to them. The higher the number, the more violent the earthquake, on a scale that goes from 1 to 10.

Earthquakes may last just a few seconds, called tremors, or they may last a few minutes. The greater the intensity of the earthquake, and the longer its duration, the more damage it can cause, especially in areas that are highly populated. The Richter scale measures only the intensity. The greater the intensity, the greater the potential damage. Some very strong earthquakes have exceeded 9 on the Richter scale. It has been estimated that in the past half-millennium, thirty-five earthquakes may have exceeded 8.5 on the Richter scale, and some have exceeded 9. However, some of them were in areas that were little populated.

Some countries are much more exposed to earthquakes than others because they are over or close to fault lines in the tectonic plates, or they host active volcanoes. About a billion people now live within 150 kilometers of volcanoes and are thus exposed to their activities. There are about 1,500 active volcanoes in the world. The San Andreas Fault, near San Francisco, is a major fault line that creates potential dangers for that city (Winchester 2005). Yellowstone is essentially a huge volcano, the eruption of which could one day create enormous damage.

There are several other fault lines around the Pacific Ocean that create a "Ring of Fire" where earthquakes often occur. There are several countries that are very exposed to potential earthquakes. These include Chile, Japan, China, Indonesia, Italy, Turkey, Iceland, the Philippines, Guatemala, and the USA. Some are around the Pacific ring where the tectonic plate of the Pacific meets those of the continents. These countries are all close to major fault lines and/or host active volcanoes. However, earthquakes can happen almost anywhere, and at any time. Cities near volcanoes can be exposed also to the ashes from volcanic eruptions, which can cause major damage and limited changes in climate. Earthquakes cannot be anticipated and, for sure, cannot be prevented.

The best protection against earthquakes is not to live in areas subject to them. However, those areas may have characteristics that make them attractive, in spite of the risks. A "global risk model" to support clients in assessing volcanic risk, and to charge some risk premiums for that protection, has recently been developed by the insurance company, Swiss Re. The model has ranked Managua, the capital of Nicaragua, as the city most exposed to volcanic "risk," among fifteen of the largest cities. It is, of course, an open question whether Swiss Re has actually measured "risk" in its precise statistical meaning (Guo et al. 2021).

The five strongest earthquakes since the mid-twentieth century have happened in Kamchatka, Soviet Union, in 1952 (9.0 on the Richter scale); Valdivia, Chile, in 1960 (9.4–9.6); Prince William Sound, Alaska, in 1964 (9.2); under the Indian Ocean, near Sumatra, Indonesia, in 2004 (9.1–9.3); and under the Pacific Ocean, in the Tohoku region, near Japan, in 2011 (9.1). There seem to have been a concentration of major earthquakes in recent years. At times, the Earth seems to become more active for no clear reason.

The most damaging or costly earthquakes, in terms of property losses, in the past fifty years have been: the 2011 Tohoku earthquake in Japan, estimated to have cost Japan $235 billion; the Great Hanshin earthquake in Japan, 1995, which cost $200 billion; and the 2008 Sichuan earthquake in China, which cost an estimated $86 billion. The deadliest recent earthquakes, in terms of human life, have been that of 1976 in Tangshan, China, which was estimated to have killed up to 700,000 people; the Ningxia-Gansu earthquake, also in China, in 1920, which was estimated to have killed 273,000; and the 2004 Indian Ocean earthquake, which, with the tsunami that it caused, killed about 228,000 people in several countries and across two continents. In Messina, Italy, on December 28, 1908, a thirty-second earthquake followed by a tsunami destroyed much of the city and killed about 150,000 people. In more recent times, the Haiti earthquake of 2010 may have killed up to 316,000 people, all in a small country, making it probably the deadliest earthquake in terms of the proportion of a country's population.

When countries become richer, they generally have more expensive structures that can be destroyed by natural disasters. Therefore, the cost of earthquakes, in terms of property damage, goes up, while that in human lives generally (though not always) goes down, because of better regulations and stronger building codes, at least in more advanced countries. To some extent, the higher costs that regulations impose can be considered insurance costs, incurred because of the expectation of future earthquakes. They would not have been encountered if there had been no expectation of future earthquakes. These costs are not easy to quantify.

7.2.2 Tsunamis

When they take place under large bodies of water, such as oceans and large seas, earthquakes can cause tsunamis – movements of enormous bodies of water caused by the energy released by underground earthquakes. The waves that are created by the earthquakes can be many meters high and can move at the speed of jetliners. They can hit coastal areas with waves that, in some cases, can reach forty meters in height. When the coastal areas are highly developed and populated, tsunamis can kill thousands of people and can do enormous damage to the structures located in those coastal areas. The 1896 Sanriku earthquake in Japan caused two tsunamis, estimated to have killed 22,000 people.

The December 26, 2004 tsunami in the Indian Ocean, near Sumatra, killed some 200,000 people in several countries. The tsunami that hit Japan in 2011, with waves estimated at thirty meters high, in a highly developed area that hosted a major atomic power plant, killed many thousands of people, did great damage to structures, estimated at $235 billion, and created a serious atomic accident. It was a major and perhaps necessary warning that atomic and other dangerous structures, including oil refineries and dangerous chemical plants, should not be built where major natural accidents are more likely to happen.

The June 2020 explosion in Beirut added chemical deposits to the list of activities that should not be placed in crowded areas where accidents can happen. But then, major natural and other accidents can happen anywhere. The probability cannot be known, but it varies from place to place. We find again the hidden presence of Frank Knight's uncertainty, the cost of which can be reduced only at very high costs.

The atomic accident in Japan caused by a tsunami followed that at Three Miles Island in Pennsylvania, on the morning of March 28, 1979. That accident, fortunately, did not have major consequences; the one in Chernobyl (then in the Soviet Union, now in Ukraine), on the morning of April 28, 1986, had enormous consequences. In both cases, the uncertainty principle had played a major role and provided future warnings for the use of atomic energy to generate electricity. Those warnings reduced the enthusiasm that had existed for the use of atomic energy. We shall return, in Chapter 8, to these atomic accidents.

7.2.3 Volcanic Eruptions

Volcanic eruptions are events that can lead to many deaths and much destruction of property, as a visit to Pompeii, near Naples, can make visually and dramatically clear. They can also change an area, as a visit to Crater Lake, in Oregon, USA, shows. Crater Lake was created by a huge hole that the eruption of a volcano created several millennia ago. The hole was progressively filled by the melting of winter snow, making it into a beautiful lake. Major volcanic eruptions can also lead to important climatic changes that can last many years. They are always existential threats to some areas.

Over the years, some countries, including Indonesia, Colombia, Japan, the Philippines, and Martinique, have experienced the deadly effect of volcanic eruptions. In Indonesia, on April 10, 1815, and again on August 26, 1883, 71,000 and 36,000 people respectively were killed by the eruption of mounts Tambora and Krakatoa. The first of these events led to a "Year Without Summer" worldwide, because of the amount of ash from the eruption, which obstructed the sun for months. In Martinique, on May 7, 1902, 30,000 people were killed when Mount Pelée erupted. More recently, 23,000 perished in Colombia, in Armero.

There have been several other eruptions over historical periods that have killed thousands of people in several other countries and have led to many changes. In 1631, Vesuvius, the same volcano that had buried Pompeii and a couple of other towns in the first century AD, erupted again, killing 3,000. And part of Naples sits on the spent crater of another large volcano. Catania is very close to the often erupting Etna that is the largest volcano in Europe. The existential risks for Naples and Catania are obvious.

In the year 536 AD, the eruption of the Ilopango volcano, in what is today El Salvador, is estimated to have killed many thousands of people; by injecting a high amount of ash containing much silica into the high atmosphere, it is also believed to have led to major and long-lasting climatic changes in both America and Europe. In Central America, these climate changes may have led to the end of the Maya civilization.

Many of the years that followed climate changes would be characterized by cold and rainy weather, by food scarcity, and by plagues. They would have a major impact on the already decaying Roman Empire, whose center had moved to Constantinople (now Istanbul). The Justinian Plague of 541–542 would come a few years later, and major migration, from food-scarce areas of Germany toward richer Italy, and Rome in particular, would lead to the end of the Roman Empire and the beginning of the Middle Ages, a period that would last several centuries. That period would be characterized by deep asceticism and the growing importance of monastic life.

Some South American civilizations – those of the Maya in Central America and the Nazca in Peru – would also collapse. Toward the end of the first millennium the climatic conditions improved dramatically for a few centuries, until a new cold age arrived in the fourteenth century, also probably caused by volcanic activities in Indonesia, Iceland, and other places.

Some recent eruptions, such as that in Iceland in 2010, led to the cancellation of flights in some areas because of the volcanic ash in the air. The Iceland eruption interrupted many European flights for several days.

There are thousands of volcanoes in the world, some on land, some under the seas. Some are dormant, but can awake at any time, as did mount St. Helens in the USA some years ago. Some are semi-active, and some are continually active. They all have the potential to create serious threats and great damage to the billion of humans who are estimated to live within 150 kilometers from them. In the USA, the volcanic area of Yellowstone is a continuing potential and major threat. Its eruption could generate unimaginable damage to large parts of the USA and the rest of the world. Keeping the area where it is located as a national park can be seen as a precaution against an eruption, because it reduces the number of people that occupy the area.

In the USA, the Geological Survey (USGS) periodically assesses the threats that US volcanoes pose for the US population and infrastructures. The USA is one of the Earth's most volcanically active countries. Since 1980 it has experienced 120 volcanic eruptions. The latest survey, released on December 19, 2018, reported that there are 161 volcanoes that pose some danger to the US population and infrastructure. Eighteen of them, in Alaska, California, Hawaii, Oregon, and Washington state, pose the highest threat. Thirty-nine others pose relatively high threats. The rest pose lower levels of threats. These threats are not risks with probabilities that can be estimated.

A National Volcano Early Warning System was established in 2005 to provide some more useful or more objective measure of the hazards that volcanoes pose. The lead author of that survey reported that "more than ten percent of the world's known active and potentially active volcanoes are within US territories," and all "pose some degree of risk to peoples and infrastructure." He added that "The ranking [in the Survey] is not a list of which volcano will erupt next [and when and with what intensity]." Therefore the Early Warning System was not a measure of statistically measured risk, a measure that could be used to determine premiums by insurance companies. Uncertainty prevented that, although the survey provided a better measure of the *perception* of risk that could guide personal decisions. More risk-averse individuals could use the warning system to assist them in deciding where to live and where to build and own infrastructures.

The largest active volcano in Europe is Mount Etna, located in Sicily very close to the cities of Catania and Taormina, among others. Although continually active and often providing spectacular sights with its small eruptions, so far it has been relatively well-behaved and has not created major disasters. But of course there is no guarantee that this civilized behavior will continue in the future.

7.3 Major Atmospheric Events

Besides earthquakes, tsunamis, and volcanic eruptions, major catastrophes may be associated with atmospheric phenomena, such as cyclones (more commonly called hurricanes or typhoons), tornadoes, and other similar atmospheric phenomena. Some of these phenomena seem to have become more frequent and more powerful in recent years, perhaps because of the progressive increase in the Earth's temperature, which increases the temperature of the oceans. The sea temperature feeds the tropical storms, transforming some of them into powerful cyclones.

7.3.1 Cyclones

Cyclones are major storms in which the speed of the wind that they create can reach very high levels. In the Atlantic Ocean and in the eastern part of the Pacific, they are commonly called hurricanes, while in the Western part of the Pacific and the Indian Ocean they are called typhoons. To become hurricanes, they must generate wind speeds that exceed 74 miles per hour; otherwise they remain tropical storms.

Hurricanes are now generally classified using a scale developed by Herbert Saffir, a civil engineer, and Robert Simpson, a meteorologist, which came into use in 1974. The scale aimed at mirroring the Richter scale, used to classify the strength of earthquakes. While the Richter scale classifies earthquakes from 1 to 10, the Saffir-Simpson scale classifies hurricanes into five categories, from the weakest (category 1) to the strongest (category 5).

The categories originally took into account not only wind speed, but also the effects of storm surge and flooding, which in some hurricanes can do the most damage, as happened in the hurricane that destroyed Galveston, Texas, in 1900 (called Isaac's storm), or the one that hit New Orleans in 2005 (Katrina), with devastating property damage and the loss of many human lives. In recent years, only wind speed has been considered in the classification, so that the scale number may not necessarily indicate the full damage that a hurricane can do, which in some cases may not be generated so much by the wind, but by water surge or flooding. Also, the length of time that hurricane winds hit a given area is very important. Hurricane Dorian, category 5, for example, tormented the Bahamas for twenty-four hours.

According to the Saffir-Simpson scale, a category 3 hurricane, with wind speeds of 178–208 kilometers per hour, can do devastating damage, while a category 4 (with wind speed of 209–251 kilometers per hour) or category 5 (with wind speeds that exceed 252 kilometers per hour) can do truly catastrophic damage. The scale has been criticized by some experts as being less informative than the Richter scale for earthquakes. As in the case of earthquakes, how long the maximum level is maintained over a given area is very important.

Reliable records of tropical cyclones have been kept since 1851, but estimates of their costs are more recent. Hurricane Andrew, for example, which hit Florida in 1992, was estimated to have done $45 billion of damage. Hurricane Katrina did much damage to New Orleans and took many human lives. Hurricane Dorian, the only level 5 hurricane, so far, to have made landfall, did enormous damage to the Bahamas in 2019. Warm sea temperature, which feeds hurricanes, can rapidly increase the speed of the wind, making it reach catastrophic levels. Wind speeds of up to 215 mph have been recorded in the East and West Pacific, and speeds of up to 190 mph have been recorded in the North Atlantic. And the temperature of the sea has kept rising, making the storms progressively more powerful.

It is only a question of time when one of these monsters will land directly on a large American city, including Miami or, possibly, New York, with what could be a catastrophic impact. In both cases, the wind destruction might be complemented by the water surge, creating casualties in numbers only seen in Asian countries in the past. That surge is being facilitated by the rise in sea level, due to the higher sea temperature and the melting of glaciers. The absence of a quantifiable risk assessment, and the uncertainty of when, or even if, such an event might happen, makes many people ignore the potential danger, and feel immune to it. It also prevents the possibility of an insurance market developing for these phenomena.

In November 2020, two very strong hurricanes, called Eta and Iota, Categories 3 and 4, respectively, came ashore, only a few miles apart and within a few days, in Nicaragua and Honduras. They hit very poor areas of those countries. A bulletin by the Latin American Program at the Wilson Center, Washington, DC, on December 2, 2020, estimated that the hurricanes had done damage to homes, infrastructure, and crops in Honduras that amounted to $10 billion, or the full national budget for 2021. The bulletin referred to the increasing impact of global warming on these countries. More than three million people in Central America had been affected by these storms. At about the same time, two other strong hurricanes hit Louisiana, also within a few days of each other; and major typhoons hit the Philippines.

The warming oceans created more strong cyclones in 2020 than in earlier years. Some of them had been accompanied by major water surges, some as high as six meters, and by seventy-six centimeters of rainfall. Statistically, the number of cyclones in 2020 was so high as to be off the charts. The hope is that this was a statistical aberration, and not a new trend. But, for sure, these events are becoming less rare and more worrisome. More powerful satellites, using artificial intelligence, are being developed, especially in Europe, to help with predictions. In future years they will make possible better weather predictions that may save lives.

Cyclones have at times led to great loss of life. The Bhola cyclone, in what is now Bangladesh, was estimated to have killed more than a half million people in 1970. The Super Typhoon Nina, in China, which, on August 7, 1975, contributed to the breaking of a major dam, killed an estimated 229,000. On April 29, 1991, another Bangladesh cyclone killed close to 140,000 people. The cyclone Nargis, in Myanmar, on May 2, 2008, killed 138,000 people. The November 14, 1977 Andhra Pradesh cyclone in India may have killed up to 50,000 people. These statistics convey some idea of the destructive power of these natural events. And the sea level is still rising, putting low areas in many countries in greater danger.

The warming of the sea and the rising of its level in recent years does not augur well for the future. And Asia may not have a monopoly on these catastrophic events. Even though the probability may be lower, these catastrophes might one day happen on the American continent. Cities such as Rio de Janeiro, Miami, New York, and others might be hit. Europe seems less exposed to these catastrophes, but it is not completely immune to them. There were some major storms in the Mediterranean Sea in 2020 that caused significant damage.

Specific, smaller areas can be hit also by tornadoes, which may destroy much property and kill many people in the areas hit. Tornadoes are unpredictable events. They can hit almost anywhere, but are much more common in some specific areas, such as Oklahoma, Missouri, and Mississippi in the USA. The people who live in those areas generally have little time to take refuge in shelters – where these are available and where they offer the needed protection. The power of tornadoes is terrifying and generally the warning time to seek protection is very limited. These events change the conditions of specific places and the lives of the people who live there. However, the damage is limited to specific areas.

Major tornadoes, which at times have killed up to a thousand people, have been experienced in Bangladesh, the United States, Russia, and even areas of the Mediterranean Sea. An obvious message is that major dams, atomic power plants, and other potentially dangerous activities should not be placed in areas that could be subject to tornadoes.

7.4 Major Floods

Since the Universal Flood in the Bible, floods have been calamities that at times have caused many deaths and much destruction. They often accompany major storms, but they may also be generated by heavy rain sustained over a long period of time within an area. Occasionally, they can be also created by the rupture of dams or, in coastal areas, by the water surge created by hurricanes that can raise the level of the sea or of rivers.

As is true for other disasters, China seems to have suffered more than its fair shares of disasters created by major floods. Floods in July 1931 are estimated to have generated casualties ranging between 500,000 and four million. Another flood of the Yangtze River in 1935 was responsible for 145,000 deaths; and a 1938 Yellow River flood caused at least half a million deaths. Other floods, in Manchuria in 1951, in the Yangtze region in 1954, and in Sichuan in 1989, generated many casualties. In more recent years, floods have continued to happen, but with less disastrous results.

Besides China, several other countries have lost many people to major floods. From September 28 to October 14, 1949, Guatemala suffered 40,000 casualties in a major flood. North Vietnam in 1971 lost an estimated 100,000 to floods in Hanoi and the Red River Delta. Other countries, such as Japan, Afghanistan, and Bangladesh, have also occasionally suffered major casualties because of floods. Most countries are affected by floods, but some are affected by major ones, those that create many casualties and much damage.

7.5 Wildfires, Heatwaves, and Landslides

Wildfires and heatwaves generally are not expected to generate major human casualties, because they are slow-moving events that often take place in less populated areas, especially in the case of wildfires. The people who live in those areas often have time to escape to safer areas, which is not the case, for example, during earthquakes, tsunamis, and floods. However, wildfires may produce major losses to housing and other structures located in the areas affected by them, as they have done in the west of the USA, especially in California, and in Australia recently, where huge areas have been destroyed.

Wildfires can occasionally generate a not insignificant number of deaths. For example, on October 8, 1871, a fire in Wisconsin was estimated to have killed as many as 2,000 people. Wildfires can be generated by natural causes, such as lightning, and perhaps more frequently today, by human actions that may lead to unintentional fires, such as throwing away a lighted cigarette in a forest or leaving a fire unattended. Another accident happened in some recent California fires, when electrical wires came into contact with very dry flammable bushes.

Because of the higher temperatures and dry conditions that have characterized some areas of the world in recent years, some regions have experienced fires of biblical dimensions. The most affected regions have been some areas in Australia, a continent that is becoming progressively dryer; the western part of the United States; the Amazon region in Brazil; and in Russian Siberia. The Australian fires that destroyed immense areas also significantly impacted the fauna of that country, killing many rare animals. Brazilian forest fires are often intentionally set by individuals who want to transform, often illegally, pristine forests into agricultural lands, or who wish to exploit natural resources that are located in the forests. These actions also deprive indigenous populations of their traditional ways of life, and deprive the world of the cooling effect that forests have on the world temperature.

The progressive deforestation of the Amazon and of other major forests in the Congo and in Borneo, forests that are considered important *lungs* for the world, because they capture carbon from the air, has become a major international concern, because of the role that they play in maintaining the Earth's ecological balance. This is one aspect, among a growing number of others, where world interests and national interests may not always go in the same direction, and where laissez-faire is not a good alternative, at least from the point of view of the world as a whole. The economic interests of specific countries and those of the world may not always point in the same direction. Alaska and the Arctic region is another such area that has been attracting the attention of private interests, because of the potential in mineral resources.

International collaboration must play a role in protecting these areas, but that collaboration often runs against powerful national or subnational interests. And nationwide interests often collide: against the interest of specific regions where the resources are located, against specific industries, and against specific groups. Protecting the purity of the environment often takes a back seat to the short-run generation of profits and jobs. At times, weak governance and corruption play important roles in allowing damaging activities.

Heatwaves have not been events that have attracted much thought in the past. However, in recent years, and in particular regions, conditions have been created that have led to truly biblical heatwaves. Some have caused the deaths of a surprisingly large number of people. What is extraordinary is that heatwaves have happened even in countries such as Russia, where one would not have expected them to occur. The new millennium has been accompanied by the highest average temperatures on record, especially in some areas. In 2010, a heatwave killed 56,000 Russians. Another in 2003 killed 70,000 people in various parts of Europe. Other heatwaves killed thousands in 2006, in Europe; and, in 2015, thousands more died in India and Japan.

When the Antarctic region experiences temperatures that can reach 21 degrees Celsius, and Siberia can experience 32 degrees Celsius, damaging heatwaves should no longer be a surprise. Like black swans, which were not supposed to exist, they have entered the realm of possibilities in the modern world. Both Antarctica and Siberia have experienced increases in average temperature of about 5 degrees Celsius in recent decades.

Finally, to complete the picture, disastrous events connected with landslides must be mentioned. In some cases, these have led to a surprising number of casualties, as, for example, in Venezuela in 1999, where a landslide was reported to have killed about 20,000 people. Some of these may be triggered by earthquakes, as in central Italy on August 24, 2016, when the small town of Matriciana was destroyed and 299 people were killed. Some are caused by sustained rain. Some landslides come in the form of avalanches, crashing down on unexpected areas, where people have lived for a long time, not expecting the danger. In some cases, in countries such as China, Peru, Venezuela, Tajikistan, and even Italy, they have led to thousands of casualties.

Once again, these disasters were not anticipated, and not being anticipated, they had not been preceded by the necessary precautions, or actions, on the part of governments, or even individuals, in relation to where to operate or build. More stringent regulations or better infrastructure might have reduced their impact. In the USA, FEMA was created by the federal government to provide some assistance to people after disasters. Again, we find the *uncertainty principle*, combined with some irrationality on the part of individuals, extracting its price in terms of human lives and property values.

8 ATOMIC DISASTERS

8.1 The Allure of Cheap Atomic Energy

While in the past most of the major disasters had had natural causes, except those due to wars and possibly some due to famines, in more recent centuries, and especially in the twentieth century, new kinds of disasters, which were nonexistent in the past, made their unwelcome appearance. Some important ones were created by the newly used atomic energy, a source of energy that had not been known in the past. Some were due to the increase in potentially dangerous industrial activities, with chemical plants, oil-refining plants, and chemical deposits located near or in cities; while others were caused by the transportation of dangerous substances through crowded cities, or their storage in populated areas.

Back in 1903, the physicist Ernest Rutherford had theorized that one day it might be possible to generate electric energy from sustained nuclear fission, which would generate heat that could heat water to generate steam, which, in turn, would drive a steam engine that would generate mechanical energy, which, in turn, would be converted into electricity. While the first major use of atomic power was destructive, the bombing of Hiroshima and Nagasaki in 1945, immediately after those events the possibility of its use to generate peaceful energy was advocated. In time, atomic energy plants would come into existence. The plants were expensive to build, but the operational costs of atomic plants, once built, were generally low – ignoring the cost of disposing of the atomic waste produced, which remained radioactive for a very long time, and uranium was abundant in the world.

From the very beginning when atomic reaction was discovered, the possibility of its use for various, peaceful purposes had been considered by experts. Besides various medical devices and similar applications, some scientists hoped that energy from the atoms could not only be a source of destruction in war, but that it could, in time, supply unlimited, cheap, clean electric energy to a world that was in great and growing need of it:

> On October 3, 1945, [two months after the bombing of Hiroshima and Nagasaki], in an address to Congress, President Truman had promoted "directing and encouraging the use of atomic energy … toward peaceful and humanitarian ends. (Segrè and Hoerlin 2016, pp. 230–251)

Experts from some private enterprises, such as Du Pont and Monsanto, who had been involved in the first nuclear chain reaction at the University of Chicago, or in the Manhattan Project, at Los Alamos, anticipated the possible future civilian use of atomic energy (Segrè and Hoerlin 2016, p. 256). The atomic bombing of Hiroshima and Nagasaki in 1945 (Wallace 2020) was followed by an extensive cover-up to hide or minimize the human costs of the bombs and the long-run dangers of atomic radiation. Lieutenant General Leslie Groves, who had directed the Manhattan Project at Los Alamos, was reported to declare that dying from radiation was "a very pleasant way to die" (Blume 2020, p. 4).

Atomic energy sources could make it possible to replace coal, petroleum, and gas, which are expensive to produce and are limited energy sources. The use of these sources also started creating significant environmental problems for the world, including the progressive warming of the Earth. Some scientific experts, industry advocates, and others from think tanks such as the Cato Institute in Washington, DC, have continued to sponsor the civilian use of atomic energy as a potentially attractive, cheap, and unlimited solution to the environmental problems that are created by the use of dirty fuels. In their view, global warming could be eliminated at low cost if enough atomic power plants were built around the world. The availability of cheap atomic energy would eliminate, or reduce, the current use of oil and coal for creating energy.

At the moment there are close to 500 atomic power plants in use in the world, some in advanced countries and others, increasingly, in less advanced and less technologically sophisticated countries. Another and more recent alternative proposed solution to those problems, which has been attracting a lot of attention, and the use of which has been rapidly increasing, is so-called *green energy*, energy derived from the sun, the wind, and, possibly, from sea waves and thermal sources, deep in the earth. The cost of using some of these alternative sources has been falling rapidly over the years, making them more economically attractive.

The first time that energy was produced, experimentally and on a very small scale by a nuclear reaction, was on September 3, 1948, at Oak Ridge, in Tennessee, USA. The second time, on a larger scale, was on December 20, 1951, at an experimental station near Arco, Idaho, USA. The first use of atomic power to generate electricity for a power grid came at the Obninsk nuclear plant in the Soviet Union in 1954. The first full-scale atomic plant opened to generate electricity was on October 17, 1956 at Calder Hall, England. In October 1957, the United Kingdom would experience one of the first significant nuclear disasters, when the Windscale fire released a significant amount of radioactive contamination in the area around Windscale.

In those years, the possibility of using the atom to generate electricity had been attracting much attention due to the work of scientists in the USA. "For example at Los Alamos [Richard Feynman] had invented a type of fast reactor for generating electric power". He had also believed "that interplanetary travel [was] now a definite possibility [with the use of atomic energy]" (Gleick 1992, p. 218). A relatively serious atomic accident that generated several deaths in 1957 in Ozyorsk, in the Soviet Union, was not reported at the time and remained secret until much later.

In the 1960s, atomic power plants started to be built in several countries, initially in countries that were technically advanced, such as the Soviet Union, the USA, the UK, France, Japan, Italy, and Switzerland. In Russia, by 1964, two such plants had come into existence. With the passing of time, atomic power plants started to be built in less technologically advanced countries, often with foreign technical assistance and direction. Generally, atomic power plants are costly to build, but cheap to run. Furthermore, the uranium needed to run them is abundant on Earth.

From the very beginning there were some accidents in these plants that were considered "minor." However, they were often important enough to have to be reported to the International Atomic Energy Agency, located in Vienna, which had been created to supervise the use of atomic energy for peaceful purposes. Some of these accidents occasionally killed some of the workers in the atomic plants, and some created minor environmental problems. However, it was argued by those who supported these activities that accidents happen in many economic activities, and not just in atomic power plants. They happen especially in plants that generate electric power, or that produce coal, petroleum, and gas. Minor accidents are a normal and unavoidable result of many modern industrial activities and they must be accepted as a necessary cost for making possible a decent, modern, standard of living. Therefore, the accidents reported in the nuclear plants were not seen as sufficient justification to slow down the creation of new atomic plants, or to reduce the number of existing plants. Modern economies have great and growing needs for energy, and these plants could deliver it more cheaply. Therefore, new plants continued to be created.

A problem that did attract some attention over the years was what to do with the residuals of the uranium used. Like human beings, atomic power plants generate residuals and these continue to be radioactive for a very long time. They cannot be disposed of, or stored, just anywhere. Isolated places had to be found, at times deep into mountains, or in other faraway places, where they could do no harm to humans or to the environment. As the amount of radioactive residuals increased with the years, so did the difficulties of finding places where they could be safely stored. It was an open question whether different countries were following similarly rigorous standards for doing so. A prevalent view was that the Soviet Union and, later, China, were less concerned than other countries with the issues of safety and potential environmental degradation.

The International Atomic Energy Agency defines nuclear accidents as events "that have led to *significant* consequences to people, the environment, or the facility" (italics added). These *significant* accidents can be caused, and most are caused, by human error. They can also be caused by the malfunctioning of some of the many parts that go into the complex atomic plant. In some cases, they can also be caused by external events that can impact a power plant directly or indirectly. These could be earthquakes, tsunamis, tornadoes, or others. They could also be created by terrorist activities or by saboteurs, perhaps using hacking techniques, as was reported to have happened in an Iranian plant in recent years. The unexpected combination of different events can at times lead to "perfect storms."

Any of the above causes can lead to either *minor* or *major* accidents. While the major accidents have been few and are the ones that have attracted much attention, it is less known that there have been literally hundreds of what have been considered "minor" accidents in atomic power plants over the years. These "minor" accidents were significant enough to have been reported to the International Atomic Energy Agency. Many of them have killed people and many have created some environmental contamination. Some of these could have easily become major accidents and some may not have been as minor as they were reported to be.

In the next sections we shall describe three major accidents that, because of their scope, had a strong "announcement effect" on the international community. Over the years they led to a progressive and significant reduction in the initial enthusiasm that had welcomed the introduction of peaceful, atomic energy. It made some countries resist the allure of cheap atomic energy. It is interesting to note that the three accidents happened in three countries that were assumed to be highly sophisticated in the use of atomic power: the United States, the Soviet Union, and Japan, in that order. Each accident resulted from a different cause, and each conveyed a different warning message to the world.

8.2 The Three Mile Island Accident

On March 28, 1979, at 6.00 a.m., an atomic reactor located at Three Mile Island in Pennsylvania, only 90 miles from Washington, DC, came close to a "critical meltdown." "The unexpected line up of a feed water cut off, a valve failure, and a control room miscalculation quickly escalated into the nearest thing to a nuclear disaster" (Gray and Rosen 2003, Preface). This accident could have been a disastrous event that, under certain atmospheric conditions, could have contaminated the nation's capital with lethal radiation. It led to the voluntary evacuation of about 149,000 people from the area. The seriousness of this accident was rated 5 on a scale of 1 to 7. The later accidents in Ukraine and in Japan would both be rated 7.

At that time, the author of this book was acquainted with one of the commissioners of the Nuclear Regulatory Commission, the US federal agency that supervises atomic plants in the USA. The commissioner was a brilliant scientist, with very strong, relevant academic credentials. In a casual conversation, a few weeks after the incident when the danger was over, he commented that what had scared him the most, during the episode, was the realization that there were no experts anywhere in the world who knew the whole power plant. All the experts that the Commission had consulted, at the time of the accident, were experts on only parts of the plant. The plant had become too complex for any human being to fully understand all the possible interactions of the many parts, in order to anticipate what could go wrong. Complexity had created an extreme version of Frank Knight's uncertainty, and had eliminated the possibility that one might comprehend the full system and be considered fully competent to deal with all of its ramifications. This complexity would play a major role in the Chernobyl accident in 1986.

The Three Mile Island accident was not the result of mistakes or of incompetence on the part of those supervising the plant. The accident pointed to a more fundamental problem more difficult to solve. It was the result of too much complexity that creates situations in both technological developments as well as in social institutions, including tax systems and government programs, that may become too difficult to control, and too difficult to fully anticipate their future functioning. From different perspectives, several experts, including archeologists, historians, and economists, have stressed the difficulties created by complexity (for example, Tainter 1988; Arthur 2015; Tanzi 2020b). Things can spin out of control in different ways in complex societies. They can also spin out of control in complex technological systems, such as atomic power plants, or machines to go into space. It should be added that there have been major incidents in atomic submarines, in satellites, and even in advanced airplanes – for example, the two Boeing 737 accidents in 2018 and the role that complexity played. All the above had used complex and difficult-to-understand machines.

The strong warning sent by the Three Mile Island incident was that, regardless of the ability of those who design atomic plants, and regardless of the training of those who run them, catastrophic incidents could happen and could be expected at some future time, especially if atomic power plants became numerous, and if, in addition to problems that could arise from their complexity, there were other factors, such as design faults, incompetence, sabotage, and natural events, that could lead to disasters.

Interestingly, the Three Mile Island incident contributed to an article published by two prominent Russian scientists, Nikolai Dollezhal and Ju. I. Koriakin, a few months after the accident, in the summer of 1979, in the Russian journal *Kommunist*. The article was entitled "Nuclear Energy: Achievements and Problems" (cited in Plokhy 2018, p. 49). They pointed out that in the USA the cost of building atomic reactors had increased several times, because of safety concerns, while this had not happened in the Soviet Union. They expressed concern about safety in Soviet plants and also about the transportation of nuclear fuel and waste within the Soviet Union. The increase in the number of atomic plants would inevitably lead to greater dangers. The article suggested that such plants should be located in far-flung places, in Siberia, and preferably near uranium deposits, and not in the European part of the Soviet Union. However, Soviet authorities considered it advantageous to build atomic plants not in isolated locations, but close to areas that needed electricity, as was the Chernobyl plant, near the large city of Kyiv.

Not surprisingly, the article was criticized by a leading Soviet nuclear expert and advocate of nuclear energy, Anatolii Alexandrov, who stressed that Soviet plants were very safe – in fact, so safe that one could be located on Red Square near the Kremlin (cited in Plokhy 2018, pp. 16–17). Alexandrov would keep pushing for the building of more atomic plants throughout the Soviet Union.

In the pages that follow, we shall describe two major atomic disasters that had more tragic consequences than the one at Three Mile Island. In at least one of them, factors besides complexity played major roles. This was the Chernobyl tragedy in Ukraine, in 1986, at a time when Ukraine was part of the Soviet Union. It is not clear if technical incompetence, during an important test, may have been a significant factor leading to this accident. But a major defect in the design of the atomic reactor was a more likely cause.

In the Fukushima disaster, in Japan, a natural, uncontrollable event, a tsunami, caused by another uncontrollable event, a major earthquake, led to an atomic disaster that had not been expected to happen. Such unexpected factors could, of course, play roles in future tragedies in other atomic plants around the world. Such atomic accidents lead to many deaths and to enormous economic damages. Some could have been even worse in the past and they could be worse still in the future.

The reported incidents sent a strong message to the world, and to the atomic energy industry, about the possible costs in human life and property of using atomic energy. Hopefully, that message was fully received by all countries that use atomic energy, or that plan to use it in the future. Clearly, the more atomic power plants there are in the world, the greater are the chances that at some point something will go unexpectedly and terribly wrong in some of them. At Chernobyl, Ukraine, and at Fukuyama, Japan, we would get some evidence of what could go wrong.

8.3 The Chernobyl Tragedy

The Chernobyl disaster took place on the night of April 26, 1986 and it released radiation equivalent to 500 Hiroshima bombs. By any standards, it would be considered an enormous disaster. It was partly the consequence of the faulty design of the power plant, and partly due to pressures by the Soviet government in Moscow, specifically conveyed by Gorbachev, then head of the Communist Party, during a long speech that he had given at the March 6, 1986 Plenary Congress of the Soviet Communist Party. That congress had taken place a few weeks before the Chernobyl accident. (See Plokhy 2018 for a painstaking, authoritative and detailed account of the history of the tragedy.)

Gorbachev's speech had called attention to the poor performance of the Soviet economy in the previous five-year plan. That admission by Gorbachev was rare at these congresses, which generally stressed positive past achievements and hid failures. Gorbachev had stressed that to reverse that poor past performance, it would be necessary in the next five-year plan to push the technological frontier, in which he assumed the Soviet Union had a comparative advantage. That push would provide a needed jolt to the Soviet economy.

He specifically mentioned the introduction of new technologies, and especially a shift from using fossil fuels, such as coal, oil, and gas, that were costly to produce and could be exported, earning needed foreign exchange, toward cheap energy, generated by atomic power, in which the Soviet Union was a leader. Gorbachev added that "in the current Five Year Plan atomic energy stations two and a half times more powerful than those in the previous Five Year Plan will come on line." These larger plants would replace "en masse" existing obsolete units (Plokhy 2018, p. 14). Gorbachev "had set the goal of more than doubling the construction of nuclear units in the course of the next Five Year Plan" (ibid., p. 39).

Gorbachev's speech had been followed by one delivered by Anatolii Alexandrov, who was the influential and powerful President of the Soviet Academy of Science, and who also headed the Institute of Nuclear Energy. The choice of Alexandrov as the second speaker, immediately after Gorbachev, emphasized the importance that atomic energy was expected to play in the Soviet Union in the next five-year plan. Alexandrov had played an important role in developing the first plants to produce atomic energy, those that would be replaced by more powerful ones. He had so much confidence in the safety of those plants that he stated that he would not hesitate to place one of them in the middle of Red Square, Moscow. The Chernobyl plant was one of these presumably safe plants. It would have to play a major role in the new planned Soviet strategy regarding energy. The Chernobyl plant was then the third most powerful nuclear power station in the whole world, and it was considered a jewel of the Soviet nuclear industry.

Among the 5,000 party members who had been listening to Gorbachev's and Alexandrov's speeches was the manager of the Chernobyl power plant, Briukhanov. He was a dedicated and serious bureaucrat and also a qualified and conscientious engineer, though his specialization was not atomic energy. Being a dedicated bureaucrat, he must have taken Gorbachev's announcement as a firm command for him and his colleagues at the plant to play their part in the promised technological push to the economy.

The Chernobyl plant was in a town in Ukraine of about 50,000 people. The town was called Pryplat, the same name as the river that went by it, and was some 150 kilometers from Kyiv, a major city. Pryplat was, in many ways, a privileged and good town to live in, because of the important atomic plant that it hosted, which gave it prestige. The town largely owed its very existence to the plant. Its inhabitants had access to many goods and services that were not available or were hard to get for most Soviet citizens. To maintain that privilege, the atomic plant had to continue to deliver, especially because of delays that had occurred in preceding years in the construction of a fifth unit for the plant. This delay had led to some not completely fair criticism of the construction manager, Kyzyma, from political higher-ups.

The pressure to deliver more energy had increased in January 1986, when Soviet Prime Minister Ryzhkov had warned that delay in delivering additional atomic energy would not be tolerated. It was a time when "everyone wanted to go nuclear," and the pressure on existing plant managers to increase production had become enormous.

Inevitably, shortcuts started to be taken, to satisfy the planned energy increase. For example, to accommodate the timing in the introduction of the new, more powerful plants, design and construction of these would need to take place at the same time. This change would reduce the time needed to build a new plant from seven to five years. But inevitably it might increase the probability of making mistakes in the plants' design. Also the cost of production of new atomic plants played a significant role. As an important, economic incentive, a new and cheaper design would replace what had probably been more expensive but safer ones.

In spite of concerns felt, but rarely openly expressed, by plant managers, about the speed of the proposed change, which was not considered prudent or, perhaps, even possible, orders came from above, and plant managers had no choice but to try to accommodate those orders as best as they could, whatever it took. Gorbachev's vision of relying on technology to accelerate the economic development of the Soviet Union, at an internationally difficult time for the Union, with atomically generated energy, had been endorsed by the 5,000 members of the Communist Party at the congress. The order became the inflexible rule of the day.

Construction on the Chernobyl plant had started in the summer of 1970, in a not too fertile land and in an unpopulated forest area in Ukraine. It was an area crossed by the River Pryplat. The water of that river would be needed to cool the nuclear reactor. The river gave its name to the sizeable town that would come into existence because of the plant. A huge amount of soil would need to be removed from the site of the plant, to create a foundation solid enough for the heavy mass of the atomic plant. The building of the plant took longer than had been expected, because of difficulties in getting some of the needed parts from vendors, and it ran into several difficulties from the beginning. It was not until December 1977 that the first reactor had become operational. The director of the plant, who was a different individual from the director of construction, would define 1977 as "the year of the birth of an energy giant on the Pryplat."

Three other units of the plant were added between December 1977 and December 1983, also with delays and considerable problems. Incompetence in construction and delays in completion were normal in the Soviet Union, and the quality of the work often left much to be desired. However, Gorbachev's five-year plan, in 1986, had to be fulfilled in the best possible way. This would create strong incentives to push under the rug problems that arose, in order to meet the promises for energy production in the five-year plan. One consequence was that quality and security were bound to suffer.

The construction of Unit 5 to be added to the Chernobyl plant's four existing units created particular problems because "the time frame had been cut from three years to two" (Plokhy 2018, p. 43). Furthermore, qualified personnel, needed equipment, and supplies were often lacking, and this created further delays. At Chernobyl the construction crews had been available, but the needed supplies often were not. The delay in the design documentation of the unit, until July 1985, had forced postponement of some of the orders for the materials and equipment needed. While some equipment had arrived in time, other essential equipment had not. Furthermore, a great deal of the hardware received was defective. For example, the metal structure for the reservoir that would store the used nuclear fuel had major defects; and the concrete panels were of the wrong size and had to be adjusted. Nevertheless, those who were charged with the construction at the plant were the ones reprimanded for the delays. At times, they were threatened with firing, if the delay were not made up in short periods. At times, this was impossible. Even in socialist economies, in spite of five-year plans, miracles did not happen.

An unauthorized newspaper article, published in the March 21, 1986 issue of *Tribuna Energetika*, written by a female journalist, had reported on some of these problems at the plant. The KGB, which oversaw the safety of what was still considered a secret technology, and the safety of the operation, had also reported on some design and construction problems. However, it was mainly the construction crew and the willingness of the manager at the plant to approve some shabby work that received much of the criticism. In any case, until March 1986, there had not been any *major* accident at the plant that could be attributed directly to construction problems.

An all-Union conference was held in Chernobyl in March 1986, attended by vendors of parts of atomic plants. The conference had gone well, and safety concerns had been minimized by those attending. The Chernobyl plant director, Briukhanov, had been away during that conference, because he had been attending the Communist Party Congress in Moscow, where Gorbachev had made his speech. For some time he had been worried about the leaking of radioactivity in some of the plant's units. The leaks had been coming from the drainage channels and from the air vents. The steam extraction units seemed to have reached the limits of their capacity, and "[t]he only effective way to deal with the problem was to stop the reactors and carry out the repairs, but that would jeopardize the fulfillment of the annual plan of electricity production" (Plokhy 2018, p. 54).

Briukhanov was faced with a classic, but not rare, dilemma. It is the dilemma at times created by uncertain alternatives with different potential, but unknown costs. In his case, there was on one hand, (a) the *likely* reprimand and criticism that he would receive from the top party officials, and perhaps even a demotion, or firing, from his prestigious position, if he stopped the plant. On the other hand, (b) there was the *uncertain* possibility of an accident happening at the plant. Until that time there had not been any serious accidents at the plant, and hopefully there might not be any in the foreseeable future. Therefore, why not hope for the best, ignore the leaks, and keep the plant operating to keep the authorities happy?

At times, the cost–benefit evaluation of a situation makes one choose what seems to be the short-run, easier alternative. This seems a normal, human, and perhaps even rational reaction. The easier alternative was to keep the plant working and to keep generating the much-needed electricity. In the meantime, Briukhanov might explore the possibility of getting some less stressful job abroad, and let someone else worry about what to do with the leaks.

At the same time, concerns about the problems encountered in completing Unit 5 of the plant reached the same journalist who had written the earlier article. Those concerns were reported in an article published in Kyiv, in *Literaturna Ukraina*. The article reported on major problems that were being faced by the construction crew at the Chernobyl power station. It mentioned that some badly needed construction materials had never arrived, and that some materials that had arrived were defective. The point of the article was that the problems experienced at the plant were not due to incompetence or laziness on the part of those who ran the construction at the plant. There had been no formal reaction to the article, which was ignored. The writer was simply considered a troublemaker, of whom there were some in the Soviet Union.

On Friday April 25, 1986, things started changing. The weather had improved a lot, the temperature had reached 70 °F, and the people of Pryplat, including the manager at the atomic plant, were looking forward to a pleasant weekend. That weekend would include picnics, for some, fishing, for others, and planting potatoes on small lots, for still others. Radioactive leaks at the Chernobyl plant had continued occurring, but they had seemed manageable. The plant was still working on schedule and was delivering the needed energy. "With an average of five minor technological accidents and equipment malfunctions per year," "the [Chernobyl] plant was considered one of the best in the industry" (Plokhy 2018, p. 63). In the previous year, the plant had exceeded by 10 percent the energy production quota for the year, and it had received praise for that result.

Because of previously scheduled plant repairs in the following months, repairs that might take several months to complete, the plant energy output for 1986 would inevitably fall, making the local authorities unhappy, at a time when more energy was badly needed. The newly appointed All Union Minister of Energy, Maiorets, was determined to significantly reduce the time that plants needed for repairs. Unit 4 at the Chernobyl plant was scheduled to shut down in April. Following the minister's orders, it was to be shut for the shortest time possible.

During the shutdown, various essential systems of the plant would be checked. One important test would be carried out *before* the shutdown. It concerned the plant's steam turbine. The test aimed at making the reactor more secure, by making the electricity go off in case of an emergency, while emergency diesel generators would take over during the shutdown, to provide the needed electricity that would allow the continuing pumping of water that was needed to cool the reactor. The problem was that there was a forty-five-second interval between the time when the electricity was shut down and the time when the generators would start working. This created a potentially serious danger.

A *theoretical solution* to the complex problem at the plant had been suggested by some engineers at a research institution in the Ukrainian city of Donetsk. The solution depended on the steam turbine generator functioning properly and continuing to generate steam for some time after the electricity had been cut off. "Energy produced by the continuing rotation of the turbine could be used to produce enough electricity for the forty-five-second gap" (Plokhy 2018, p. 64). "The shutting down of Plant Four could provide a test of whether the suggested, theoretical solution was correct. But to conduct the test, the automatic shutdown mechanism would have to be disabled to simulate a power failure and the blackout of the plant. There was a risk that the reactor might go out of control during the test itself" (ibid.). However, this risk was considered minor by the experts.

This was a classic example in which *theoretical and untested* solutions were applied to not fully understood systems or situations. It was not a case of incompetence, but simply one in which humans were faced by complexity that created uncertainty, and uncertainty created risks that could not be measured. There is also a tendency to put trust in those who are supposed to know more. Those in charge of the tests at Chernobyl were highly trained engineers. The problem that they would encounter was that reactors, like humans, at times, do not behave as expected. It was a situation similar to that faced when a car, unexpectedly, keeps accelerating, regardless of the action of the driver.

A few years earlier, a reactor near Leningrad had had such an experience, during a test similar to the one that would be tried at Chernobyl. The problem that had occurred in Leningrad had not been fully understood and it had led to some minor changes to reactors, including Unit 4 at Chernobyl. One is reminded here of the experience encountered by the engineers at Boeing, who had tested the Boeing 737 MAX.

The test was planned for April 24 at 10 p.m. Control rods would be inserted into the core of the reactor to reduce the intensity of the nuclear reaction. Some rods were kept available for possible later use, if needed. However, the number of rods available had not been considered important by the experts conducting the test, when the system of emergency water supply to the reactor had been disabled, around 2 p.m. A related factor was a failure in another power plant in Ukraine that provided electricity to Kyiv. At that time, there had been a request that the Chernobyl plant delay, until the evening, the shutting down of the Chernobyl reactor, in order not to reduce electricity for Kyiv.

What followed, during the complex test of shutting down one of the reactors, was a sequence of (a) conflicting instructions; (b) unclear guidelines for some of the personnel on what to do; (c) the unavailability of some needed individuals who could not be reached when needed; and (d) simply confusion among the twenty people involved in the test. These factors led to delays in some decisions and to mistakes in others. It was not a question of clear incompetence, because the individuals involved were, for the large part, highly trained and competent individuals. Rather, it was one of those situations typically created by new and complex problems. It was a situation created at times by different understanding among the actors on what needed to be done. There were reportedly 4,000 indicators that needed to be monitored during the operation. The time for the test was stretched well beyond the two hours that had been expected. Complexity, confusion, and, what later turned out to have been some mistakes, came together to lead to what would be a perfect storm and a monumental tragedy.

The process of shutting down the reactor by inserting the rods was continued, but if the reactor were completely shut down, the test of the turbine, which had been planned for a long time, would have to be abandoned. There was some disagreement as to how much the power level could be reduced without danger. Soon, several critical indicators started to move in the wrong direction. What happened next is described in dramatic fashion by Plokhy (2018), in a chapter entitled "Explosion." After the test (which had lasted thirty-six seconds) was completed, the power level of the reactor went out of control and the power kept rising. An emergency button, which should have shut down the reactor, was pushed, but the power output of the reactor still kept rising. There seemed to be nothing to slow down the reactor. There was a large increase in hot steam and there was no place for it to go.

There was, first, a strange roar from the plant, which was followed by a big explosion that threw the roof of Unit 4 into the air. The roof landed on top of the reactor, without, however, sealing it. Radiation could and did escape on a large scale. "[The] panoply of safety systems [in the plant] had been considered idiot-proof [by the experts who had designed it]. No textbook that [they] had read [had] suggested that reactors could explode." At first, "they thought that there had been a earthquake. It took them a while to realize that it was a man-made earthquake" (Plokhy 2018, p. 85). A large amount of radioactivity was sent into the air. It would spread over a large area and would even reach Scandinavian countries. This would likely become the biggest, peacetime, manmade disaster in the history of the world.

The repercussions of this disaster would be wide, but at the beginning no one knew just how bad the situation was. The minutes or hours after the explosion would create situations for those living through it that would make Dante's Inferno look like a nice place. Confusion, sheer terror, physical pain from burns, nausea and vomiting due to exposure to radioactive poisoning, would combine to create a level of hell for those who lived through it that perhaps nobody had ever experienced before, with the possible exception of the victims of the atomic bombing of Hiroshima and Nagasaki in 1945.

In spite of the often heroic behavior by many during the emergency, some of the plant employees would later suffer from guilty feelings for what had happened. Why did this happen when they had done everything the way it was supposed to be done by the experts who had considered the plant safe? Had they made mistakes? What had they done wrong? The idea that the problem was not their performance, but that of a technology that was not well-understood, and that had become too complex to be fully understood and controlled, was difficult for many to accept. Some of them would die a few days later, carrying with them that feeling of personal guilt for what they might have caused.

After the explosion, radiation around the plant, and soon in the city nearby, reached very high levels, and some were so high that they could not be registered by the available measuring instruments. The idea of evacuating the city started to be contemplated, but was at first dismissed as being guided more by panic than by necessity. Some party officials argued that the radiation levels were still too low to justify evacuation, and wanted to wait for party officials to visit the city to make a decision. In the kind of hierarchical society that existed in the Soviet Union, important decisions were made by those higher up who had the power to make them, and not necessarily by those who had the information. In turn, those who had the power were often reluctant to make decisions that they might later regret for having made, or that might turn out to have been the wrong ones. This often led to the postponement of some urgent decisions, and to the attempt to pass the buck to someone else.

The General Secretary of the Communist Party of the Soviet Union, Mikhail Gorbachev, in the early morning of April 26, had been informed that there had been an accident at the Chernobyl atomic plant. However, he was not told about the scope of the accident. A commission was created to look into the accident. The members of the commission flew from Moscow to Pryplat. The assumption continued to be that this was just one of the many accidents that happened annually at atomic plants in the Soviet Union, and that the plant would quickly be repaired and would return to full operation.

When the members of the commission reached the plant, they soon realized that the accident was not a routine one, but was far more serious. They also immediately ran into high and dangerous radiation, but they continued to stick to their belief that atomic plants were safe and that the accident was not a major one and could be contained.

Slowly, the members of the commission came to realize how serious the situation really was, even though some of them continued to want to minimize it, both in their minds and in the announcements to be made.

The immediate concerns were about the need to evacuate the city, and the possibility of a new explosion at the plant. No city had been evacuated in the Soviet Union for any cause since World War II, and there was a desire to avoid making such a drastic decision, and to continue to believe that it might not be necessary and that the danger might be exaggerated.

A helicopter flight over the plant would convince two of the most highly trained experts of the commission, who had come from Moscow, that the situation was critical. The graphite was still burning in the turbine and it needed to be extinguished. But how to do it? The two experts realized that a meltdown had occurred at the plant and that much radioactivity was being spread from the plant to areas around it, including the town nearby. There were conflicting views on what needed to be done, or on what *could* be done at the plant.

Finally, it was concluded that the town of 50,000 people might have to be evacuated. At 9 p.m., "[t]hree powerful explosions illuminated the dark sky above Unit 4" (Plokhy 2018, p. 133). The danger for Pryplat increased, because radiation was rising fast. Yet still nobody wanted to take responsibility for ordering the evacuation of the town. Finally, between 10 and 11 p.m., the order to evacuate the town the next day came from higher up, and preparations began for buses and trains.

Many of the firefighters and other people who had been at the plant were taken to hospitals, where some efforts were made to treat them for the effects of the high radiation. Some of those more exposed were flown to Moscow, where there was more expertise on how to deal with high radiation. The question was raised about the possible danger for Kyiv, which was 130 kilometers away. Again, uncertainty continued to reign, in the presence of a very complex situation. As had happened in the past during pandemics, the unseen radiation acted in the same way as the invisible viruses, which could kill without being seen. Some people had started dying of excess radiation. Many would die later. The buses that would come to pick up the residents of the town would be exposed to radiation and would carry it to other places.

While the evacuation of the town was going on, the question of how to stabilize the atomic plant became a major preoccupation for the relevant experts. The idea of dropping bags full of sand from helicopters on the damaged reactor was contemplated. The objective was to seal the reactor, and sealing it might stop the radiation. The logistics of how to do it were studied. Various logistical problems had to be dealt with. When the dropping of sand bags from helicopters started, about 80 percent of the bags dropped missed the reactor because the hole in the roof above the reactor was small. In the operation, many of the pilots were exposed to much radiation. Some became sick and very tired days later. Some started realizing that their mission was suicidal, but they continued in the operation. The process would continue for eight days. Many of the pilots ended up in hospital and some would die.

There were questions whether the dropping of sandbags was the right strategy. Nobody truly knew what was going on inside the reactor. Could the dropping of sandbags make the situation worse? There was much uncertainty. Some tests indicated that the reactor was alive and that it could explode again at any time. Another explosion might contaminate a large part of Europe.

"It was then decided that the helicopters would drop not only sand but also clay, lead, and boron into the opening of the reactor. Sand was needed to extinguish the graphite fire, lead to lower the temperature of the burning graphite, and boron and clay to prevent a chain reaction" (Plokhy 2018, p. 163). But again, there was no certainty that this would work. Some of the experts in Moscow "were reluctant to endorse the idea," and some were convinced that there was no possibility of a chain reaction. But the possibility of a new explosion remained for some of the experts.

On the morning of April 28, Michael Gorbachev was informed that Unit 4 of the Chernobyl atomic plant needed to be buried. Huge amounts of sand and boron were dropped on the plant during many dangerous helicopter flights that put the pilots in great danger. The radiation emitted started falling and kept falling. But was this due to the airdrops? Changes in the wind direction spread the radiation that was already in the air in different directions, putting different areas in danger. A ten-kilometer zone around the plant was created, from where people would be resettled in addition to those in Pryplat, but many people were still needed in Pryplat to help with the shutdown operation.

Many of the proactive devices needed (respirators and dosimeters) were often not available and neither were medicines to deal with radiation sickness. Once again, many of those involved stoically faced the risks of becoming contaminated. An attitude similar to that of individuals who have refused to wear masks during the Covid-19 pandemic was shown by many. What you cannot see cannot kill you, and you cannot show your weakness. Some of the people in the area kept tilling their land during the emergency. All assumed that the difficulties would be temporary. But high radiation readings kept moving further away from the plant and approached Kyiv, where radiation soon reached high levels. It became clear that the emergency would not be limited to Pryplat.

In spite of the scope of the tragedy, official Soviet government sources remained largely silent about it, and there was no free press or civil society that could provide the information. Another relatively major atomic accident had happened in the closed city of Ozyorsk, in the Urals, in 1957, which had required the resettlement of 12,000 people and had put many more in danger due to the radiation. At that time, policies had been developed on how to keep these accidents as secret as possible. Those policies would be applied to the Chernobyl accident, but this time it was more difficult to keep the information secret. Because of the amount of radiation released, and the fact that the accident was much closer to populated areas in Western Europe, the accident could not be kept secret. High levels of radiation soon reached Scandinavian countries and beyond, and concerned Swedes would press the Russians for information. A terse and limited announcement was made in the Soviet news, but the world already knew much more about the accident. On April 29, reporting on the accident described it as "the worst nuclear disaster in world history" and predicted that it would have a high economic impact.

On May 1, an important labor day celebration in the Soviet Union and in Europe, a big parade had been planned in Kyiv. It was to be attended by thousands of people. However, the radiation had reached very high levels, and it would threaten those who attended the celebration. But cancelling it would have been politically dangerous for those who would make the decision. It would also send a signal to the world that the Chernobyl incident had been more serious than the Soviet government had wanted to convey. Just as with President Trump's handling of the Covid pandemic, they did not want to create panic. The consequence was that many of those who took part in the parade would in time pay a high personal price for having done so, and the Soviet government would also pay a high political price in terms of lost credibility.

Soon friction increased between Moscow authorities and Kyiv authorities (as developed in the USA in 2020 between the federal government and the governments of several states). Moscow continued to be more concerned about the impact of the crisis on agricultural production, and on whether agricultural quotas would be filled, than on human beings. Radiation was not assumed to affect crops. However, some officials in Moscow had started to fully comprehend the enormity of the disaster.

There continued to be discrepancies between the number of people hospitalized as reported by Moscow and as reported by Kyiv. There were also divergent statements on whether the hospitals were fully equipped to deal with the growing number of patients. The number of affected children kept increasing. Official newspapers ceased reporting the number of casualties and Moscow continued to attempt to maintain a monopoly over the flow of information.

In the following days, which included Easter Sunday, radiation levels kept rising and would soon reach astronomical levels. The radioactive map around the plant was extended to thirty kilometers, but radiation kept on rising, well beyond the thirty-kilometer perimeter. Where was the increase in radiation coming from? Leading nuclear scientists were uncertain about its origin. This uncertainty would challenge the views that had been accepted by many, including even some religious people, that Soviet science was infallible and that it did not make mistakes.

As time passed, it was becoming evident that powerful Soviet science could not fix the Chernobyl problem that it had created itself. Soon, some started fearing that the Chernobyl disaster might become a global disaster, even one that could make "Europe as a whole ... a wasteland" (Plokhy 2018, p. 198). This could happen any time. The uncertainty that had existed in scientific knowledge was becoming increasingly apparent. This uncertainty added to that created by institutional confusion, on the role of different institutions.

The heat within the power plant kept rising, the radiation level kept going up, and the leaves of the trees in the forest near Pryplat started turning red because of the high radiation that they were absorbing. There started to be talk of the possibility of what was called the China syndrome, the possibility that radiation would contaminate the Dnieper River and, in turn, world water tables. But because of the complexity of the situation, no one seemed to know what to do.

The large amount of water in the basement of the plant was one of the major concerns to the experts, because the rise in the temperature of the plant could increase the steam pressure and make the plant explode. Firemen were given the suicidal task of trying to drain the radioactive water. Some capitalistic financial incentives (significant amounts of money) were authorized by Moscow for the firemen who would be involved in this very dangerous operation. It had also been decided to freeze the area beneath the reactor, to prevent it from breaking through its foundation and contaminating the water table with radiation. The use of financial incentives was a radical departure from communist thinking, and they may not have been necessary because of the natural dedication of many workers and their community spirit.

Concern about the rising level of radiation in Kyiv was leading many of its residents to leave the city. Gorbachev became increasingly concerned about the reputational cost of that development for the Soviet Union. Attempts to shift responsibility between the Ukrainian authorities and those in Moscow continued. "Two weeks after the explosion, the organization of the whole effort to deal with the disaster was anything but clear" (Plokhy 2018, p. 217).

The lives of many of those dealing with the effort were put in great danger by exposure to the high radiation. Those charged with removing radioactive debris from the plant came to be called *biorobots*; but they were not robots, but human beings. Some would survive only days after the operations. Some 600,000 individuals, in addition to 340,000 military personnel, would in time be mobilized from all over the Soviet Union and would be put to various tasks related to the Chernobyl accident. Some of them would have to cover themselves with lead protection that they themselves manufactured, to try to protect themselves from the radiation. The Soviet Union would prove very effective at channeling huge numbers of individuals to a single and well-specified task, just as it had done in fighting Germany during World War II (Tanzi 2021). But at times, confusion continued to reign.

The heroic actions of many and the spirit of cooperation that prevailed were reported and praised in the news media and in official pronouncements. But what was increasingly called the danger of the "China syndrome" continued to be a great unofficial preoccupation for the experts. The idea of building a concrete platform, called a sarcophagus, to permanently cover the atomic plant was eventually considered and endorsed by the International Atomic Energy Agency in Vienna, which had sent observers to the plant.

The bad news of firemen and miners dying continued to be strictly controlled and censored in local press releases and was hidden from the Soviet population at large. However, acts of heroism and altruism by firemen and others were widely reported. The number of deaths and of those contaminated by radiation were not reported. The major concerns for the Soviet authorities in Moscow remained the prevention of domestic panic and the damage that the news could do to the reputation of the Soviet Union abroad.

The war of words with the western press, and especially with the United States government, continued, in both official statements and in articles in the news. However, the more time passed, the more difficult it became to hide the true scope of the tragedy. Jokes started to circulate, especially in Ukraine, that conveyed the growing popular skepticism about official statements. One such joke told about a Chernobyl man and a Kyivan man who met in heaven. The Kyivan man asked the other: "What brought you here?" "Radiation," was the reply. "What brought you here?" "Information." Eventually, Gorbachev would realize that the propaganda war was being lost, and he would adopt a policy of transparency, called "glasnost." That change would eventually lead to the breaking up of the Soviet Union and would start the long, difficult process of transition of the Soviet Republics to different political and economic systems.

The next face of the tragedy would be the attempt to bury the exploded reactor, in order to try to end permanently the spread of radiation. This would not be an easy enterprise and it was one that had to be done as soon as possible, to contain the number of casualties and the economic costs. A very experienced, old, able, and energetic individual, Yefim Slavsky, was given the difficult and enormous task that was to be performed in a highly contaminated environment. Military men would help with decontamination and construction of the "sarcophagus." Many thousands of military and civilian men would be involved in this operation. Many technical difficulties were encountered, but, in time, the "sarcophagus" was built and the attention of the authorities would shift to the search for someone to blame for the disaster.

The official view continued to be that, if there had been a disaster, someone must have been responsible. The whole system could not admit to having been responsible, by using faulty atomic reactors. The experience was a repeat of the Stalin trials of the 1930s, when people were shot for presumed mistakes (Hosking 1992; Getty and Naumov 2010). It was easier and politically convenient to blame some of the lower-level technicians who had performed the experiment, who may or may not have made some mistakes during the frantic hours when they had tried to shut down the reactor. Some of these individuals were found guilty and were condemned to various years of forced labor in Siberian gulags.

8.4 The Fukushima Daiichi Nuclear Disaster

The Fukushima Daiichi nuclear disaster, in Japan, is the other major, atomic disaster experienced, so far, in the nuclear age. This disaster happened in one of the most technologically advanced countries in the world, and in one that is legendary for the reputation of its citizens in being very careful about following rules, and in producing much-admired and technologically advanced products, such as cars and cameras, which are considered as reliable as they can be. The plant had been designed by a very experienced American enterprise, General Electric, and had used the latest techniques. It was built and run by TEPCO, the Tokyo Electric Power Company, also a very experienced company.

The Fukushima Daiichi atomic power plant was one of the largest such plants in the world. It consisted of six light boiling water reactors. It had been specifically designed to withstand earthquakes, because the plant was built in a country and an area subject to earthquakes. There had been major concerns about placing atomic energy plants in a country such as Japan that was subject to major earthquakes.

In 1994, Japanese author Katsuhiko Ishibashi had published a book entitled *A Seismologist Warns*, which had become a bestseller. The book had warned about "nuclear earthquake disasters." These concerns, presumably, had led to the use of specific safety measures supposed to protect against such accidents. In the Fukushima Daiichi disaster there had been no question that different behavior by the technicians who were charged with running the plant during the accident would have made a difference. However, there would later be many questions on whether some safety measures had been compromised during the construction of the plant and on behavior *after* the accident.

Later evaluations of the accident would conclude that the original plant designers had failed in not carrying out some proper risk assessments when the plant was built, and there had been questions about some aspects related to safety that had been raised by mid-level technicians at General Electric. The ministry that supervised the atomic energy industry in Japan, the Ministry of Economy, Trade, and Industry, had also failed in providing proper supervision to the operation of the plant.

A reason for this failure may have been the existence of a conflict of interest. That ministry was both *regulator* and *promoter* of the Japanese atomic energy industry. This double role must inevitably have created a conflict of interest for the ministry, a conflict that, to some extent, was similar to the one that had existed in the Soviet Union before the Chernobyl disaster. Additionally, fears of inviting lawsuits by residents in the area where the reactor was built, which could have stopped, or at least delayed, the project, had been a factor in discouraging the Tokyo

Electric Power Company from addressing some necessary security measures that would have alerted those who lived in the area.

After the accident, TEPCO would admit that "announcing information about uncertain risks would [have created] anxiety" among the population. Furthermore, risks of tsunamis higher than twenty meters that could flood the plant, which had been suggested as a possibility by several sources, were considered highly "uncertain" and were dismissed by TEPCO, as such risks often are. We find here another example of a combination of different and apparently unrelated factors, which, when combined in an often unpredictable way, can create an environment, or conditions, that can lead to "perfect storms."

In a pronouncement made some time after the disaster, in March 2012, the prime minister of Japan would say that the government had been partly responsible for the tragedy, and that the problem had been that the officials who had made decisions had believed in "technological infallibility." We see here a reflection of the thinking that had existed in the Soviet Union. The prime minister of Japan, at the time of the disaster, admitted that in a country exposed to tsunamis, an atomic power plant should not have been built so close to shore.

Other cultural and institutional factors were mentioned by other political figures and by critics as having contributed to the tragedy. One of these was the reluctance by subordinates, especially in some societies, to give bad news to those above them (see Gladwell 2008, ch. 7, for a description of this problem). Delays in reacting to some information and poor communication among relevant parties also played roles. Some of these were especially relevant in decisions about evacuating people from the contaminated area, after the scope of the disaster and the level of the radiation being released in the air started to become clear. The radiation soon reached levels so high that, as had happened at Chernobyl, they were not believed. It is often easier to disbelieve unpleasant news. A report on the accident in the British journal, *The Economist*, after the event, would be particularly critical of the behavior of the operating company (Nice 2011).

If one can attribute disasters directly to "Acts of God," the Fukushima disaster might qualify as one of those "Acts." If a mistake is to be found in this disaster, it is that Acts of God do happen in the real world, and the possibility of their happening, even if it seems remote, should not be ignored. This observation would seem to be particularly relevant, especially when decisions are made on where to locate dangerous human activities, such as atomic plants, large dams, or other similarly, potentially dangerous ones, such as oil refineries and deposits of dangerous chemicals. This is, again, an area where uncertainty can and occasionally does play a role, one that can be good or, at times, bad.

In an earlier chapter, we surveyed some natural disasters and showed that some of them, though not predictable in a precise statistical sense, were likely to happen in some geographical areas, *at some time* in the future. It would thus seem rational to avoid placing dangerous human activities in areas potentially subject to these dangers. However, the potentially dangerous areas may have other important immediate attractions and, in the presence of these attractions, the potential negative, but uncertain impact of natural disasters (on human-made activities, and especially on dangerous ones), may attract less attention than it should.

When it is difficult to measure the risk statistically, the dangers tend to be ignored, more so than those that can be measured. This may be considered a form of irrationality. Those who make the original decisions, especially when the individuals have some vested interest in the activities, tend to become more optimistic about future prospects. This is likely to have happened when the Fukushima plant was built. The combination of a major earthquake and an unusually strong tsunami must have been considered one of these highly unlikely Acts of God from which there is no protection, and that therefore can be ignored.

The Fukushima Daiichi nuclear disaster happened at 2.46 p.m., on March 11, 2011, when a very rare, level 9 earthquake took place under the sea, near the island of Honshu. When the earthquake occurred, three of the plant's units, units 1, 2, and 3, were in operation, but units 4, 5, and 6 were not. The earthquake immediately shut off the electricity to the operating units, as it would be expected to do. And, as expected, emergency diesel generators started operating, to keep the cooling systems in operation. They kept operating as they had been designed and expected to do. However, what had not been expected was that the tsunami that followed the earthquake a short time later would hit the plant, at the expected great speed, but with a wave fourteen meters high. Such a wave had not been expected in the security plans. The plant was ten meters above the level of the sea on the coast, a level which had been considered safe from normal tsunamis. Ironically, the level of the coastline had been significantly lowered, from about thirty meters to ten meters, during the building of the plant, to create easier access to the plant from the sea. Given that lower level, there was no safety mechanism to protect the plant from the impact of such a high tsunami. Other changes that had not been reported to the proper supervisors had also been made during construction.

The tsunami flooded the buildings that hosted the six turbines, disabling the diesel generators that had been expected to continue generating the energy necessary to keep cooling the reactors. Some of the reactors started to overheat. This would lead to the meltdowns that followed in some of them. The meltdowns were followed by unexpected hydrogen-air chemical explosions, and by much radiation generation. A large amount of radioactive waste had to be dumped in the ocean, creating later problems, such as fish that could not be eaten because of high radiation. The operations to stabilize the situation would continue for months, or even years, after the event.

After the accident, it became difficult to determine how much of the molten fuel had remained in the containment vessel and how much had worked its way into the ground below it. Various unexpected developments kept taking place in the units of the plant for several months, including in the units that had not been working on the day of the tsunami. Because of the complexity of the situation, various tests and simulations produced different estimates on the question of how much melting of the core had taken place. However, it became clear that there had been a significant amount of melting of nuclear fuel. That melting had produced, and would continue to produce for a very long time, a great amount of radiation to the environment around the nuclear plant. This required the evacuation of many thousands people who had been living in the area around the plant.

During the first days of the meltdown there had been no release of information on the meltdown of three of the plants nor of the amount of radiation that the plant was spreading in the area. Furthermore, the government had decided that radiation in the ocean would not be measured.

As had happened in Chernobyl, there would be debates between local authorities, which believed that the lives of local citizens had been ignored, and national authorities and the managers of the plant. The lack of information on radiation levels meant that many of the local residents who had been evacuated were sent to areas that were equally radiated. It was later revealed that, during the disaster, the officials of TEPCO had been instructed not to use the term "meltdown" in describing what was taking place in order not to create panic. Some would describe this as a cover-up, and any differences in reactions between

Chernobyl and Fukushima would become more difficult to identify. As had been the case in Chernobyl, evacuation came much later than it should have, and the delay may have cost many lives.

Between the earthquake and the tsunami, more than a million buildings had been destroyed and 470,000 people had to be evacuated. The accident at the plant would be *directly* responsible for the evacuation of 154,000 persons. The others would be evacuated because of the high radiation level. The economic and social costs of the accident and the earthquake would be astronomical. The direct economic costs alone would be assessed at $235 billion. But many costs, including reputational costs, could not be measured. Recently, the Swiss Re insurance company rated the disaster as the costliest in the history of the world.

This event, like the Chernobyl accident, was rated 7, the highest category for atomic disasters. The event at Three Mile Island had been rated a 5. While 18,500 people had died as a direct result of the earthquake and tsunami, there were many unanswered questions about how many would be killed by radiation-induced cancers in later years. As at Chernobyl, a large area around the plant at Fukushima would be declared permanently uninhabitable, and parts of the Pacific Ocean contaminated by radiation would be restricted for fishing. The leaking of radiation from the storage tank into the ocean would continue for some time. An underground ice wall aimed at blocking the flow of groundwater into the reactor was created.

It was as if the earth had become permanently smaller and less valuable. Today, in 2021, there is an ongoing debate on what to do with the huge amount of contaminated water that is still stored in tanks. The managers of the plant would like to release it in the ocean, claiming that this would be safe. Environmentalists, fishermen, ordinary citizens, and Koreans (South Koreans in particular), due to their proximity to the disaster, are strongly opposed to it.

Some countries recommended to their citizens living in Tokyo, to leave that city while the radiation there was high. High radiation would be registered on the west coast of the USA and in the eastern part of Russia. The radiation in the sea around the plant would be spread widely by strong currents. For some time, the drinking water in Tokyo would register high levels of radiation. A lot of uncertainty was created and continues to exist in several areas, so that the full cost of the accident may never be known.

In September 2015, a major typhoon complicated the situation and caused further evacuation. Conflicting measurements about radiation and their effects on health continued to cause debates and questions about the safety assurances given by some agencies. (For some evaluation of this incident, see Blandford and Sagan 2016.) Some time after the event, a Japanese government commission declared that the accident had been partly caused by human errors.

This accident turned attitudes against the use of nuclear energy in many countries. The early enthusiasm vis-à-vis that use, which had assumed that cheap and safe energy could be obtained from atomic energy, was followed by deeper skepticism (Caldicott 2014). Several countries stopped relying on this source of energy, even though some individuals and pressure groups have continued to advocate it as an easy solution to the problem of climate change. In Europe, France has remained an important exception, having continued to be a major user of atomic energy, so far without any reported accident. Some think tanks, such as the Cato Institute, have continued to recommend its use, and so has Bill Gates in a recent book (Gates 2021a).

The negative attitude vis-à-vis atomic energy has continued in the USA and elsewhere, in spite of reported, important technical progress or future likely progress that is making, or is promising to make, atomic plants less expensive and more flexible. These innovations include modular reactors that are more efficient, and advanced non-light water reactors, including molten-salt reactors. For the time being, the plan is still to retire some existing plants, thus reducing the amount of energy generated by nuclear plants in the USA.

Combined, the three atomic accidents reported above indicate that the complexity of atomic plants could always create the possibility of human errors, which could lead to catastrophic consequences. Human errors could occasionally combine with natural events to precipitate unanticipated disasters, as happened in Japan. The errors can be reduced by technical improvements, but they cannot be totally eliminated.

The Fukushima disaster indicated that as long as there are natural events (earthquakes, tsunamis, tornadoes, cyclones, major wildfires, and other such occurrences) that can hit any place on Earth, atomic plants will always be subject to some dangers. Acts of terrorism could also precipitate nuclear disasters. For example, imagine what would have happened if one of the planes hijacked by terrorists on September 11, 2001, had been directed against the atomic plant at Three Mile Island?

The conclusion must be that the only completely safe atomic plant is one that is never built. However, it must be recognized that no activity can ever be completely safe. It is always a matter of degree and of cost–benefit calculations. In the case of atomic energy, immediate or short-term benefits must be evaluated against possible future, uncertain costs. There may come a time when that evaluation may lead, once again, to the use of atomic energy.

On February 13, 2021, two related news stories reminded us of the difficulty of the above evaluation. The first was a level 7 earthquake in the Fukushima region, which, fortunately, did not damage the atomic plant. The second was an audit by the US Department of Energy, Office of Inspector General (DOE-OIG), which found that the nation's top nuclear laboratory, the National Nuclear Security Administration, which is home to the atomic bomb and hosts the world's largest science and technology labs, was at risk of major wildfires because of very severe drought conditions and poor management of the forests in the areas. Furthermore, a huge, unusual winter storm in Texas would show that some electricity grids could also be badly damaged by severe natural events. They had been built ignoring such uncertain events.

Clearly, the combination of uncertain natural events and manmade dangerous activities can occasionally create unanticipated, unpleasant situations. That combination deserves more attention when decisions are made as to where to place those activities and how to build them. The option of not building is always present, but at a cost.

9 INDUSTRIAL DISASTERS

9.1 Introduction

While the Industrial Revolution brought lots of benefits to mankind, and freed many humans, at least for some centuries, from the Malthusian trap, it also created many manmade disasters that had not existed before. Some of these were minor, but some led to significant loss of life and property, or damage to the environment. These accidents happen because of incompetence, ignorance, the complexity of new technologies, unexpected consequences of some of them, and also because of greed by some, which makes them ignore dangers, especially when the dangers affect others, particularly unknown strangers.

Many of the disasters are the consequence of placing potentially dangerous activities near areas where people live. Some of them, occasionally, can be connected with natural events. From the above perspective, there is often some kind of original sin behind these events, such as that committed by governments that ignored community welfare and allowed these activities to take place, especially near populated areas.

It may not be a coincidence that in the USA many of these recent accidents seem to take place in Texas, a state that seems more relaxed in the application of regulations than, say, California or Massachusetts. Regulations are the major tool that governments have available to reduce accidents. They reduce the personal liberty of some individuals, as libertarians stress, but they increase the safety of the community as a whole. So that there is often a "trade-off" between these two objectives. Some governments give more importance to one over the other. And some enforce regulations more effectively than others. We shall report on only a few of these accidents, especially on those that have caused many casualties, or major environmental costs. Wikipedia provides a useful list of many of these industrial disasters.

9.2 Transportation Disasters

Some major industrial disasters have been connected with the transportation of dangerous substances, such as explosives, chemicals, and petroleum products. These disasters could not have happened before the Industrial Revolution, when these substances did not exist. Some of them have killed hundreds or even thousands of individuals, as, for example, did the explosion of a ship in the port of Halifax, Canada, on December 8, 1917. The ship was loaded with explosives to be delivered to France, and the explosion killed 2,000 people and injured 9,000 more. A similar explosion in Port Chicago, California, on July 17, 1944, killed 320. An explosion on a ship carrying ammonium nitrate fertilizers, on April 16, 1947, in Texas City, killed at least 578 people and injured some 3,500 others. This is considered the worst industrial disaster in the USA. On July 28, 1948, a chemical tank wagon exploded in Ludwigshfen, Germany, killing 207 people, injuring 3,818, and damaging 3,132 buildings.

Some of these transportation accidents also created major environmental problems, for example: the March 1967 shipwreck of the *Torrey Canyon* supertanker off the coast of Cornwall, England; the March 16, 1978 *Amoco Cadiz* sinking near the northwest coast of France; the oil spill of the Ixtoc 1 exploratory oil well of June 3, 1979; the July 6, 1988 Piper Alpha disaster on a North Sea production platform, which killed 167 men and created insured losses of US$ 3.4 billion; and the *Exxon Valdez* oil spill of March 24, 1989. On October 20, 2010, British Petroleum's oil-drilling platform Deepwater Horizon, operating in the Macondo Prospect in the Gulf of Mexico, exploded, killing some workers and generating lots of environmental damage and much damage to the fishing industry in a large area. BP had to pay billions in penalties.

9.3 Industrial-Natural Disasters

Some major industrial disasters have been connected with, or at least partly caused by, natural events. Industrial activities have occasionally combined with natural events to create situations that led to disasters. This was the case, recently, when electrical wires over forests that had become very dry caused major fires in California, killing many people and destroying many properties. In some cases, dams connected with industrial activities were damaged, due to landslides or heavy rain that caused the dams to break and flood the areas below them. This happened in Italy with the Vajont Dam, in October 1963. It led to the destruction of several small towns downhill, and the death of about 2,000 people. It also occurred in the collapse, in August 1975, of the Banqiao Dam, in China, which led to the immediate death of some 100,000 people and to far more death, due to the famine that followed. The dam, built during the Cultural Revolution, had been of poor quality, so the tragedy was not entirely unexpected.

There have been many examples of the spreading of dangerous chemicals over populated areas, by enterprises, which have created deaths and other problems, just as radiation does in nuclear accidents. Perhaps the most serious of these disasters was the one that occurred in Bhopal, India, at a Union Carbide India Limited plant on December 3, 1984. An uncontrolled reaction in a tank that contained poisonous methyl isocyanate led to the release of a large amount of the poisonous gas in the atmosphere around the plant. This resulted in immediate or later deaths estimated at between 3,700 and 16,000. It also led to major health problems for people and animals in a very large area around Bhopal, with these problems lasting for several years.

A somewhat similar incident had occurred in the USA in Donora, a small city in Pennsylvania, thirty-nine kilometers from Pittsburgh, on October 27, 1948. The incident has been described as one of the worst air pollution disasters in US history. It occurred in a plant run by US Steel. It was caused by an unusual combination of fog and smog that had trapped sulfuric acid, nitrogen dioxide, fluorine, and other poisonous gases in the air above Donora. The gases would normally have been dispersed in the air by normal air circulation, but the unusual weather conditions impeded this dispersion. The poisonous smog led to significant respiratory problems and other health problems for people in the area. It killed twenty people immediately, but many more later, and caused major respiratory problems for at least 7,000, in a town of just 14,000.

Because of the unusual weather circumstances that had prevailed during the event, lawyers representing US Steel in court proceedings argued that the tragedy had been an "Act of God," caused by "freak weather conditions," and not by the activities of the plant. Therefore, the enterprise could not be considered culpable. Obviously, the accident would not have happened if the plant had not been in the town. The plant was closed in 1966 (Davis 2002).

122 PANDEMICS AND OTHER DISASTERS

This accident contributed to raise the sensitivities of Americans to the dangers of industrial pollution. It also indicated that some complex circumstances that are difficult to anticipate and plan for make it difficult to attribute blame, or to anticipate some disastrous events in particular places and circumstances. Lawyers for companies involved in such accidents have often been clever in finding justifications for these events.

The Trump Administration would show much less concern for these environmental considerations. Many of the previously imposed regulations on industrial activities were removed or relaxed during the Trump years. Often the science behind regulations would be questioned, and some of the scientists who had been behind them would be reassigned or dismissed.

Another major accident that was caused by circumstances similar to those in Donora occurred in London in 1952, and resulted in the death of an estimated 12,000 people. The deaths were the result of the "Great Smog of London," a deep fog caused by the combination of coal combustion and diesel exhaust. Coal-fired thermal power plants release sulfur dioxide, nitrogen oxide, mercury, and other substances that are hazardous to human health (Bogmans and Mengyi Li 2020). The Great Smog of London would lead to the passing of the Clear Air Act 1956 in the UK.

Many deaths are likely to be caused by the high pollution produced by the burning of coal in Beijing and in Delhi, over the years. The burning of coal is now generally considered a great environmental hazard.

9.4 Storage of Dangerous Materials

The storing in populated areas of products that can explode has often been a cause of disaster. One such disaster happened on August 4, 2020, in Beirut, Lebanon, when a large deposit of ammonium nitrate, which had been stored for years in a warehouse near the harbor, caught fire and exploded. The enormous explosion destroyed or damaged many buildings in the city, killed about 200 people, and injured more than 6,000. It largely destroyed the port.

Many similar explosions had occurred over the years in several countries. Some of them were due to the storage of dangerous substances; some were due to the explosion of oil refineries; some to leaks in pipes carrying gasoline or gas; others to explosions in firework factories.

9.5 Mining Accidents

Not surprisingly, from the earliest times when mines were opened to provide access to valuable minerals, there have been many accidents in them. Some of these have been major and have cost many lives. The worst such accident, in England, occurred on December 12, 1866 in Barnsley, West Riding of Yorkshire, killing 361 miners. The worst mining accident in the UK occurred in Senghenydd, Wales, on October 14, 1913. It killed 439 workers. Another bad accident was that in the Welsh village of Aberfan, on October 21, 1966, which killed 116 children and 28 adults in a school. It was caused by the collapse of a colliery spoil tip built on a mountain slope that contained 23,000 cubic meters of waste from the chemical extraction of coal. The tip had been thirty-four meters high and it was on a spring that was saturated by heavy rain and collapsed, destroying a school full of children. It was caused by a combination of rules not observed and a natural event (heavy rain) not expected to happen. Because of the many young children killed, it had a big impact and led to significant legislation.

The worst mining accident in continental Europe occurred on March 10, 1906, in Courrières, France, when 1,099 people died, including many children, who, at that time, were often used in these works. In Japan, in Kyushu, on December 15, 1914, 687 people were killed in the worst such accident in the country. In Belgium, in the town of Marcinelle, on August 8, 1956, a fire in a mine killed 262, mainly Italian immigrant workers.

A serious mining storage accident happened in January 2019, in Minas Gerais, in Brazil, at the Corrego do Feijao mine, near the town of Bramadinho. A storage dam, which contained twelve million cubic meters of mining waste, broke, destroying everything in its path, killing 270 people, and causing a major environmental disaster. The storing of the waste had been a cheap way to deal with that waste for the mining company.

There have been many similar disasters in other parts of the world. Many more of these major disasters occurred in the earlier years of the Industrial Revolution, when laissez faire governments played no role in enforcing safety standards, including prohibiting the use of children in these dangerous activities. Children had often been used in mines. In more recent years, better techniques and more stringent government regulations have reduced, but far from eliminated, these accidents.

In countries where the role of government has remained weak, or in federal countries such as the USA, where some regions have fewer regulations, and where lobbies and/or local interests are strong, such as West Virginia and Texas, these accidents have continued, and they are likely to continue to occur in the future.

10 GUIDING ECONOMIC PRINCIPLES FOR DISASTERS

Given the many disasters and catastrophes that, over the centuries, have visited countries, killed many people, and damaged economies, disasters that were only described in small part in previous chapters, one would expect that the field of economics, largely developed over the past couple of centuries, would have paid some attention to them. It is strange to observe that this has not been the case.

The main body of theoretical economics that came into existence mainly a century or so ago, and which, in some essential way, has remained unchanged until now, except for the recognition that there are business cycles that mean economic developments are not always smooth, and there are various factors that make the real economy different from the theoretical paradigm, economics has mostly ignored the existence of *uncertain*, catastrophic events, as compared with events that are *risky*.

Modern economics was developed around the implicit notion of smooth-developing, efficient, and regular economic changes, character-ized mainly by competitive forces, and by markets that guide the behav-ior of the participants, pushing them toward actions that, over the long run, presumably, promote optimal results and maximize public welfare. This was the economics that received the most explicit description and support in the work of great economists such as Alfred Marshall and the Classical and Neoclassical Schools, and, later, with some marginal differ-ences among them, in the work of Milton Friedman, Paul Samuelson, Ludwig von Mises, George Stigler, and others.

After the Great Depression of the 1930s, and the work of Keynes on economic fluctuations, there was some recognition, on the part of many, but not all, economists, that there are business cycles that, with some frequent but uncertain regularity, affect economies, and that might justify interventions by governments to deal with them

(Solimano 2020). The possibility that natural or manmade catastrophes might occasionally interfere with the theoretical description of how economies operate was largely ignored. Countries and enterprises were not expected or advised to prepare for occasional, major, random shocks, and to make some preparations for the possibility of their coming. These preparations might help to reduce the damaging effects of these events when they do occur.

As a consequence of the above, no economic principles were developed on what to do in *anticipation* of random, but possible, future disasters, and also what to do when they become a reality. On the contrary, some of the principles that were stressed by the literature, and were expected to be followed, by both governments and private enterprises, were likely to become obstacles to actions, before and during catastrophes, that had remained *uncertain* until they happened, but that had had some concrete possibility of occurring, as, for example, earthquakes in California, hurricanes in Miami, tsunamis in Japan, or pandemics anywhere.

Uncertain events continued to play an important role in the real world, but a very marginal one in economic theory and economic decisions, when compared with *risky* events, events for which the risk could be statistically determined. The latter could be handled with the assistance of the well-developed insurance industry, which had become an integral and important part of the market economy over the past two centuries. Or they could be handled with some government programs, such as public pensions and public health. Risk attracted significant attention, uncertainty did not.

The government programs against personal risks (public health, public pensions, etc.) continued to be opposed by libertarians who believed in the power of the market to provide private options (such as private pensions and private health insurance), in which individuals could acquire protection against future risks by paying some premiums, or by accumulating personal assets to be used in retirement or during illnesses. Chilean-style pension systems became popular in the 1980s and were adopted by several countries.

In spite of its theoretical importance, Frank Knight's insight about the role of uncertainty, even in pension systems, continued to be ignored, or to play a very marginal role in guiding or influencing government policies, and/or the behavior of individuals and enterprises. Many pension systems are underfunded and will leave pensioners with little income when they retire.

Consider, first, the guiding rules that were expected to influence the behavior of governments in democratic countries with market economies. Governments were expected to keep public spending and tax levels low and, until the most recent years in which some have called for a greater role for public debt, to keep their public balances low and in equilibrium. When budgetary equilibrium became difficult to maintain, countries were expected to follow some legislated, fiscal rules, rules that limited their degree of freedom.

This, for example, was the case with the rules imposed on member countries by the European Monetary Union's Maastricht Growth and Stability Pact. That "pact" aimed at limiting the budget deficits to 3 percent of GDP, and public debt to 60 percent. It was also the case with the equilibrium imposed by the balanced budget rules that are supposed to guide individual states within the USA.

Governments that would spend significant amounts of money in anticipation of random, uncertain catastrophes, say, by creating more hospital beds in anticipation of possible, future pandemics, or that would build stronger protections against floods or earthquakes by creating better protective structures, would risk losing the election. They would be accused of having "wasted" money by some or many citizens.

Only statistically quantifiable *risks*, such as those faced by individuals who reach retirement age and require pensions, or some other form of old-age assistance, would receive some official attention. However, as mentioned, pension funds based on retirement laws have often remained underfunded, as they are for US public pensions. Public health systems are still opposed in some countries. Also, infrastructure that would likely be needed in future years has continued to receive less attention than many think that they should have. There has been clear reluctance in many countries to finance these future needs with current taxes.

The problem with the above behavior is that when a disastrous, random event (such as the Covid 19 pandemic) occurs and destroys many jobs, lowers tax revenue, and/or pushes up some government spending to protect workers who have lost jobs and incomes, and to prevent many enterprises from going broke, the government budget soon diverges from the budgetary rules. This happened on a major scale in 2020, in the countries of the European Monetary Union and among the US subnational governments. The US federal budget was not constrained by such rules and its deficit could increase sharply without breaking any rule.

Governments have been at a loss as to what to do because there were no shared economic principles to guide them during the pandemic. In some cases, even regulations that, if they had been followed, might have helped to make the pandemic less painful, had been weakened by past governments' policies or behavior, which had stressed short-run needs and had largely ignored the long run. The long run will now be associated with huge public debts that, somehow, will have to be financed or dealt with. Some economists have dismissed the future difficulties created by high debts, as the IMF seems to be doing in the face of the impact of the Covid pandemic on fiscal deficits.

Governments should be reminded of Adam Smith's (1937 [1776]) warning, that

all states ... have on some occasion played this very juggling trick [of replacing tax revenue with borrowing] ... When national debts have ... been accumulated to a certain degree, there is scarce ... a single instance of their having been fairly and completely paid. The liberalization of public revenue ... has always been brought by bankruptcy: some an avowed one, but always a real one.

Smith's warning has been challenged by some economists in recent years. They have argued, essentially, that the world has changed and public debt is no longer the danger that was once assumed to be. In 2020, the share of public debt to GDP was estimated to be 97.6 percent for the whole world, 98.1 percent for the eurozone, 122.7 percent for advanced countries, and 128.7 percent for the USA. It will be much higher in 2021.

One wonders, for example, how Italy will service, or retire, a public debt that, at the end of 2020, had reached 157.5 percent of its GDP, when the country already had a very high tax burden and slow growth. What will be the impact of the $1.9 trillion US Covid relief package that was passed in March 2021, which is expected to be totally financed by debt? The high debts that were accumulated during World War II, at very low rates, and with long maturities, were partly dealt with by inflation rates that exceeded the low interest rates on the debt, and by high growth years. The maturity *structure* of the US federal debt has remained remarkably low (65 months in 2020), in spite of the low rates, and in spite of the rate of growth of the debt. An increase in real rates would immediately sharply increase interest payments, in a situation where fiscal deficits are already high and growth rates are modest.

There are some possible *theoretical* explanations for the reasons why possible, but uncertain, future disasters are ignored, and why there is a tendency to focus on the short run, besides Keynes' rather flippant comment that "in the long run we are all dead!" As Mises commented on this statement, while he basically agreed with Keynes, he added that "unfortunately nearly all of us outlive the short run" (Mises 2005, p. 130).

The first explanation is that what is not statistically quantifiable is not an *insurable* risk. As an *uncertain*, non-insurable future event, there is, perhaps, an irrational human tendency to simply ignore it. A second explanation might be that the attention given to the short run may have been influenced by the fact that the economic principles that were developed in the past came about when the average life expectancy of humans was relatively low, say thirty to forty years. The shorter the life expectancy, the more the short run becomes important, compared with the future. Major catastrophes are less likely to occur during a shorter time span than they are during a longer period.

As life expectancy becomes longer, the chance of experiencing a catastrophic event during a person's life span becomes greater, making Mises' observation more relevant. The fact that in several countries today (Sweden, Japan, Spain, Italy) life expectancy has become much longer (it exceeds eighty years and many live up to a hundred years) may have made people pay more attention to the longer run, and also to possible, but uncertain, future catastrophes. Among these, there is the "mother of all catastrophes," global warming and its effects on life and nature, which will be discussed in the following chapters. Dealing with global warming will require the intervention of many governments, and also the coordination of many of their actions, in order to be successful.

A third, possible, but more speculative, explanation is that the more attention a country's population pays to the individuals who are currently living, and especially to the individual liberties of those individuals, as compared to the interests or welfare of the whole community and of future generations, the less concern there will be, among its members, about the future and about the individuals of the generations that will follow.

Concern for the future requires some, or more, altruism that, when it is pronounced, extends across generations. A more altruistic and caring society is more likely to pay attention to phenomena such as global warming, the biological diversity of the Earth, and the safety of future generations, made up of individuals who are not yet born, and who do not yet vote, than an individualistic society, which may see greed by some of its living members as a desirable trait, a trait that presumably makes the economy grow faster.

Part III

Climate Change and Global Warming

11 WHEN THE EARTH BECAME MAN'S PRIVATE PROPERTY

In the past couple of centuries, and especially since the 1980s, the physical environment has not only been shaping human life but also, perhaps for the first time since the human race appeared on Earth, through their many activities, actions, and growing numbers, humans have been significantly shaping the natural environment, and not always in desirable, sustainable ways (McKibben 1989; Smil 2021). James Calvin Taylor, a classics scholar at Harvard, has reported that two millennia ago the Roman natural historian Pliny the Elder, in his encyclopedic *Natural History*, had already expressed some concerns about the negative impacts that human activities, especially through quarries, were having on the natural environment.

Significant *social* costs are being created by human activities, costs that often are not reflected, or fully reflected, in market prices. These costs have become progressively more important and, increasingly, have diverged from those that would be reflected in correct market prices, providing implicit and often very large subsidies to those who produce, or consume, the products and services that contribute to environmental costs. (See Clements et al. 2013 for some estimates of energy subsidies.)

The problem is not just limited to the market prices of *particular* fossil fuels, such as coal and petroleum, which are those that attract much attention; it is a more general problem. It is difficult to identify all the products, all the services, and all the human activities that create environmental costs broadly defined, and not just climate change. Those costs may also involve excessive use of land or water, as in the case of hamburgers.

It is also difficult to determine the specific prices that should be corrected, because of the implicit subsidies that the users of those products receive, due to the costs that they impose on the environment. For example, it may be difficult for a normal person to comprehend that the consumption of milk, or beef, creates social costs that are not reflected in their market prices. Correcting fully the prices of coal, or petroleum, by using carbon taxes, will help, but it will not correct the market prices of milk and beef.

In the past half-century we entered an *Anthropocentric Era*, an era when human beings were clearly at the center of the world in which they lived, on Earth (see, especially, Smil 2021). They are shaping that world as if it were their private property, rather than the other way around, as had largely been the case for millennia, when they had shared the Earth with all the other animals and species, and had left relatively few traces on it. Humans are no longer sharing the physical world fairly with other species. Rather, they are monopolizing that world for their well-being and selfish interest. Economics, and especially price theory, has not fully recognized, or has been slow to fully recognize, this change.

At first, humans started changing only the areas of the regions in which they lived – for example, with quarries, the introduction of new crops, new agricultural methods, the domestication of some animals and the killing of others, the building of small dams and other small irrigation projects. Progressively, their actions started to influence the whole world, having an impact on other species, on diversity, on the climate, and in other important ways. It took some time to recognize that humans could have such an effect on the natural world. The whole world became the private possession of human beings, a possession that could be "used and abused", as for any private property, and as they saw fit, to improve their existence. This process accelerated and took different dimensions during and after the Industrial Revolution.

Forests and wilderness areas were progressively reduced in size, and so was the diversity that had existed in the flora and fauna. Plants that could more easily feed humans, such as wheat, corn, rice, and potatoes, replaced wild plants. Some of these new plants were brought from far away from where they were now grown, as was the case for potatoes, corn, and tomatoes. Some of these new plants would be genetically modified, in time, with possible, but not always predictable, long-run effects. Also, animals that could feed humans, especially chickens, sheep, pigs, and cows, progressively and significantly replaced the many wild and untamed animal (wolves, lions, tigers, elephants, bears, bison, and buffaloes) that had freely roamed the wilderness areas of the Earth in the past.

A recent book (Smil 2021) has provided some data (obviously not precise statistics, but informed guesses) as to the extent to which human beings have changed the Earth in recent decades, especially in North

America since the 1980s. Around the year 1800 in North America, the weight of mammals in the wild (bison, buffaloes, and others) exceeded that of domesticated mammals reared for food (cows and others). By 1900, the total weight of domesticated mammals was twice that of wild ones; and by around 2000, it was twenty times greater. By that time, the Earth had largely become a farm. Cultivated areas had grown enormously; Columbus would not have recognized the land he had discovered 500 years earlier.

The above changes might be seen, and progressively came to be seen, as a gain for humans and a loss for nature's diversity. While it is easy to determine the short-run benefits of these changes for humans, making it possible for the human population to keep growing and for humans to live better and longer lives, it is more difficult to determine the long-run implications of these changes, *for the whole Earth.*

The meat that we now eat is either produced in conditions that are often highly unsanitary and require the use of hormones and other medicines (as in the case of commercially raised chickens), or that require a large amount of land (as for cows and sheep). A reduction in the consumption of beef by humans would create extra space for other crops that could also feed humans, and would do so often at lower environmental costs. However, beef is frequently seen as a superior food, so that higher average income levels around the world, and larger populations, lead to higher demand for beef and, consequently, to more land allocated to the raising of cows. One consequence of this is more climate change, because of the required replacement of forests with grassland and also, importantly, because of the fact that the digestive processes of some livestock, especially cows, emit large amounts of methane gas, which is particularly bad for the environment.

It has been reported that there are now some 1.4–1.5 billion cows in the world, about one for every five humans. According to the United Nations Food and Agricultural Organization, that livestock accounts for about 15 percent of global greenhouse gas emissions, with 40 percent of that coming from methane emission from the cows' digestive systems. Each cow is reported to produce around 100 kilograms of carbon per year. This is a significant amount that could be reduced by eating less meat (Schlossberg 2020).

Two related positive developments may be worth reporting. One is the recent introduction of beef substitutes, such as "vegan beef" and "vegan burgers," which may progressively reduce the rate of growth in the

consumption of real beef and of other meat products. Some leading restaurants in the USA are becoming vegetarian. The second is some recent
developments in the feeding of cows. It has been reported that different
feeds may significantly reduce methane emission by cows. Unfortunately,
this kind of sustainable feed is scarce, and it is an open question how soon
the use of this seed could make a noticeable difference. Milk substitutes are
also being introduced. Recent research indicates that cutting methane
emissions could be an effective way to reduce global warming.

There are also some experiments, in California and some other places,
to farm food that would generate less carbon and even develop agriculture that might help reverse the effect of climate change, by drawing
carbon from the air and storing it in the roots of the plants. Cutting
methane emission would have a significant impact on slowing global
warming because, while methane is more damaging than other fuels, it
stays less time in the atmosphere than greenhouse gases from other
fuels. There are also experiments in producing crops with less water
and fewer fertilizers and insecticides. All these experiments point to
the ingenuity of humans and have the potential to contribute to the
fight against global warming and other environmental problems.
However, it might take a long time before these experiments are scaled
up in order to have a significant impact on the billions of farms in the
world, and time is of the essence in the race against global warming.

The Earth's diversity, in both fauna and flora, has suffered significantly over recent decades, making the world biologically poorer
(Dasgupta 2021). Additionally, because of the impact of some human
actions (building of dams; use of plastic that ends up in rivers and seas;
irrigation and use of artificial fertilizers) that pollute bodies of fresh
water and kill the sea plants and coral reefs in coastal areas where the
sunlight can reach the seabed, fish, which in the past had been abundant
in many of these coastal areas and in rivers and lakes, have become
much less so. Coral reefs have been progressively dying, creating "dead
zones" in the seas. We may not be fully aware of it, but much of the fish
that we now eat increasingly comes from fish farms, where chemicals
are needed because of some pollution of the water.

Perhaps some mention should be made at this point of a movement
that started in the USA more than a century ago and spread later to other
countries. This environmental movement aimed at protecting some pristine and unusually beautiful areas from human exploitation, keeping
these areas (National Parks), as far as possible, unchanged by human

actions. In these areas, most human activities are prevented and the existing fauna and flora are protected. These are the National Parks that now exist, especially in the USA, but also in other countries, and they are protected from commercial activities. However, their raison d'être is still to provide pleasure to humans, and crowding may change them in time. Today, there are many such parks in the world, providing great pleasure to visitors and protection to the local environment. The creation of these parks, however, often had to overwhelm very strong opposition from local and other vested interests, which saw these areas solely for the potential commercial value they could generate.

Climate change may be expected to attract and is attracting more attention, especially in countries that focus more on the whole community, than in those that put more emphasis on the economic freedom of the individuals who live in them at that time. This might explain why Scandinavian and some other European countries have been paying more attention to climate change than countries that are more focused on the economic freedom of individuals. This seems to have been the case in the USA during the Trump Administration, when prosecutions for environmental crimes, such as violation of the Clean Water Act and the Clean Air Act, significantly decreased. The Biden Administration has promised a change.

The above, of course, are partly theoretical speculations. They may or may not be correct, or important. In the USA, a change in administration has suddenly brought a different *official*, if not necessarily a popular, attitude toward environmental issues. Hopefully, the official change will get the popular support that it needs, and it will be sustained in future years, without being watered down by the pressure of vested interests.

The behavior of private enterprises in countries with market economies has continued to follow principles that stress short-run objectives and pay little attention to the long run. Environmental costs were and are often ignored, as for example in mining activities. The more an enterprise operates in a competitive market, the more it is compelled to keep its (private) costs low, to remain competitive. To do so, it has to keep wages low (and, if possible, to ignore environmental costs that it may generate). It can do this by reducing the number of workers that it employs, say, by replacing them with robots, by squeezing their wages, by reducing the power of labor unions, and by ignoring social responsibilities. The enterprises have to keep inventories low, relying on timely deliveries, and "just in time" inventory techniques.

When recessions come, as they periodically do, the enterprises that operate in these competitive markets lay off workers and reduce their total wage bill as much as possible. This was and has continued to be what American companies did and were expected and allowed to do, pushing up the unemployment rate. It may be interesting to report that Japanese companies, which, perhaps, operate in what may be a more altruistic, or more community-centered, society, with a different implicit social contract, tend to retain more of their workers during bad times, using profits that had not been distributed in the good years. As a consequence, the unemployment rate fluctuates significantly less in Japan than it does in the USA.

American companies also pay much higher compensation to their managers than most other countries, and they distribute more of their profits to their shareholders. They also often use their profits to buy their own shares, rather than to make real investments, or to retain workers during hard times. This behavior leads to higher unrealized and untaxed capital gains for shareholders. It also contributes to less even wealth distribution.

This behavior was partly inspired, and justified, by the influential article by Milton Friedman (1970), published in the *New York Times Magazine*. The article had argued that the only responsibility that private enterprises have, or should have, is to maximize returns to their shareholders. They do not have any social responsibilities, including that of minimizing their reliance on dirty fuels. This is a code of behavior for a society that emphasizes individualism and short-run economic objectives, rather than one that aims at the long-run welfare of whole communities.

This kind of society is likely to pay less attention to phenomena such as climate change and biological diversity, and to increasingly uneven income distribution. These are phenomena that inevitably require policies that give importance to the welfare of whole communities more than to that of individual members. Phenomena such as these have grown in importance, especially since the 1980s, and it has become increasingly difficult to ignore them.

Friedman also opposed the use of government regulation that plays, or should play, a role in environmental issues (Nelson 2020, pp. 221–222). His views and those of other influential members of the "Chicago School" played a significant role in shaping the "market fundamentalism" that became popular in the 1980s and later years, especially in the USA and the UK, and, through them, influenced several other countries, especially those countries that had been part of the Soviet Union and that had started a transition from central planning to a market economy. Market fundamentalism generally opposed larger government roles, even in connection to roles that the government ought to play in dealing with environmental issues.

In recent years, the US Trump Administration progressively weakened, or eliminated, many environmental regulations that had been introduced in earlier years and showed no interest in problems created by climate change. At the same time, it introduced high tariffs on imports of solar panels, used in utility-scale power generation, making the generation of green energy in the USA more expensive because there were no domestic alternatives for some of those panels.

There is a clear need, today, to rethink some of the above economic principles, to make them more consistent with current developments and needs in the world in which we live. Perhaps, there is also a need to save the market economy from attacks coming from populist forces, forces that do not like the way they see that market working, and do not see how it is helping everyone, as it had been claimed that it would. A recent report has found that in several important countries, including the USA and China, four out of five respondents to surveys indicated unhappiness about the way the economic system has been working (Wike et al. 2017).

The market economy needs some intelligent monitoring, and some essential corrections, including that of paying more attention to social costs and equity results. It does not need to be replaced by central planning, but, definitely, it needs come correction. In countries that have been able to make necessary corrections, such as Scandinavian countries, the market has continued to perform well its allocation and distributive roles, and personal liberties and economic incentives have not been dramatically reduced, as some had feared they would be. According to the most recent surveys, these countries have continued to be at the top of several relevant indices of productivity, performance, labor participation, and even economic liberty. This has not been true for the USA, the UK, and others, where the corrections have been insufficient.

The new economic thinking, which should replace that of the past, should not assume the smooth and orderly path of economic developments visualized by evolution and by smoothly working economies, as was theorized by the classic economists and by economists from the Chicago and Austrian Schools. Such economies were assumed to operate smoothly and to work with well-working, or even perfectly working, markets, without concern about potential catastrophes. Disasters, pandemics, and other catastrophic events, including those associated with climate change, were considered so rare that they could be ignored. The same was the case for the possible impact of human activity on the environment, activities that could make market prices differ significantly from social prices (Bostrom and Circovic 2008).

If global warming and other slowly developing catastrophes, both of a biological and natural origin, associated with climate change (which, in turn, is assumed to be the consequence of human activity) become concrete phenomena, as most reputable scientists now believe that they have already become, it would be wise to begin to react to them, and to stop acting as if they did not exist. We would do better to start developing what could be called a *disasters economics*, one that fully incorporates uncertain, but possible, future disasters in its analyses and policies, and to pay attention to the full impact of human activity on the natural world. If we are not able to do that, the economic principles which, to some extent, have guided behavior and policies in the past, will no longer be useful principles. They could clearly become economic *fables*.

Interestingly, on January 27, 2021, the President of the European Commission, Ursula von der Leyen, announced that the EU would create a biodefense preparedness program to prepare against future health crises similar to the Covid 19 pandemic. The program would seek to prepare for future pandemics by discovering and preparing for known and emerging pathogens, and by developing experimental vaccines, in collaboration with the private sector's leading pharmaceutical entities and leading research groups. Long-run financing would be made available to these entities, to allow them to engage in relevant *fundamental* research that, because such research cannot be patented, does not have an immediate market value (IMF News Report, January 27, 2021). This would seem to be an attempt to deal with future uncertain dangers, and to be better prepared to respond to some of them that are likely and expected to become more frequent, such as pandemics and epidemics.

In the chapters that follow, we shall address more directly the impact that human activities are having on the world around us, and the extent to which we humans are changing the natural world that we inherited, and which, in the past, we had shared with other species. As Saint Francis stressed, eight centuries ago, and as the current pope, who bears the same name, has continued to affirm, the other species are also God's creatures and they deserve protection and living space as much as humans do.

12 EARLY CONCERNS ABOUT THE ENVIRONMENT

12.1 Introduction

Part II of this book dealt with major disasters, pandemics and other catastrophic events that, at various times and in some places, had brought death and destruction for human beings, and other species. In many, but not in all of them, governments, with better administrators and more financial resources, could have helped at least in dealing with the consequences of the disasters, when they happened, or, perhaps, even in anticipating them, by making some preparations for their possible coming.

In all fairness, however, the governments of the past could not have done much to prevent the disasters from happening, or dealing with their consequences when they happened. In addition to their lack of administrative and financial resources, the kind of disasters that we described in the previous pages were mostly, truly, "Acts of God." They were events that could not have been anticipated with any useful degree of precision about timing or scope.

This and the following chapters will deal in part with a somewhat different situation, with what a knowledgeable author has called "A Story of the Future" (Wallace-Wells 2019). It is a story that has been developing, slowly but unmistakably, under our own eyes. It is a story for which we have been unable, *so far*, to change its course sufficiently to guarantee, or hope for, a happier ending. This is the story of ongoing climate change and the worrisome global warming that it is generating.

Without major and urgent changes, an increasing number of experts believe that, if not contained, in the long run, global warming might make the earth largely, or partly, "uninhabitable," as we know it. In its extreme form, climate change might even lead to a sixth extinction, one in which most of the species on Earth disappear, as has happened five times previously, in the millions of years of the Earth's existence

(Kolbert 2014). There is already evidence of a significant reduction in diversity, as some species have become extinct, and many more are running the same risk.

This unhappy development would not happen in a very distant future, millions of years from now, as past extinctions have. Rather, it might happen as soon as a few generations into the future. Many experts believe that it is already slowly happening and that it can be seen with our own eyes, if we are not myopic. Furthermore, it could not be argued that it would be an "Act of God," because it is clearly an act that we humans have been creating, with our normal, or routine, daily activities, often without realizing it.

The "story of the future" is a saga developing at a pace that may still be too slow for some to fully appreciate the likely longer-run consequences of ignoring what is going on; or to help promote an urgent wake up call, accompanied by concrete actions, by both national governments and international organizations, to try to change what might be the final and truly tragic destination. There would be less of an excuse that this disaster was an "unexpected random event" and that it was so unpredictable that it could not have been anticipated. This would be far from the truth.

12.2 Climate Changes in Past Centuries

As mentioned in previous chapters, over many centuries, some regions of the world had experienced occasional changes in their climate due to various natural causes, including, especially, volcanic eruptions and, possibly, solar activities. At times, those changes created difficulties for the people living through those years and in those regions. At other times they may have been beneficial.

For example, the years before the Black, or Bubonic, Plague of 1346–52, in Europe, were reported to have been unusually cold and rainy. These factors had reduced the production of food in Europe and, probably, also in Asia. That reduction may have contributed to create environmental and economic conditions that had become favorable to plagues. On the other hand, the first two centuries of the second millennium were reported to have been unusually warm, leading to more food production and to the introduction of some new techniques in agriculture that had increased food production (Cipolla 1994). According to some historians, the warmer climate might have made it easier for north

European navigators, especially the Vikings, to reach Iceland, Greenland, and even the North American continent, centuries before Columbus' trips. At that time, these places might have been warmer and, because of that, greener and more welcoming (Morison 1971). This might explain the name that was given to *Green*land.

The seventeenth century and the early part of the eighteenth century were also reported to have been unusually cold. In some of those years, the Venetian Laguna was reported to have frozen, during winter months, due to the unusually low temperature. Once again, economic conditions, at least in European countries, which in those years were also damaged by several wars, must have deteriorated, leading to reduced food production, frequent epidemics, and a reduction in the average height of the populations, a reduction that, as some recent biometric studies have reported, accompanies poor diet and food scarcity experienced by whole populations over long periods. It has been reported that the soldiers who fought for Napoleon, around 1800, were rather short (Fogel and Harris 2011; Tanzi 2018c). The Malthusian constraint on population growth had returned to be fully operational in those years. As a consequence, there was less population growth than there would be in the period after 1800 (Kuznets 1966; Cipolla 1994).

During the first half of the nineteenth century, the climate changed and the Industrial Revolution started to bring some limited, positive improvement to the standard of living of a few countries, and especially for some social classes. As time passed, a growing share of the population of the countries undergoing that "Revolution" started to experience increases in their incomes. The "enclosure movements" of land that had been used as "commons" and to which, previously, there had been free access, led to *private* agricultural use. This created personal incentives that, in turn, led to more production in the "enclosed" lands. More food could be created, leading to faster population growth. Agricultural production in newly populated distant lands in the Americas and Australia also contributed to increased food production.

12.3 The Industrial Revolution and the Need for Energy

The Industrial Revolution brought Watt's steam engine and many other mechanical inventions, and increasing demands for mechanical energy to run the newly invented machines. Human muscles were no longer sufficient to run some of these machines, and some replaced human muscles with mechanical energy, increasing labor productivity. Interestingly, at times, they also replaced what had been efficient "green energy uses," such as the windmills and sailing boats that had existed. When Columbus discovered America, and Magellan went round the world for the first time, they did it with ships that depended on the energy provided by wind. Many of these ships were later replaced by steamships, which used fossil fuels.

The new energy was initially supplied mainly by coal, where this was available, and by running water from rivers and creeks. The regions that had these energy sources in abundance initially benefited the most and grew more rapidly than those that did not have them. Some areas in England, Scotland, Germany, and some other places were the early beneficiaries because they had coal and other energy sources in abundance. From the early years of the Industrial Revolution until the time when electricity became widespread and, later, when petroleum and natural gas were also used (and, later still, atomic energy), coal remained the dominant energy source.

In some activities, such as steel- and cement-making, and in countries such as China, Australia, India, and some others, coal has continued to be a major energy source, until today. "[S]teel-making ... alone accounts for about 7 percent of global greenhouse gas emissions" (*Financial Times* 2021). The greater availability and affordability of coal has continued to make it a much-used fuel. *The Economist* (2020) reported that in spite of significant reductions in the use of coal in America and Europe in recent years (by 34 percent since 2009), coal still accounts for 27 percent of total energy used. In 2019, fossil fuels accounted for 71 percent of EU energy use, according to Eurostat (Products Eurostat News, February 4, 2021). In France, which makes greater use of atomic energy than other countries, that proportion is significantly lower. Coal still accounts for 40 percent of global electricity production (Liu and Bansal 2016).

Mining companies and power plants have been facing mounting, popular pressures to improve their targets to better comply with green energy requirements by capturing more of the carbon that they release. Several of them have made commitments to become cleaner and eventually neutral, with regard to the generation of dirty emissions, but within periods that normally extend *thirty years or more into the future* (*The Economist* 2020; *Financial Times* 2021). The problem is that by that time, following the example of the past thirty years, the Earth's temperature may have risen to dangerous levels. For example, the

European Green Deal is a plan to "decarbonize" the European Union by 2050 (Di Bonifacio and Stagnaro 2021), and the Green New Deal that has recently been introduced in the US House and Senate does not have more ambitious goals.

In the years that followed the beginning of the Industrial Revolution, years that saw the increasing use of electricity, then generated by the power of running water and by the burning of coal, coal had also powered steamships and trains, means of transportation that, in a rapidly integrating and globalizing world, were growing in importance before planes became common. The use of coal would later be accompanied, or challenged, by that of petroleum, to power some new machines that needed energy, such as cars, buses, and planes, for which coal could not be used.

For a while in the past half-century, nuclear energy played a growing role in generating electricity, until the atomic disasters, described in an earlier chapter, reduced the use of that energy source in many (but not all) countries.

More recently, what have been called "green energy sources," energy generated by the sun, the wind, sea waves, and thermal sources deep inside the Earth, have become increasingly cheaper and more important. For example, in the USA, in 2020, wind provided 9 percent of total energy use. Recently, it has been providing all the energy used by the Empire State Building in New York City and by many other buildings. The use of these sources is likely to continue and intensify.

In addition to the above green energy sources, which are already in growing use in many countries, the future may also see the use of more ambitious and technically more advanced ones, such as those from hydrogen and, perhaps, from energy obtained from atomic fusion. There is now much research in the area of hydrogen energy, including in Europe, Dubai, and the UAE. The generation of hydrogen sources might not be completely clean. It would come in different colors, reflecting how environmentally clean it is, with blue hydrogen being the desirable goal.

Atomic fusion is a far more ambitious goal. That goal is being pursued by multiple countries and a very expensive experiment that has been under way in Provence, France. It involves scientists and financial contributions from thirty-five countries. The goal of this scientific experiment would be nothing less ambitious than reproducing on Earth, on a small scale, the process that produces energy in the Sun. While the theory of how this happens is more or less understood (the atoms are squeezed together at enormous force, making them fuse and releasing heat at enormously high temperatures), the engineering challenges of producing a machine that would do this on Earth are extraordinary.

A machine that was first designed in the 1950s in the Soviet Union (Tokamat) is providing the basic design. However, producing such an enormous machine, with the degree of precision needed, and assembling in Provence all the large components produced in different and faraway places, makes it, perhaps, the most complex experiment ever carried out on Earth. If successful, this would be a game changer for energy production. At some future date, it would generate unlimited sources of green energy. However, it must be realized that, given the complexity of the undertaking, there remains much uncertainty about the timing and the success of the outcome. Nevertheless, this is a remarkable attempt at global cooperation that has received less attention than it should have.

There is also some research going on in the UK to use the energy that can be extracted from regular tidal waves and for newly designed sailing boats that would use the wind to power them. In some recent experiments, it has been shown that these ships can be as fast and efficient as steamships and would be much more energy-efficient. Also, wind turbines placed offshore have started to be installed. There are also some proposals to spread foils in the atmosphere that would block some of the Sun's rays, as some volcanic eruptions have occasionally done.

The world makes great use of most of the now available energy sources. Except for hydroelectric energy and, more recently, solar and wind power, the energy used is obtained from sources that burn carbon that releases greenhouse gases. Those gases remain in the atmosphere for a very long time and create the *greenhouse effect*, which increases the average world temperature. In the case of atomic energy, now obtained from fission, which does not burn carbon, its use leaves radioactive residuals that have to be disposed of safely, creating different difficulties. Additionally, it may lead to the atomic disasters that were described in an earlier chapter.

As mentioned, France has continued to make greater use of energy from atomic fission than other countries, so far without any major, known accident. There is also some hope that *blue* hydrogen will become available in the not too distant future; and also for traditional, but safer atomic power plants, which might make atomic plants attractive sources of energy once again.

12.4 The Cumulative Effect of Carbon in the Atmosphere

It has been estimated that from the start of the Industrial Revolution until 2020, about 1.4 trillion tons of carbon has been released in the atmosphere that surrounds the Earth. That atmosphere determines the average climatic equilibrium of the Earth. For many thousands of years, the average temperature of the *whole* Earth has been estimated to have changed relatively little. However, after the beginning of the Industrial Revolution, and especially since the 1980s, in some years, the average temperature of the Earth has been significantly higher. In more recent decades, the Earth's temperature has been rising at a pace considered worrisome by many scientists.

So far, the average Earth temperature has been estimated to have risen by about 1.1 degrees Celsius above the level it had in 1880. Furthermore, "more than half of the carbon exhaled in the atmosphere by the burning of fossil fuels has been emitted in just the past three decades" (Wallace-Wells 2019, p. 4). Those decades, and especially the last one, have been the warmest on record, causing increasing difficulties and raising insurance costs, and concerns about the future. Some cities were particularly affected, and in 2020 the temperature inside the Arctic Circle reached 38 degrees Celsius, and in Antarctica close to 20 degrees Celsius. The World Health Organization has estimated that between 1998 and 2017, more than 166,000 people were killed by excessive heat.

Carbon remains in the air for a very long time, unless it is absorbed by growing trees or other sources, and it creates the greenhouse effect, which traps the heat from the sun, preventing it from being dispersed in space. This leads to the progressively rising temperatures on the Earth's surface that have been observed.

Unlike natural gas and petroleum, coal is *concentrated* carbon and, because of this, when it is burned, it releases a great deal more greenhouse gas, the carbon dioxide that leads to global warming. Coal accounts for a larger amount of the carbon dioxide in the air than does petroleum, which has also been contributing to it on a large scale; and coal continues to be abundant and cheap. Methane gas has the same bad effect as coal, but it remains in the air for less time.

In spite of the increasing use of *greener* sources of energy in recent years, due to their falling prices and to government subsidies in some countries, coal still accounts for 39 percent of the total use of fossil fuels, and

44 percent of global greenhouse gas emissions. Its use is, thus, still a very important contributor to the reported increase of the world temperature. For that reason, unless it can be made *green*, coal should be the first energy source that should be banned, or made very expensive by carbon taxes.

Financing for coal and, to some extent, for petroleum, has become more difficult. For example, the Asian Development Bank has announced that it will no longer finance power plants that use coal. Some other financing sources have adopted similar policies. However, coal is not and should not be considered solely responsible for global warming, because there are other culprits, and coal continues to be necessary to produce steel and cement.

As mentioned earlier, the average temperature of the Earth has been increasing at a pace considered worrisome by many scientists, especially since the 1980s. Without significant and relatively rapid reductions in the use of dirty energy sources, and a reduction in deforestation, which has been reducing the capacity of trees to absorb carbon from the air, the average temperature is expected to continue to rise and could rise by 1.5 degrees Celsius or more by 2050. This rise could lead to the disastrous environmental consequences that will be described later. This development will not happen in a distant future, "when we are all dead," to use Keynes' famous definition of the long run. It might happen much sooner. To a significant extent, it is already happening, even though many humans do not yet show a full awareness of, or concern about, it.

The use of coal and other polluting energy sources is continuing in the present day, and it is expected to continue, especially in Asia and in many middle-income and poor countries. Forests continue to be burned or destroyed to accommodate economic activities. These actions continue to add a lot of carbon to the atmosphere, carbon that will continue to trap heat and contribute to the intensification of the phenomenon of global warming, as many serious climate scientists believe, and as the UN has continued to stress.

The latest *State of the Global Climate 2020* report, issued by the UN's World Meteorological Organization in 2021 states that "we are on the verge of the abyss," and the Secretary General of the UN, António Guterres, affirmed that "we have no time to waste, climate disruption is here." We should not be ignoring what science and reliable scientists are loudly telling us. In 2020, greenhouse gas concentration continued to increase in spite of the impact of the pandemic that reduced many activities, including travel worldwide.

In earlier years, especially during the second phase of the Industrial Revolution, in the decades around 1900, the countries that today are among the most economically advanced made great use of coal, and contributed the most to the increase of carbon in the atmosphere. In later years, they started to shift to other less but still dirty energy sources, especially petroleum, natural gas, and, in the past half-century, atomic energy, until the arrival of green energy, which does not add carbon to the atmosphere.

However, in some of these advanced countries, including the USA, Russia, and Australia, the shift to green energy, so far, has not gone far or fast enough, and the use of coal and petroleum has continued. These countries, therefore, share some significant responsibility for the global warming that the Earth has been experiencing in recent decades. They should bear some of the extra costs of dealing with the problem. They could do this by shifting more rapidly to green energy sources, and also by subsidizing some use of green energy in the poorer countries, encouraging the planting of trees, and discouraging the destruction of forests. However, it would be a mistake to attribute to these countries the full responsibility of the recent climate changes. Others share in the responsibility. Because of the size of their economies, the USA and China are the major responsible countries, increasingly accompanied by India.

In the 1970s, reliance on coal increased: (a) because of energy security concerns, especially during and after the oil crisis that dramatically raised the price of oil and made coal relatively cheaper; (b) because of the increase in electrification in many developing countries that required coal to run the power plants that generated electricity; and, especially, (c) because of faster economic growth and higher income levels in some large countries, especially China and, increasingly, India and some other countries that required more steel and cement production and consumption.

Higher incomes lead to increasing use of air conditioning, of cars, of refrigerators, of air travel, of computers and of various other electrical appliances that rich countries use and that individuals with higher incomes in emerging markets want to use and are now using. Today, China alone accounts for about half of global coal consumption, and India, which also has been growing fast, accounts for another significant share. Both of these countries now produce and use many cars and much cement and steel. They have large and growing middle classes, with rising incomes, who want modern facilities and a modern way of life, including travel. Therefore, the polluters are no longer just the advanced countries, although some of the latter do contribute significantly to it, including the United States. Much of the carbon in the air has been added in recent decades and will continue to be added in the years to come.

The generation of electricity and the production and consumption of steel and cement remain major reasons for the use of coal, and many developing countries are a long way from satisfying their need for electricity and for reducing their use of coal. Countries that do not produce steel import it from those that do. And those that produce it do not always use the most efficient methods to do so. There have been proposals to tax steel and cement when they are imported.

Higher average temperatures in the world, and rising incomes and population in many countries, can be expected to continue to fuel the increasing demand for electricity in future years, associated with the use of air conditioning, house heating, refrigerators, and many other electrical appliances. Some of this electricity will continue to be generated by cheap fossil fuels, and will continue to put greenhouse gas into the atmosphere, contributing to further increases in the average temperature of the planet. That temperature, which is already much higher than it should be, could continue to rise and could reach dangerous and irreversible levels, if current tends continue.

The current view of experts is that an increase in the Earth's temperature by about 2 degrees Celsius would be the extreme, permissible level that could be tolerated by adaptation, requiring costly and urgent measures to adjust to it, and to keep the world temperature at or below that level. This, however, may be an optimistic view, because such temperatures would create major and growing problems, as the current lower temperature is already creating. Higher temperatures could lead to real catastrophes, as the UN has been warning.

12.5 Other Environmental Problems

Global warming is not the sole environmental problem that the world faces, even though it is the most serious. The growing world population, combined with much higher average personal incomes for that population, especially since the 1980s, has led to some important changes in preferred diets and to a much larger increase in the demand for food in general, and especially for particular foods. It has also led to different ways of handling the food, including the growing use of plastic.

12.5.1 Problems Created by Pesticides and Fertilizers in Agriculture

There has been an increase in the production and consumption of particular agricultural crops, such as rice, wheat, corn, soybeans, and potatoes. The additional production of these crops has required more agricultural land and the use of artificial fertilizers and pesticides, to increase production and to protect crops from insects. Fertilizers and pesticides allow greater production, but they also contribute to polluting the land, rivers, lakes, and seas.

Several decades ago, new varieties of wheat and rice were developed in a research laboratory in what was called a *green revolution*, a revolution in genetically modified agricultural seeds. New ways of producing crops were introduced. American agronomists were often behind some of these developments that were copied in many other countries, especially in developing countries. They were resisted in Europe, leading to some trade friction between the European Union and US exporters, who resented the restrictions imposed on the export of some US agricultural crops that Americans considered safe.

The green revolution was credited with having saved millions of human lives, which would have been threatened by famine, in India and some other places. However, the use of fertilizers and pesticides progressively contributed to some environmental problems, by polluting land and water sources. It was for these reasons that the European Commission had put up obstacles to the import from the USA of these "genetically modified seeds" and of crops produced using them. Additionally, the green revolution made possible a large increase in the world population, an increase that is continuing today in developing countries.

12.5.2 Problems Created by Plastic Products

In addition to the problems that were created by pesticides, fertilizers, and other chemicals in past decades, the invention and increasing use of plastic in daily activities has created other problems. Plastic was definitely a great invention and its use made human life more comfortable. It also probably reduced some infections by making the handling and storage of foods safer. However, used plastic material (as well as other garbage) must be discarded, such as drinks in plastic containers. The discarding of plastic has been creating increasing environmental problems, because the discarded material often ends up in rivers and seas, and, with increasing frequency, it is found in the stomachs of dead whales, dolphins, and other fish. Plastic has also covered important coastal areas, areas that had provided nutrients to sea organisms, damaging the growth of sea plants and reducing the nutrients that support sea creatures. Plastic objects, some from China, have even made their way to the pristine environment of the Galápagos.

Until recent years, discarded plastic products had been often exported by some advanced countries to less advanced ones, including China, Indonesia, and the Philippines. The importing countries were left with the problem of how to dispose of them. They did not usually do a good job of disposing of them safely. Corruption and criminal groups played some role in the disposal of used plastic and other garbage in some countries.

In more recent years, the situation started to change. In 2018, China stopped the role that it had played in recycling other countries' used plastic products. Some other countries, such as the Philippines, sent back the ships that were carrying those products. Those who had been exporting these products had to find other ways of disposing of them. For example, Italy has had significant problems and recently has been exporting used plastic to Bulgaria, where criminal elements have been reported to play some role.

So far, progress in what to do with these materials has been limited, and the problems have continued to grow. Only 15 percent of the plastic produced annually is reported to be recycled. Much of the rest ends up being burned, at times to produce energy, or is discarded abusively, in various ways. Sooner or later, much of it makes its way into water sources. It has been estimated that in twenty years' time, the plastic that ends up in the seas will triple, to about 29 million metric tons per year. Many beaches have already been overwhelmed by plastic (Hassey et al. 2021).

The problems range from the need to separate plastic products from other garbage at the time of domestic disposal, in countries where these systems have been introduced, to deciding what to do with it once it has been separated, and determining who should bear the cost of disposing of it in ways that would not affect the environment. Should it be the users or the producers of plastic? If the producers, how can we estimate and make them pay for the environmental costs they generate, using the "polluter pays principle?"

Plastic is one among many examples of innovations that, when they were introduced, were welcomed as great inventions. For sure, plastic simplified and improved the quality of human life. Its social costs would appear only later and they would be increasingly significant.

A representative of Greenpeace, Hiroaki Odachi, reported that Japan, a country that has made a major effort to separate the collection of plastic from other garbage, collects and isolates between 70 and 90 percent of the million tons of plastic waste generated each year in that country; 56 percent of it is incinerated, thus contributing to greenhouse problems. The rest is supposed to be recycled: 10 percent of the recycling is done domestically, while the rest is shipped overseas, leaving the disposal problem to other, generally poorer countries.

A webcast of March 30, 2021 by the Wilson Center in Washington, DC reported "On the Frontline of Indonesia's Plastic Waste Crisis." It reported that "only 10 percent of Indonesia's yearly 6.8 million tons of plastic waste is recycled," and nearly half is burned or dumped. The country is "responsible for 10 percent of global plastic leakage into the ocean, second only to China." A collaborative action plan has been set up to reduce marine plastic litter in collaboration with USAID.

Chemicals and plastic may be generating other problems as well. A potentially important one, reported in a recent book (Swan 2021) and supported by many studies, is that some of these commonly used products, by interfering with normal hormonal functions, including those of estrogen and testosterone, may be putting the future of the human race at risk, at least in rich countries, by raising human infertility. The book reports that from 1973 to 2011, in Western or rich countries, the total sperm count of the average man had fallen by 59 percent, reducing the number of births. Some of these countries, Russia, Italy, and Japan, have been experiencing a significant decline in their populations for some years. In the USA, the fall in births is a more recent phenomenon that was accelerated by the pandemic in 2020.

The conclusion is that future generations, especially in advanced countries, are likely to have fewer and perhaps too few children in the years to come. However, a very recent study, at Harvard's GenderSci Lab, has questioned the results of the original studies (Aggarwal-Schifellite 2021a). Clearly, there is some uncertainty in the above result and, as in other areas, coordinated global action would be needed to deal with this potential problem, if it is a real problem. Migration might help to bring some balance, but coordination among countries would be unlikely and migration brings other problems. We find here another example of the unintended and unanticipated consequences of some actions by humans, actions whose original aim may be to improve standards of living.

Some experts have started worrying about the long-run implications of some recent technological developments, as, for example, those associated with artificial intelligence. What will happen when machines become smarter than humans? Will artificial intelligence end up helping us or damaging us? Will humans continue being in charge? Some of these pertinent questions have been addressed in an important book by Oxford philosopher Nick Bostrom (2014). One conclusion is that it is often impossible to predict the long-run effects of new technologies.

12.5.3 Demand for Superior Food Products

The increase in total world population (at least for the next few decades), accompanied by the expected increases in average incomes, has led not only to a growing demand for food in general (and for plastic and fossil fuels), but also for foods preferred by higher-income earners. Some foods are considered superior, so that as average income rises, the general demand for these foods also increases. Meat and fish products are often preferred by higher-income individuals, including chicken, pork, lamb, and, especially, beef, along with salmon and lobster, which are also much desired. Higher incomes lead to increased demand for these foods. Americans consume on average 220 pounds of meat per capita every year, and people in other countries might like to imitate that consumption.

The production of some of these foods requires much land, especially land to support cows and sheep that eat grass. In some areas, 1.5 hectares of grassland are reported to be needed to support a single cow. As the need for this land has increased, the land has been progressively taken away from areas that had been forests, savannas, and grassland, which had been available to other animal and plant species. This has created the equivalent of an "enclosure movement" on a global scale, one somewhat similar to the "enclosure movement" that took place in the nineteenth century in England and other places, when humans privatized, or "enclosed," on a larger scale, land over which some had acquired property rights. Previously, that land had been shared with other species or with other people, as "common" land, or "commons." The reduction of wilderness areas has inevitably had an impact on biological diversity, which, according to the UN and other sources, is being reduced at a fast rate, leaving less land for other species to use.

Some of the animals that feed humans today, especially cows, through their digestive systems, generate a significant amount of methane gas, a gas that contributes to the greenhouse effect. They also generate ammonia and hydrogen sulfide, which produce bad odors. The odors have been estimated to cause 17,000 deaths yearly (Washington Post 2021, p. A26).

The UN has estimated that between 20 and 30 percent of the total greenhouse effect now originates from these animal sources. This is in addition to that generated by the reduction of forests. Therefore, the consumption of meat by humans not only reduces the land that had been available to other species, and which had contributed to the diversity of the Earth, but also contributes significantly to global warming, by reducing forest areas and by the emission of methane gas by cows and other domestic animals. Some movement has begun to reduce the consumption of meat products, leading, as expected, to some strong reactions on the part of those who produce meat.

The increases in population in future years, and the increases in average incomes now taking place in China, India, Africa and other countries, are likely to intensify these damaging environmental trends in future years. The world population has been projected by the UN to approach 10 billion in 2050, and 11 billion by 2100, with significant changes among regions. The Indian population will overtake that of China by 2027. Most of the increase will come from Africa and will have a major impact on the demand for food. The US will lose its third place in population to Nigeria, and the Democratic Republic of the Congo, Ethiopia, Tanzania, and Egypt will overtake Brazil, Bangladesh, Russia, and Mexico.

The high demand for seafood, especially for certain fish, has also led to commercial overfishing, using modern techniques that often damage the seabed. This overfishing and some of the modern techniques used have been sharply criticized by environmentalists, who fear that the amount of fish in the sea is being fast reduced by overfishing and by an inability to enforce global rules on a global resource that has continued to have characteristics of being a "common" resource, without effectively enforceable rules. In several countries, criminal gangs have taken control of activities connected with the disposal of garbage; they do not follow established legal rules. And different countries have shown different interests with regard to protecting the seas. There continues to be an attitude that the oceans are too big to be affected by human actions, and that they should continue to have the characteristics of "commons," equally and freely accessible to everyone.

The increasing use of chemicals in fish farms is also creating growing problems and much of the fish that we now buy is coming from
these farms.

12.6 The Problem of Ozone Depletion

A problem somewhat similar in effect to that of plastic began to be
created about a century ago, but it was noted in the 1970s. It was found
that some chemical agents (chlorofluorocarbons, HCFCs, halons) that
were being used in several domestic products, and which had made life
easier for humans (such as manufactured halocarbon refrigerants, solv-
ents, and propellants), had been depleting the ozone layer in the atmosphere, and were contributing to the formation of ozone holes and of
springtime polar tropospheric ozone depletion. The ozone layer, which is
16 to 40 kilometers up in the Earth's stratosphere, prevents the most
harmful wavelength of the sun's rays from passing through the atmosphere. Therefore, it protects humans from these dangerous ultraviolet
rays that can cause skin cancer and other health risks, such as blindness
and cataracts. They can also hurt plants and animals.

As often happens in such cases, these bad effects were initially challenged and denied by representatives of the chemical companies that had
developed and were producing the damaging chemicals, such as DuPont
and Union Carbide. The ozone depletion theory was initially described by
them as "a science fiction tale ... a load of rubbish." But papers published by scientists, some at the University of California, Berkeley, eventually influenced public opinion, including that of President Reagan,
who had had skin cancer on his nose, and Prime Minister Thatcher,
who had a chemistry degree. The scientists who had raised the alarm
had originally been accused of being KGB agents, who wanted to destroy
the US capitalist system and replace it with the feared "socialism."

Oregon was the first American state to ban the use of the damaging
substances. In 1987, countries eventually adopted the Montreal Protocol,
which banned the ozone-depleting chemicals. The Protocol took effect in
1989. Soon, the ozone hole that had appeared over Antarctica started
shrinking. It is estimated that by 2065 the ozone hole will return to the
level it had before 1980.

The Montreal Protocol has been considered an example of an important
international environmental agreement. However, some of the new chemicals that have replaced the old ones, especially some hydrofluorocarbons,

are pollutants many times more damaging than carbon. Also, some chemicals now widely used in hairsprays and cosmetics are considered major contributors to global warming. Therefore, the battle against global warming must be fought on many fronts. New international protocols will be needed to reduce the use of these various pollutants. The bottom line is that there are many products besides coal and petroleum that generate externalities that are not good for the environment, and the greater reliance on green energy is only one part of the fight for a better environment.

12.7 Market Prices and Social Costs

Taxes on carbon emissions generated by the burning of fossil fuels have been strongly advocated by various economists in recent years (Nordhaus 2013). These taxes would make the use of such sources more expensive and also more efficient. Taxes are generally preferred to regulation by economists because they are less restrictive instruments and can be used more flexibly. Carbon taxes would aim at removing the enormous implicit subsidies that the users of fossil fuels receive (Clements et al. 2013). The subsidies are caused by the fact that the market prices of these fuels are too low, because they do not include the social costs that their use imposes on the environment and on society, through the carbon emissions that they put into the atmosphere, and in some other ways, including their effect on health.

Less attention has been paid to the fact that the market prices of some of these fossil fuels also do not include some direct environmental costs (and impacts on health), in addition to their greenhouse effects. Examples of such costs are the ugliness of mountains that have been cropped, as some mining enterprises have done in order to allow the easier extraction of coal or other minerals from mines; the contamination of rivers, caused by coal mines and other mines; oil spills in the sea; and the "black lungs" illnesses experienced by coal miners.

If carbon taxes were correctly estimated and properly used, they would remove the implicit subsidies that the users of dirty fuels receive, bringing the private costs of using coal and other polluting energy sources more closely in line with the true, total, social costs in the use of these energy sources. This would have a significant impact on policies. However, it may not be easy to determine the correct level of the social costs that dirty energy sources impose on the world. Those costs may have increased with time, as more greenhouse effects were generated. In the USA, the Biden Administration has raised the level of those costs by about seven times the level assumed by the previous administration.

The coal and petroleum industries generate many jobs, in many poor areas, such as West Virginia in the USA, and similar areas in other countries, including Australia and the UK. These jobs are socially important to those areas. Therefore, there are strong, local, vested interests that oppose, and will continue to oppose, the use of carbon taxes or some regulations. Furthermore, national governments have not been able to efficiently and widely redistribute the social benefits, in terms of a better environment, of stopping the production of coal and other dirty energy sources. Such redistribution would make those policies easier and more equitable to use, and not just more efficient. An example is a recent UK decision to allow the first deep coal mine in decades (the Cumbria mine) in a poor region, against existing UK environmental policy. Job creation was given precedence over environmental considerations. (The decision is being reviewed at time of writing.)

The private enterprises that produce petroleum and coal have invested large amounts of money (trillions of dollars) in these sources over the years. Not surprisingly, to protect those investments, these enterprises have been active, and often successful, in casting doubt in many minds about the connection that exists between the use of fossil fuels and climate change. Originally, they had questioned the validity of the temperature measurements, arguing that the temperature of cities had distorted the average annual temperatures of the planet, because cities tend to have higher temperatures, and often measurements are taken in cities. Later, they had to agree that there might have been some increases in the Earth's average temperature (that there had been some climate change), but they insisted that it was due to natural causes, not to human actions. They could point out that climate changes had happened at various times, in some areas, in the past, which had had little to do with human activities.

Their strong lobbying power has often been powerful enough to prevent significant changes in some countries (the USA, India, Russia, Australia, and some others) in the production and use of dirty sources of energy. The important social and political short-run objective of maintaining high growth and fuller employment, especially in poor areas and in countries with still lower-than-average incomes, such as India and China, has been a factor that has contributed to the continued use of coal. The goal of economic growth continues to guide economic policies in most countries (Shiller 2012).

Especially in the USA, in recent years, there has been a *shale oil revolution* that has generated a lot of natural gas extracted from rocks fragmented deep in the Earth, using various chemicals. This recent energy revolution has led to much higher production of natural gas and to a significant reduction, in the USA, in the import of oil and the use of coal, contributing to a reduction in the price of the latter.

It has also generated some significant social costs, including the contamination of underground water sources in some areas, and some health and other environmental problems, including the generation of small earthquakes in some US areas and states, such as Oklahoma. Once again, the full social costs of producing shale oil or gas are not being captured by the prices at which those energy sources are being produced and used. Shale oil production also generates methane gas, which is more polluting than coal.

As mentioned earlier, the production of meat is accompanied by significant social costs that are not captured in the prices that consumers pay when they buy meat. Taxes aimed at correcting for environmental costs ought to extend to the consumption of meat and some related products, such as milk and cheese, and especially to the price of beef.

12.8 Green Energy to the Rescue?

On the positive side, in many countries, including, especially, China, the USA, and several European countries, such as the UK, Germany, and Denmark, new and increasingly competitive "green energy sources" are being generated and used and, as we have seen, others are on the horizon. In some of these sources, energy is derived directly from the sun and the wind. These green energy sources are favorable to the environment, and their use has been increasing rapidly in recent years, replacing, in part, the dirty energy sources.

In the USA, greenhouse gas emissions created by power plants reached their highest level in 2007. Then emissions started to fall. By 2020, they had fallen significantly. The same, but less significantly, happened to the greenhouse gases emitted by transportation. For the latter, the increase in vehicle use, over the years, was balanced by their increasing efficiency in mileage, and, more recently, by the use of electric vehicles. These do not emit greenhouse gases, but use electricity, which may still depend on coal burning. In future years, most vehicles may run on electricity, hopefully generated by green sources. However, the manufacture of the vehicles will still require steel or aluminum, the production of which will generate greenhouse gas.

The net total greenhouse gases put in the atmosphere annually, by the USA and the rest of the world, is still growing, at a significant, though falling rate of increase. Therefore, greenhouse gases in the atmosphere are still rising and will remain high and will even increase for many years to come, thus continuing to increase greenhouse gases and increase world temperatures.

The increasing use of electric cars and of green energy has started to make a difference in *net* emissions, in the USA and in several other countries, especially when the electric energy that they use is not generated by the burning of coal. Cars, and even planes, that may run on solar panels are also being studied, but they may still be a long way off in the future. All this, undoubtedly, is potentially good news. Unfortunately, it may still not be sufficiently good news. At current levels, the USA and other countries are still *adding* a lot of greenhouse gases every year to the already high amount that is already in the atmosphere, and they will continue to do so for many years to come, unless techniques are discovered that actually remove them from the atmosphere in sufficient amounts to compensate for new additions.

The world is still a long way from the time when there will be a *zero net addition* to greenhouse gases that are already in the atmosphere. And that zero net addition will still leave a lot of greenhouse gas in the air, which will keep the Earth's temperature high. An analogy may help us to understand the problem. If someone who does not know how to swim is drowning where the water is 100 meters deep and rescuers manage to pull that person to where the water is only 20 meters deep, the person may still drown.

Until the time is reached when the greenhouse gas in the atmosphere starts *falling*, the US and other countries will continue to be net contributors to climate change. They will still add carbon to the atmosphere, carbon that will continue to contribute to the increase in global warming (see Bullard 2020, for some data). The carbon in the air should not only not be increased, it should be reduced, for a safer future.

In some countries, the new, green technologies have made and are making a significant difference in reducing the net amount of carbon being added to the atmosphere. Some countries are close to becoming zero *net* polluters. The UK has reduced the annual release of carbon by more than 12 percent in a few years. Significant reductions have been reported in some other countries, such as Greece and Spain. "Denmark aspires to become one of the most climate friendly countries in the world" (Batini and Segoviano 2021). It plans to reduce greenhouse gas emissions by 70 percent by 2030. This trend is important and welcomed, but it needs to be accelerated, and it needs to involve far more countries. While this trend reduces the carbon that is *added* in the air, it does nor reduce the carbon that is already up there, which may remain in the atmosphere for a very long time and which has already been creating difficulties.

The cost of generating electricity by using solar panels has fallen by about 80 percent in the past ten years, and by even more in some favorable locations, such as the Middle East and India. That trend is likely to continue. The cost of generating electricity from the wind is also down, about 60 percent, and the cost of batteries, to store the electricity produced by the sun and the wind, is 85 percent cheaper. "We now know that total decarbonisation is *technically* feasible at very low cost." "Over the long term, humanity does not face a trade-off but a clear win-win. *But we must invest to get there, and ... the amounts* [to be invested] *seem huge*" (Turner 2020, italics added). Adair Turner chairs the UK Energy Transition Commission and is knowledgeable in this area.

The question is, how long is the long run, and what can happen between now and when we get there? Equally importantly, how many countries will be able to afford and will be willing to meet these huge costs? And will the process of getting there be fast enough, before the greenhouse effect becomes more serious, or even catastrophic? Optimism can easily lead to complacency and to slow policy actions. A positive but slow trend may not be sufficient to take the world to a safe landing, or at least to one in which, with some affordable, short-run adaptation, humans can survive the worst effects of climate change, and life will remain not too different from what we have known in recent decades.

Green energy obtained from the sun and the wind has become, and is likely to continue to be, progressively cheaper. The reduction in price is leading to an increasing share of total energy use. While this change is taking place, billions of people are being added to the world population, especially in poorer countries. Many of them will likely have higher incomes than they would have had in the past. They will want to have cars, air conditioning, televisions, electrical appliances, and many other gadgets that use electricity and that have made life in richer countries more comfortable. Many will want to travel and see the world, as millions of richer, middle-class Chinese people have been doing in recent years, before the pandemic. It has also been estimated by the International Energy Agency that some 900 million individuals still live in "energy poverty" – that is, without access to energy (Birol 2007). All these will increase the demand for energy, pushing it well above current levels. The world will also continue to need steel and cement, the production of which is a major source of carbon in the air.

Whether the substitution of dirty energy with clean energy will come fast enough to prevent potentially very damaging climatic changes remains to be seen. For sure, without effective and universal acceptance of the need for change, and without strong coordinated policies among many countries, haphazard and scattered measures, along with independent private actions, will help, but may not help enough. They may not be introduced fast enough to prevent bad future outcomes.

The fight for a world without global warming is a fight for a *global* "public good," and public goods are generally produced by government actions and by global solutions. However, we do not have a global government that can promote such solutions. Therefore, national governments must continue to fight that fight, as well as they are capable of doing, and some are more capable than others, and more willing to participate in global agreements. Hopefully, the next global meeting on climate change, in Glasgow, November 2021, will signal some concrete progress.

As the conclusion of a recent report has put it, referring to the USA: "2020 has been quite a year. The [USA] has seen record-breaking wildfires, hurricanes, floods and tornadoes, prompting governments, insurers and property owners to think of new ways to mitigate risk and make our neighborhoods more resilient." "By understanding the risk these events pose . . . we can better plan for a catastrophic tomorrow" (CoreLogic 2021).

The US National Oceanic and Atmospheric Administration has estimated that in 2020 there were twenty-two separate billion-dollar climate-induced events in the USA. The previous record for a single year was sixteen. Air pollution is also affecting life expectancy in major cities. Other countries were not spared these extreme events. In the future we may have lower life expectancies and lower birth rates, in at least some countries. Japan, Italy, Russia, and several other more advanced countries are already experiencing fast-falling populations.

Only governments could coordinate globally the needed plans to deal with this problem, as they did with the ozone problem. It is an illusion to believe that spontaneous actions by free individuals or by uncoordinated individual governments would be capable of doing what is needed. However, the actions of some governments may make things worse. The year 2021 started with winter storms of record-breaking severity in Texas, a state that has been allergic to regulation and indifferent to climate change. The record storm created historic problems and revealed the poor preparation by that state for events that are becoming, and are likely to become, less rare. In this lack of preparation Texas is not alone.

The reports cited earlier provided a list of some of the worst climate disasters in US history. They include Hurricane Katrina in August 2005, which cost $125 billion and caused 1,833 deaths; Hurricane Harvey in August 2017, which cost $125 billion and caused more than 100 deaths; Hurricane Maria in September 2017, which cost $90 billion and caused 3,059 deaths; and Hurricanes Sandy and Irma in October 2012 and September 2017, which cost $70 billion and $50 billion respectively, and that caused 233 and 97 deaths. The concentration of very destructive hurricanes in more recent years is evident.

12.9 Different Impacts of Climate Change among Countries

A difficulty in promoting sufficient, international, coordinated policies in the absence of a global government, but in the presence of hundreds of different countries and governments, is that the mid-run impact of climate change on different countries and on different social groups is not the same. Some countries may see it as being to their advantage to let other countries introduce the needed changes, especially if these changes require costly investments. They can remain classic "free riders." Some will continue to oppose drastic measures on grounds that they restrain individual freedom.

It should be recalled that in the USA, some individuals even objected to the use of more efficient electric light bulbs, some years ago, when these became available. They saw their use as a restriction on their personal liberty. Some have continued to object to the use of face masks and vaccination as protections against the Covid 19 pandemic. The assumption of rationality on the part of individuals may not be a guarantee that the policies that science judges to be the best will be accepted by everyone, and in the necessary time. Some individuals define rationality differently from others, and the rate at which individuals discount future costs and benefits tends to be different among different people.

In the medium run, some countries, especially Russia and Canada, are likely to gain, as countries, from climatic change, because of their location, and because of the fact that they are both major producers of dirty fuels. Some poorer countries will not have the money necessary to make the costly switch to green energy from their already existing coal-fueled plants, which were paid for in the past, to costly but more efficient new plants that require new investment. This change may happen in the long run, but the long run may be too far in the future to stop global warming. During the transition time, many bad things might happen. Rich countries, directly or through international institutions, should help poorer countries, by financing some of the needed changes. And even within the countries that will benefit from global warming, some groups, such as the Inuit tribes who had lived in parts of Canada and Greenland, may be forced to change a way of life that they might have preferred.

12.10 Concluding Remarks

The bottom line is that it may be a cruel illusion to believe that private actions, helped by some important technological changes, will, automatically and quickly, solve the ongoing global warming problem. Or that adoption by independently operating single agents of greener energy will make us deal *in time* with the future negative impact of climate change. These reactions are likely to help, but they are not likely to help sufficiently and in the needed time. The consequences might be too tragic to allow a continuation of current trends. The conclusion of a study conducted at Harvard, with the collaboration of various British universities (Burrows 2021), has reported that, in 2018, 18 percent of total global deaths were caused by damaging matter released in the air by the burning of fossil fuels.

Unlike other disasters, climate change is an event that is easy to ignore in the short run, because it does not happen suddenly. However, it is too frightening to ignore over the long run, and to simply hope that it will not become disastrous for the planet and its creatures; or to hope that with some spontaneous adaptation, everything will be okay. *Global* dangers require *global* solutions, and dealing with global public "bads" requires *coordinated*, global government decisions. The coordinated and effective actions of many governments will be needed, in addition to the ingenuity of individuals.

Those public actions will need to be accompanied by serious *and enforceable* global agreements. The time for effective global cooperation should not be delayed. International organizations, including the UN and those created at Bretton Woods and later, were formed precisely for the purpose of facilitating global cooperation. They should be more active than they have been so far, and more global in following interests.

Whether global agreements will rise quickly enough to the needed level to prevent the *worst* effects of global warming remains the proverbial $64,000 question. To a significant extent, the answer to that question may determine the future of life on Earth, as we have known it, and that of the human race and of other species that have considered the blue planet their permanent home. In the coming years, we will stress that all species are linked by a common destiny and that they are all guests of the same habitat. The more we get away from the interests of specific groups or individuals, and the more we take a global and world community perspective, the greater appears to be the need for some global, coordinated actions.

13 FROM ENVIRONMENTAL CONCERNS TO CLIMATE CHANGE

13.1 Growing Environmental Concerns in Past Years

Some concerns about the impact that increasing human activities and the growing world population might be having on the Earth, the blue sphere that hosts humans and billions of other species, started to be expressed in the 1950s. At that time, lead in the gasoline used by cars, which were becoming larger and were inefficient in their gasoline consumption, started to attract attention. The lead was seen to pollute the air, especially in large and less well-ventilated cities. That gasoline use started to be seen as potentially damaging to human health. On hot summer days, the sky was, at times, partly obscured by the air pollution created by the many cars using leaded gasoline.

This was seen as a mostly localized pollution problem. Questions started to be asked about the effect that the lead in the air might have on humans, and especially on young children. There was increasing pressure on car makers to make cars more efficient by changing their design, their size, and their engines. These changes would reduce pollution and also oil imports. Diesel cars started to be prohibited. There was the usual, strong opposition to the regulations that some states, especially California, were imposing on car-makers, to induce them to produce cars that would be more efficient and less polluting.

Over subsequent years, the efficiency of cars increased a great deal, because of improved styling and mechanical improvements to engines. Many gasoline stations closed because of the reduction in gasoline use, and the quality of the air generally improved. There was no sign that these regulatory measures had reduced individual liberties, as some had argued that they would. However, they had improved individual health and air quality.

In 1962, a marine biologist named Rachel Carson, who had published some popular books on the beauty of the seas, published a new book called *Silent Spring*. It became a much-discussed bestseller. The book attracted attention, especially from those who had started to worry about the increasing number of people in the world to be fed, and about the little-monitored and controlled impact that some industrial activities and some chemicals were having on the planet. At that time, the population of the world was around 3 billion, less than half of what it is today, and a third of what it is projected to be in future decades. A major concern seemed to be how these many people would be fed.

The individuals who first worried about these problems called themselves *environmentalists*. They started to form associations with those who shared the common objective of defending the Earth's environment. They were often ridiculed as being leftist, and being against individual freedom and capitalism. Population growth became a major concern, and some countries, such as China, introduced regulations (such as "one couple, one child") to reduce population growth.

Carson had written especially about the impact that the increasing use of pesticides and other, recently developed chemical substances that were used in agriculture, was having on the quality of land and of water in rivers, springs, and lakes, sources that in the past had provided people with clean drinking water and an ample supply of fish. Carson argued that some chemicals were damaging the water sources and were depriving them of oxygen – oxygen that is important to sustain the nutrients in the water that feed the fish and that sustain marine life. She criticized the chemical industry for minimizing the problem and for spreading what she considered false information about the safety of some of their products. Perhaps, in part, because of the impact of Carson's book, in 1970, with an executive order, President Nixon created the Environmental Protection Agency (EPA), and in 1972, the US Congress passed the Clean Water Act.

With the passing of time, the Clean Water Act would be challenged and watered down by some US administrations, and by pressure coming from some Members of Congress, who were lobbied and financed by the affected private enterprises in their jurisdictions. They expressed concern about profits, short-term economic growth, loss of jobs and of economic freedom, and were much less interested in a clean environment. President Reagan and, later, President Trump would be particularly indifferent, or even antagonistic, to environmental concerns. Reagan would famously state that "conservation means that you are cold in winter," which he did not consider a favorable prospect. And Trump considered concerns about climate change as being against the interests of the United States.

The Trump Administration had promoted the scaling down, or even the removal, of many regulations that had been introduced in previous years and some environmental crimes went unpunished. The science behind those regulations and the scientists who pushed for them were challenged, and some of the scientists were removed, silenced, or forced to quit. Government reports were censored for any references to global warming. There was more freedom for polluters.

A clean environment is, obviously, a *global* public good. It is a good that is not generated automatically by private actions that continue to be directed in favor of specific interests. The public interest must prevail over damaging private interests. In the absence of a global government, some coordination by the governments of many countries is needed and it must be especially supported by the largest countries. The problem is that a dirtier environment is often associated with economic benefits accruing to enterprises that can reduce their costs by disposing, at low costs for them, of potentially dangerous chemicals and other substances in creeks and rivers, and by storing them in dams or other storage areas, or simply dumping them on the environment. Many mining and other enterprises did this in the past with impunity, and some have continued to do it in the present, especially when they think they can get away with it, as they have done in Brazil and in Syria, for example, in recent years, and as they did routinely in most countries in the past.

In 1970, the Jones and Laughlin Steel Corporation in the USA was sued for discharging large amounts of cyanide into the Cuyahoga River, near Cleveland, Ohio. The danger that the disposal of chemicals such as arsenic and cyanide in drinking water might create for children and others continued to be challenged by well-financed representatives of big enterprises. At times, the science behind some regulatory decisions was questioned, because it was still less than absolutely definitive about those dangerous effects. This uncertainty was exploited to challenge some regulations, and to take up critical and adversarial positions vis-à-vis some proposed regulations.

Some lakes and rivers were being contaminated, and in 1969 the Cuyahoga River had even "caught fire" because of the many chemicals that were being discharged into it, leading to a public outcry. There were cases of towns or areas where the population could no longer drink publicly provided or underground water because of contamination.

To save money, some towns had switched to dirtier water sources. Some lakes, such as Lake Erie in the USA, started developing algae that were considered toxic to humans, preventing the use of the lake for recreational purposes. In the Soviet Union, which seemed to be particularly indifferent to environmental issues, some large lakes were run dry by the diversion of water sources for irrigation purposes.

In 2020, the US Environmental Policy Administration (EPA) announced that a cost–benefit analysis would be applied to the enforcement of the Clean Water Act. This implied that there are economic benefits associated with less clean water that may be considered more important than the provision of clean water and, presumably, of better public health. By stressing the *costs* of a cleaner environment and minimizing the benefits of a regulation (say, clean water), the EPA would acquire the power to reduce or weaken many regulations, as it had been doing during the 2017–20 years. More "economic liberty" was acquired by the polluters, at the cost of a dirtier environment for the citizens. Not surprisingly, the same administration would ignore the issue of global warming, having withdrawn from the 2016 Paris Agreement, an accord that had tried to establish some voluntary guidelines for countries and that President Trump had immediately declared as being damaging to the interests of America.

It should be recalled, from previous chapters, that by the time Carson published her book, there had already been some major environmental disasters involving chemical plants, and a debate had started about the claimed safety of cigarette smoking and of some new chemicals. Attitudes had begun to change, and the quality of the environment had started to be seen, at least by some, as a superior good, one whose importance and the demand for which increased more than proportionally with higher incomes. When one is starving, he/she worries less about the environment and more about how to fill the stomach. Carson's book had called attention to a specific, though widespread, problem, rather than to a general, environmental problem, as climate change would later become.

If Carson had been writing today, she might have written another book, which could have been called *Silent Seas*. It would describe not the beauty of the seas, but the problems that acidity, plastic materials, and higher temperatures are creating for the seas and the creatures that live in them. Some areas of the seas and of other bodies of water have become *dead zones*, where, because of a lack of oxygen in the water, there are no living organisms, including coral reefs, and no fish. The death of many coral reefs has attracted increasing attention in recent years, especially in Australia. Whales, dolphins, and other creatures, with increasing frequency, are being found dead, because of plastic objects that they have ingested. And plastic objects have even reached the Galápagos.

Polar bears and other species that live in the very cold regions of the Arctic have been losing much of their natural habitat because of the melting of the ice that had covered the water. Concerns have also been raised about the ecosystem of the American "Great Lakes," which hold "six quadrillion gallons of freshwater that our planet needs to survive" (Folger and Ladzinsli 2020, *National Geographic* cover story). Developments in the Great Lakes, in rainforests, and in savannas and grasslands have shown the great ecological interconnectivity that exists among different organisms, about which we may have been less aware in the past, or to which we paid less attention. Biological diversity is an important, global public good.

Huge areas of previously pristine forests and grasslands have been converted into directly productive land, to feed humans or to provide them with raw materials and minerals for their economic activities. Activities such as mining and logging have often displaced primitive tribes and many animal species that depended on those areas for their existence. The new activities have also polluted large areas. The rights of the people and of the animals who had lived in those areas have been ignored, as they have been considered not important enough to stop human progress. Human progress continues to be seen from an exclusively narrow economic development perspective, and not as a zero sum game, as it often is, between humans and other species.

Glaciers have been melting at an increasingly fast pace in Greenland, Iceland, the Arctic, and, especially, in the Antarctic regions, and also in the Himalayas, the Andes, and the Alps, slowly contributing to the rising sea level, a development that has started to create some difficulties for some of the world's large metropolises and areas located at sea level. To protect these cities from the effects of the rising sea will require huge and increasing resources. For example, the US Center for Climate Integrity and Resilient Analytics has estimated that the twenty-two vulnerable coastal states would need to spend $400 billion over twenty years to protect the most vulnerable areas.

Also, the glaciers feed important rivers which, by providing needed water, make living conditions possible for billions of people (rivers such as the Ganges, the Mekong, the Nile, and the Colorado). They risk becoming progressively dryer because of the melting of the glaciers that used to feed them. This melting could create unimaginable difficulties for the people who depend on that water (Gates 2021a). This is not a future and *uncertain* problem. To a considerable extent, it is already happening. It has started to lead to increasing migration from some such areas. It also represents "a change in our practice of mourning and remembrance, a change in how we understand our history," as Sarah Dimick put it in the *Harvard Gazette* (Aggarwal-Schifellite 2021b).

The Arctic regions today are the fastest warming areas on Earth. They are also some of the places where the interdependence of nature and human activities is, perhaps, most obvious. The melting of the ice that had covered the sea in the Arctic, previously allowing many animals to live on the ice, is making that large body of water navigable, creating important economic benefits for Russia and some other countries. However, it is also having an important, indirect effect on global warming, because the loss of the ice cover for the large body of water is eliminating the cooling effect that the ice had provided, by deflecting the sun's rays during the summer months, when the sun shines twenty-four hours a day. Because of the melting of the ice cover, the sun is warming the water in the Arctic Sea at a fast pace.

Reliable data indicate that the average annual temperature of the polar regions has been increasing at a much faster rate than in other regions of the planet. An important side effect of this is that the polar regions are having less of a cooling impact on the rest of the planet than they had in the past. Another important effect is that many of the animals that had lived on the ice, such as polar bears and others, are fast losing their living space and facing existential difficulties (Spohr and Hamilton 2021).

The increase in temperature in Siberia is making that immense region a more pleasant place to live in for its scarce (about four million) population, and is expanding the land that Russia can use for agricultural purposes. However, it is also warming the *permafrost*, the land that had been permanently frozen and had been unavailable for agricultural use. The warming of the permafrost is releasing into the atmosphere large amounts of methane gas, a gas that contributes a lot to the greenhouse effect and to global warming. This is an effect that the use of green energy, to replace coal and petroleum, cannot eliminate and must compensate for, as long as the world temperature remains high enough to continue, or to accelerate, the melting of the permafrost.

13.2 Growing Awareness about Connectivity

Since Carson wrote her bestselling and influential book, we have become increasingly aware of the connectivity that exists among the various parts of the planet, and among the various species and organisms that share the Earth with humans as their habitat. In spite of their importance, human beings do not have, or should not have, an exclusive monopoly over the use of the planet. The Earth is not their private property. When concerns about the environment started to increase, sixty or so years ago, there was much less awareness of the importance of, and concern about, this connectivity.

In 1970, the Editors of *Fortune* magazine published a small book by the title *The Environment: A National Mission for the Seventies*. The book contained thirteen essays written by informed individuals, all dealing with various issues related to the environment. Of particular interest was a "Statement by President Nixon," which made some very important observations. Nixon's essay cited de Tocqueville, who, after his trip to America, a century and a half earlier, had written that America had been lucky to receive from God "a boundless continent." However, Nixon continued, "the abundance that has helped to make America great … has too often worked to … [make] us careless. Many Americans have taken our resources for granted and have relied, without reflection, on their continued plenty. Many have failed to imagine a time when the air and water would lose their sparkling quality" (Editors of *Fortune* 1970, p. 11). Nixon added: "Our generation has inherited the results of our carelessness;" "[s]trong government action would be required — at the Federal state and local level." He called this action a "crusade" (ibid., p. 12), and defined the quality of the environment as "not only a national" but also an "*international* concern" (ibid., p. 13; italics added).

Considering that the above statements were made more than fifty years ago, and by a Republican President, they were extraordinarily ahead of their time, especially when one compares them with those made by some government officials in recent years, including by a recent US president of the same party as Nixon; and considering what has been happening to the environment around the world since that time. Clearly, Nixon was well ahead of his time, or the world was well behind his, and he may have been the US president most concerned about the environment until 2021.

In the 1970s there were growing concerns about the impact that many dams, some of them very large, built for irrigation and to provide electricity to less developed areas of the USA, were having on the environment, in previously pristine areas, and on the fish population of rivers. Originally, these dams, such as the Hoover Dam, had been admired mainly as marvels of engineering, and as great contributors to human welfare. Today, there are an estimated 58,000 dams around the world that have significantly changed the original flow of water, presumably in favor of humans.

When the relationship between economic growth and environmental decay started to attract the attention of a growing number of environmentalists and some economists, views about the beneficial effects of these dams started to change. As the title of a book published at about that time put it: the *solution* to low income levels and to poverty, i.e. economic growth, had started to be seen as the *problem* (Barkley and Seckler 1972). That solution would continue to be a problem. Today, large dams on rivers that cross different countries often attract great controversy, or even threaten wars, as the dam on the Nile, in Ethiopia, has been doing. Dams are one important and visible way in which humans have changed the natural world.

In the 1970s there was increasing attention and support by some experts, and even by some economists, to the idea of a self-sustaining world, one that would remain naturally balanced without economic growth, as are virgin forests. (See the interesting essays in a 1973 book, *The No-Growth Society*, edited by Olson and Landsberg.) Of course, there were many unanswered questions about how that no-growth world would be achieved and maintained, and what its implications would be. (See, especially, the essay by Kenneth Boulding in Olson and Landsberg 1973.)

Another environmental concern that attracted considerable attention in the 1970s was the possibility that, if economic growth at the time continued, the world would eventually run out of some important natural resources, including coal and petroleum, which were assumed to be in limited supply (Ehrlich and Erlich 1972). The oil crisis of the 1970s gave some credence to this possibility at the time.

The *Club of Rome* came into existence in those years. That Club included individuals who believed that population growth needed to be reduced, and that the world, as a whole, should aim at zero economic growth, accompanied by policies aimed at making the distribution of the world's and of individual nations' incomes more equal, to make zero growth more acceptable, or even possible. This would require important and radical redistribution policies, both across and within countries.

Since that time, (a) the world population has more than doubled, and is expected to triple and reach nine billion in the next generation; (b) world GDP has grown much more than world population; (c) petroleum and other resources, so far, have *not* become as expensive or as scarce as they had been forecast to become in the 1970s; (d) the distribution of *world income* has become more equal, because of the fast growth of previously very poor and very populated countries, such as China, India, Bangladesh, Indonesia, and the Philippines (Milanovic 2005). That fast growth in previously poor countries lifted hundreds of millions of individuals out of extreme poverty, while making the distribution of income for the world as a whole less unequal.

At least up to 2020, there has been little evidence of the growing scarcity of fifty basic commodities, according to an index published by Gale Pooley and Marian Tupy (2021) for the Cato Institute. But the fifty commodities may not be fully representative, and the situation might quickly change.

However, the distribution of income *within* many important countries (USA, China, India, Russia, Brazil, UK, etc.) has become less equal, raising questions about, and providing less support for, a no-growth world. There has not been evidence of a change in the prevalent thinking that has continued to favor economic growth and the opportunities that it provides to increase standards of living. And the assumption has continued to be that basic commodities will continue to grow in line with growing needs.

The "market fundamentalist" policies, which have become fashionable in many countries since the 1980s, were a call for economic efficiency and economic growth, not a call for better income distribution and a more sustainable environment. The expectation was and continues to be that more efficiency would lead to faster growth, that economic growth is desirable, and that "trickle-down" would benefit everyone. The goal was to make everyone consume more.

The fiscal and monetary policies of many countries have continued to be directed toward the promotion of economic growth, with the notable, but trivial exception of Bhutan, a country that officially made the growth of Gross National *Happiness*, and not of Gross Domestic *Product*, the goal of its national policies. Bhutan's example attracted some initial attention, but it has not been followed by any other country, in spite of the publicity and support that it received from some popular economists (Stiglitz, Sen, and others) and from some important political figures, some years ago. The pursuit of growth has continued to be more important than that of happiness for economic policy.

13.3 From Environmental Concerns to Climate Change

In earlier decades, environmental concerns had been related to specific environmental issues and problems. In more recent decades, attention has turned to climate change, and especially to global warming. It turned to the impact that humans might be having on the Earth's temperature and climate. As far back as 1896, a Swedish chemist, Svante Arrhenius, had theorized that an increase in greenhouse gases in the atmosphere, caused by the burning of wood, coal and some other fuels, might in time lead to higher temperatures for the planet. That possibility was largely ignored, until the 1990s.

The year 1988 had seen an unusually severe drought in the USA. The drought led to a Senate Hearing. In testimony presented at that hearing, the scientist James R. Hansen forcefully and convincingly argued that human activity was likely to be responsible for the higher temperature and possibly for the drought. He linked droughts to the increase in greenhouse gases that had been taking place from the time when large amounts of dirty fuels (coal, petroleum, and others) had been used to generate energy, since the beginning of the Industrial Revolution.

Hansen's testimony led to strong denials from representatives of the coal and petroleum companies. However, it also attracted a lot of media attention. A speech the same year (on September 27, 1988) by Margaret Thatcher to the UK Royal Society, which also showed concern about climate change, contributed to making climate change a topic worthy of media attention. Thatcher's speech had been directed at advocating the use of atomic energy in the UK, which in her view would not generate greenhouse effects. Her speech had been mainly in support of more use of atomic plants.

Hansen's testimony was followed, some years later, by the screening of former US Vice President Al Gore's documentary, *An Inconvenient Truth*, and, in 2006, by the publication of the scholarly, 700-page UK study, *The Stern Review: The Economics of Climate Change* (Stern 2006). That well-documented study attracted a lot of media and scholarly attention (inter alia, Nordhaus 2007; Weitzman 2007).

In 2015, NASA scientists reported that carbon dioxide in the atmosphere had been increasing well beyond past levels, and that half of the carbon dioxide released when fossil fuels are burned remains in the atmosphere for thousands of years. An estimated fifty-one billion tons of greenhouse gases are released into the atmosphere each year. As Bill Gates would put it, in a lecture given at Harvard in February 2021, "the CO_2 accumulates like water in a bathtub that is already almost full. When [the water] hits a certain level, it overflows and, in the case of climate, it tips" (Gates 2021b). It is the sum of all the CO_2 in the atmosphere since the Industrial Age that determines the rise in the temperature. This means that, even a sharp reduction of *new* emissions would not reduce the existing temperature for a very long time.

The above reports and announcements made global warming a popular, though still highly controversial, topic for the media, and especially for the public, in the years that followed. This would lead to the 2016 Paris Agreement, coordinated by the UN, which aimed at encouraging global collaboration and national actions in introducing measures that would mitigate global warming.

In the USA, much skepticism has remained about global warming among large sections of the population, and generally there has been less interest in the issue than in other rich countries, especially in Europe. Some individuals have continued to believe that solar and volcanic activities or other phenomena have been behind climate change, not the burning of fossil fuels. Representatives of the fossil fuel industry have continued to question the statistics and have remained skeptical, even though recent public pressure to make their performance "greener" has increased, and has led to some promises by the industry to do better in future years. "Green coal" has remained an important goal, and the generation of green energy and the possibility of creating "green hydrogen" have been attracting increasing attention. Sources of financing have tightened for projects aimed at generating dirty fuels.

13.4 Climate Change and Income Distribution

It is wealthier individuals who increasingly account for, or benefit from, a disproportionate share of the growth of GDP, and for the actions and spending that have led to climate change. Climate change and its impact for global warming has become a major concern. In terms of importance, it has replaced past concerns about running out of natural resources. The environmental problem of the 1970s has reappeared under a different and more worrisome guise, as *global warming*, a change in the climate that, in the view of some experts, if not stopped, threatens to make the earth *uninhabitable* in the long run, possibly bringing a *sixth extinction* of the species on Earth.

Experts may be wrong about this worry, at least for the short and medium run. But their predictions are so worrisome that they cannot be dismissed, because of the uncertainty that accompanies them. Suppose that the experts are not wrong? Uncertainty creates some irrationality that makes some or many individuals ignore that possibility, especially in the presence of more urgent needs faced by many humans that distract them from longer-run problems, which may occur when they are no longer alive. Concern about global warming requires some altruism, especially vis-à-vis those who will be living in future generations, and also with regard to other species; and because global warming will affect different individuals at different times.

As a recent newspaper article put it, "the emissions [that contribute to global warming] attributable to the richest 1 percent of the global population account for more than double those of the poorest 50 percent" (Dennis et al. 2020, p. A3). US emissions per capita are estimated to be 75 percent above those of China. This means that the distribution of living standards plays a large role.

The year 2020 was the warmest year on record so far, in a decade that was also the warmest, according to the UN World Meteorological Organization. The increase in the Earth's temperature started around 1940 and accelerated after 1980. The year 2020 also experienced the most active hurricane season in the Atlantic and a very active typhoon season in the Pacific and Indian Oceans. Cyclone Amphan, in the Bay of Bengal, in May 2020, displaced almost five million people and cost an estimated $13 billion. Five other cyclones cost at least $5 billion each.

The cyclone seasons have started earlier and are lasting longer than in the past. In January 2021, California experienced torrential rains brought about by slow-moving "atmospheric rivers," which can carry enormous amounts of water and caused mudslides and brought misery to areas that, earlier, had experienced forest fires because of the drought, fires that can also generate toxic fumes.

In February 2021, the US experienced record-breaking winter storms that left large areas of Texas without electricity and without drinking water, during extremely cold temperatures, threatening the lives of many residents. Indifference to climate change and the power of the fossil fuel industry in Texas had played a role in the regulatory framework that contributed to that result, and in the design of the little protected electricity grid.

Firefighters in the west of the United States, in Australia, and even in Siberia, had to fight enormous, horrific, and highly destructive fires in 2020. Other areas have not been spared by very destructive storms. South Sudan, for example, experienced one of the worst floods on record, which destroyed much of the country's annual crop. Through major storms, floods, and even locust invasions in Africa, climate change is generating, or contributing to, major and increasing pain in various parts of the world. The year 2020 was a very costly one for insurance companies, which had seen rising costs over the past decade. The Covid 19 pandemic added to the misery, and some other dangerous viruses, such as Ebola, reappeared in Africa. In 2020, life expectancy in the USA was reported to have fallen, and it probably also fell in other parts of the world.

The distribution of income *within countries* can be seen as a major environmental, and not just as a political and social, problem. It is a problem with obvious consequences for the growth of the global average temperature. This implies that it will be more difficult to address the problem of global warming, without addressing not only economic growth, but also the increasingly uneven income distribution of that growth. The environmental traces that people with high incomes leave on Mother Earth have become more visible and more damaging than those left by the poor. It is not just population growth that is the problem, but, increasingly, the increase in average income, accompanied by the uneven distribution of higher incomes.

This means that the share of properly measured total "income" that the top one percent gets and uses is much larger, when the unmeasured social costs that it imposes on the Earth (the subsidies they implicitly receive through the use of cheap carbon and petroleum, and in other ways) are taken into account. Those subsidies go disproportionally to high-income groups. "Market fundamentalism," through its likely impact on income distribution, has clearly been a contributor to global warming.

In 2020, while many so-called "essential workers" had to deal with the consequences of the pandemic and also with the loss of their jobs and of their "essential income," the world's 500 richest individuals added $1.8 trillion to their total wealth. They experienced an increase equivalent to 31 percent of their wealth, according to the Bloomberg Billionaires Index. They and other rich individuals have continued to do very well, so far, in 2021, because of the booming stock market. This is not the "trickle-down" that the prevailing economic paradigm had promised. In 2020–21, while millions of workers have suffered, the richest have enjoyed record stock market gains. This could not be seen as good publicity for the prevailing economic paradigm, and it may have implications for long-run developments.

The available statistics seem to indicate that the countries that have been more concerned about the environment and, in recent years, have started to take some serious measures to deal with the bad effects of climate change, such as the UK, Denmark, Finland, Sweden, Germany, the Netherlands, and Norway, are mostly (though not all) countries with more even income distribution. On the other hand, countries that have shown more indifference to climate change, are often countries with high Gini coefficients. The USA, Russia, China, India, Brazil, and Mexico are among them. This may not be a coincidence.

Whether the Earth can continue to support current and likely future increases in consumption by humans (especially the consumption by billions more individuals, with higher incomes), without major changes, should become a major and urgent question for policy. It implies that income distribution within countries must be seen, and must become, part of the ecological problem, and part of the solution to the global warming problem.

This, of course, will make the solution more difficult, because richer individuals have more control over policies, and are those who have invested much money in the enterprises that produce dirty energy. Some negative reactions have already begun to the policy changes proposed by the recently installed Biden Administration in the USA, concerning the environment and tax changes, and such reactions can be expected to intensify. In 2021, the USA rejoined the Paris Agreement and will be a full actor in the November 2021 meeting in Glasgow.

Hopefully, more democratic institutions and wisely corrected market economies would still be part of the desirable solution, preventing more radical alternatives that would rely exclusively on uncoordinated top-down solutions. The solution requires major policy changes in market economies, not necessarily a radical paradigm change. We do not want to go back to central planning, Soviet style. The danger is that resistance to reasonable changes may, in the long run, bring less desirable populist changes in countries that rely on democratic elections.

14 FROM CLIMATE CHANGE TO GLOBAL WARMING

14.1 Short- and Medium-Run Scenarios

The impact that climate change has, or will have, on humans can be assessed from an immediate, or short-run, perspective, or from a longer-run one. That impact can be significantly different from the one that the same higher average world temperature might have if sustained over a long time. Both the temperature level and the length of time over which a given level is sustained are likely to be important determinants. Additionally, the direct, short-run impact of climate change on the human race might be significantly different from the direct impact that it may have on the Earth's ecological diversity, created by evolution over millions of years.

That diversity made the Earth the diverse, fascinating, and beautiful place that it is. Humans were an important part of it, but they were not the only important species. Some religions, such as Buddhism, give a lot of importance to other species, as have some Christian saints in the past, such as Saint Francis. In this chapter, we pay attention to these two different perspectives. In a later section of this chapter, we shall focus briefly on what could be called a bad, or worst, scenario. It is the scenario that might be created by a higher, but still not very high temperature, sustained over a long period. It would approach, but would not reach, a truly catastrophic scenario, one that an average world temperature increase significantly higher than, say, 2 degrees Celsius, would likely create. We could call that the "nightmare," or the "uninhabitable earth," scenario.

The immediate, or short-run effects of climate change can not only be different from the long-run effects, they can also differ significantly between different regions of the world, and different countries, favoring or damaging some more than others. For a few important countries, the short-run effects of a higher average temperature might be largely beneficial, and might even be welcomed by those who live in those countries. Such countries include Russia, Canada, Iceland, and parts of Alaska, the north of Scandinavia, and the Patagonian parts of Argentina and Chile.

The above countries and areas have extensive territories located in regions in the far north or the far south. Those territories had been too cold in the past to sustain much in the way of productive agricultural activities, before the recent climate change, which has raised their average temperature enough to bring large extensions of land into possible agricultural use, and has made life more pleasant for those who live there. This, for example, has been reported to be happening in Siberia.

As a recent article in the *New York Times Magazine* put it: "A great transformation is now underway in the eastern half of Russia," where "for centuries the vast majority of the land [had] been impossible to farm." The spring now comes earlier and "rainstorms are now stronger" (Lustgarten 2020, p. 26). The average annual temperature has been moving toward an *optimum level* for agriculture that, according to the Proceedings of the US National Academy of Science, is between 52 and 59 degrees Fahrenheit.

Russian crops are likely to increase in the next few decades, while they may fall in many other parts of the world. Russia has already become the largest exporter of wheat in the world, while in the past it had experienced several famines. Russia and Canada will be able to capitalize on climate change because they are far from the Tropics, and are not affected (or at least, are less so) by the more frequent and more powerful storms, droughts, and heatwaves that climate change has been bringing to countries and territories closer to the Equator.

Russia and some other countries will also benefit from the fact that the melting of ice in the Arctic Ocean is opening trade routes that had been impossible to navigate until now. Those trade routes will dramatically reduce the time taken to travel by ship from the North Pacific to the North Atlantic, and vice versa, and will also reduce the time taken to reach the Mediterranean regions. It might also increase congestion in the Bering Strait, with the accompanying danger of accidents. To reduce or avoid these accidents will require some global cooperation. Some attempts are likely to be made by some countries, especially Russia, to establish sovereignty over certain areas and natural resources in the Arctic, leading to global frictions.

However, for the countries that host the overwhelming share of the world population, especially those located in Southeast Asia and parts of

Africa and America, the effects of climate change will be anything but benign. "These countries [will] have to deal with rising sea, with droughts, and with an overheating climate. By 2070, more than three billion people will find themselves living outside the optimal climate for human life, forcing billions of migrants to press northward, mostly into the United States and Europe" (Lustgarten 2020, p. 26).

The world will definitely become different from the one we have known. How different is difficult to tell. Different areas of the United States and of the world will be affected in different ways, by the rising of the sea level, by intensifying storms, by heatwaves, by massive wildfires, and by droughts that might cause intense water shortages in some areas, such as in the west and the Midwest of the USA. There are several large cities by the sea that will be affected by the rising sea level.

Researchers at Rutgers University have estimated that the sea level in the New Jersey area has been rising by about 2.5 cm every eight years, and that it may rise by about 43 cm by 2050.

Some recent research at Harvard has concluded that the melting of the Antarctic ice sheet will raise the level of the sea by 30 percent more than had been estimated previously (Siliezar 2021). Several other recent simulations, by various experts in different countries, published in *Nature* (Hooijer and Vernimmen 2021), have reached divergent conclusions about how much the sea might rise by. They all agree that the melting of ice, especially in Antarctica, could significantly raise the sea level. However, some have argued that part of the ice melting could be neutralized by a continuing accumulation of snow over the huge area of Antarctica. At the same time, the possibility that large glaciers could detach themselves from the continental shelf and fall into the sea, creating faster melting, remains a worrisome possibility that is increased by higher temperatures. If that did happen on a large scale, the level of the sea might rise more significantly than predicted by some estimates, and might submerge many cities and greatly reduce land areas.

The rise in sea level will lead to significant migration, within several countries and between countries, and to great expense in an effort to protect the affected cities from the rising water, and from stronger storms. The damage from storms, fires, and droughts, and the costs of adaptation and insurance premiums, have already been going up significantly. They will continue to rise, making it more expensive and less pleasant to live in some cities and in some areas. While this might be taking place within the United States, "Canada [may] move into the ecological sweet spot for civilization," and it may benefit significantly from climate change (Lustgarten 2020, p. 27). The same is likely to be true for Russia.

In conclusion, some countries and some territories within large countries might benefit from the warming trend, while others will suffer. The countries that will suffer have far larger populations. As a consequence, there will be large migratory movements, with the inevitable social and economic problems that large-scale migration, especially across countries, often causes (Gates 2021a). Some of these movements have already started.

14.2 Should Humans Remain at Center Stage?

The above is a human-centered perspective on climate change. It puts the Earth at the exclusive use of humans, and ignores what is happening to other species, assuming that that is not important. Another view would be one that looked at climate change from a broader perspective, one that gave importance to all species.

There is now overwhelming evidence that large areas of the rainforests (in the Amazon, the Congo, Papua New Guinea, Borneo, Western Samoa, and other forest areas) have been cleared to accommodate agricultural and mining developments in what had been virgin forests (Piotrowski 2019). These changes have inevitably destroyed the habitats of many indigenous tribes who had lived in those forests, tribes who had contributed to the diversity of the human race and human culture. These changes have also destroyed the habitat for many indigenous animals and plant species, slowly advancing the time when the sixth extinction, feared by Elizabeth Kolbert (2014), might become a possibility. The move toward higher average incomes for humans, and toward more similar and higher consumption patterns, is a move toward a standardized human being, the creation of a kind of human robot (a "robot man") that would have gained increasingly standardized consumption for humans, but would have lost some of the earlier diversity that the Earth had enjoyed.

Other areas, such as the savannas in Africa, parts of the Arctic, and grassland areas in other regions of the world, are also being changed by human incursion, or by the changes that humans have been bringing to those areas. Many indigenous animals in those areas have been facing very difficult times. Just think of what happened to the bison and the buffaloes in the American Midwest, or to elephants and other animals in Africa; or what is happening to polar bears. These changes have been occurring right under our eyes. The climatic change that is taking place has been a major contributor, if not always the only one.

Even if the Earth's temperature does not increase much further than it has done so far, and if it stays at the current historically high level, an average level estimated to be a little more than one degree Celsius above what it had been for a long time, the above processes are likely to continue and to intensify. But the temperature is likely to increase still further in the years to come, if new green technologies are not introduced quickly and widely enough, and if other changes are not made that absorb the carbon that is already in the air.

The open question is whether the substitution of green energy for dirty energy can happen spontaneously and fast enough, without major government intervention, and without global cooperation. The optimists think that it can. Better-informed realists continue to have reasonable doubts. The current reality is that most of the desirable changes are planned by countries or by fossil enterprises *for decades in the future*. Though desirable, these changes might come too late. Furthermore, some of the changes remain optional so far, and they are not being endorsed with similar general enthusiasm or firm commitments.

14.3 Worrisome Possible Future Developments

In this section we describe a possible scenario, one that might be created within a couple of generations or, say, by the year 2100, at a time when some of the people who are already born today, our children and grandchildren, might be still alive, given current life expectancies. On the way there, life on Earth would become progressively more difficult to live in for some, and more dangerous for many. This scenario would make Mother Earth a less welcoming place for humans and for other species, than they had previously considered it to be (Nordhaus 2013).

Future developments could bring changes that would be so damaging that there may be a natural human tendency to dismiss and ignore them, as President Trump and members of his Administration, as well as the President of Brazil, had done. Some would consider such a scenario as the script for a horror movie, and not a realistic forecast. However, in the face of growing scientific evidence that suggests that this scenario may be becoming more realistic, a typical reaction might still be the normal, though irrational, one of dismissing it, while continuing to focus on the day's problems and hope for the best.

As was argued in Chapter 2, on the distinction between risk and uncertainty, the above is often the reaction of many humans when confronted with highly unpleasant, but still uncertain, future events. It is a reaction that *behavioral economics* might discover in its experiments, if it has not already done so. Irrationality makes people dismiss future, bad outcomes, when these are still highly uncertain. This may help us to comprehend how highly trained, and presumably decent, Boeing engineers could have dismissed the possibility of catastrophic failures in their new plane, the 737 MAX, and let it fly. One would not wish to believe that they did this knowingly and intentionally, as fully rational individuals.

The evidence from current developments, and the writing of many serious and informed experts, should make us pay more attention to future scenarios, which, while still uncertain, are becoming increasingly plausible. These scenarios may become less uncertain if fundamental, and not just marginal, changes, are not made, and soon, in the way humans have been behaving and have been abusing the Earth. An acceleration of economic growth in future years, which remains an important goal of most governments, and the wish of most humans to consume more, combined with the estimated, projected increase in billions of the world's population, are likely to make that scenario increasingly realistic, in the absence of major and radical, not just cosmetic, changes.

Just imagine a continuation of the trend toward a higher average temperature than the Earth has been experiencing in the past decade; or, more realistically, a further increase in that temperature, because of:

(a) *net addition* of greenhouse gases that human activities will continue to generate and add to the gases already in the atmosphere;

(b) the continuation of the burning of forest areas, created by wildfires due to dry weather conditions, by illegal human actions, or even by government policies;

(c) the continuing emission of methane gas, released by the (now existing) 1.4–1.5 billion cows, a number that is likely to increase, due to the growth in population and the increasing demand for beef that is likely to accompany population and income growth – a demand that might be slowed down or contained by the recent increase in vegetarian diets and the introduction of vegan "beef" and other vegetable substitutes for real meat in advanced countries;

(d) the melting of the permafrost taking place in Siberia and other places, which releases methane gas;

(e) activities connected with the extraction of shale oil; and

(f) the impact that the loss of ice cover in the Arctic Ocean is having and will continue to have on the speed at which the Sun is adding heat to the water temperature in the Arctic region and changing that region's temperature.

All of the above developments are already taking place, and will continue to take place, unless they are stopped somehow, and some of them cannot be stopped. They will keep the Earth's temperature high and may raise it beyond the 2 degree level considered crucial, unless *urgent* and *drastic* actions are taken.

This crisis is not likely to resolve itself with the help of the free market and with spontaneous free market innovations, as some continue to believe that it will. Some ongoing market choices, and some new technological developments, are definitely likely to help and are helping. They may slow down the trend, but they may not be sufficient to stop, or reverse, the temperature rise soon enough.

The *progressive* replacement of dirty energy by green energy, a replacement that has been taking place at an increasing pace in several countries in recent years, may slow down the rate at which the Earth's temperature increases, by reducing the *rate* at which greenhouse gas is being *added* to the atmosphere. However, it will not reduce the *level* of the greenhouse gas that is already up there, and some increase will continue to come from various sources (methane from permafrost and from cows, carbon from continued use of fossil fuels to produce steel and cement, etc.). These sources of greenhouse gas cannot be stopped, or are difficult to control. That carbon that is already in the atmosphere is likely to continue for a long time to have a warming effect on the Earth's temperature.

The planting of billions of trees that would absorb carbon from the atmosphere would clearly be beneficial. So would better protection of existing forests and the shifting of human diets away from meat and other animal products. Also, and importantly, because this is already feasible with available technology, a greater use of atomic energy might help, as shown by France's example. All of these measures, in addition to a fast increase in the use of green energy and other innovations, would be beneficial in preventing the situation from going from bad to worse.

However, except for the planting of billions of trees and more use of atomic energy (which would come with the serious risks mentioned earlier), and, possibly, the development of totally new technologies capable of actually *subtracting* carbon from the air on a large scale and storing it in the ground, as new trees would), all the changes will simply slow down the temperature increase. They will not reverse that increase. Major developments in blue hydrogen, in atomic fission, and in other areas could be helpful, if they came early enough.

As a consequence of the above, many of the already observed bad effects of climate change are likely to persist, even if at a hopefully not worse pace. Some will become more damaging, especially if the *reduction* in new emissions of greenhouse gases does not take place soon and fast. In the next section, we consider some of the likely bad effects of the already existing situation. These bad effects could easily become worse in later years.

14.4 Possible Future Climate Changes

Let us consider, first, the warming of the oceans and its consequences. That warming took place over many years and is not likely to start to reverse itself as long as the Arctic Ocean remains uncovered by ice and continues to absorb more heat, and as long as the Earth's temperature remains higher than in the past. Even then, it would take a long time for the sea temperature to return to past levels. The warming of the sea expands the water volume, contributing to some of the observed rise in sea level. The high temperature will continue to feed this expanding process. The warming of the seas also creates more evaporation, thus contributing to more frequent and stronger storms, especially in some areas, but reducing slightly the rise in sea level.

Some recent scientific evidence, published in the journal *Nature Geoscience*, has indicated that the change in the water temperature and in the salinity of the sea water, due to the melting of glaciers, is disrupting the age-old circulation of currents in the Atlantic Ocean (see, e.g., Rahmstorf 2002; Caesar et al. 2018). Those currents had kept the north of Europe warmer than it should be, given its northern latitude. These changes in sea currents are significant and worrisome developments, but their longer-run consequences are not clear at this time.

The glaciers that cover Antarctica, Greenland, parts of Iceland, and the Arctic region, are, in some places, hundreds of meters thick. They were created over thousands, or millions of years. Their creation, in the distant past, had reduced the level of the oceans by hundreds of meters, expanding the dry land. Therefore, the observed melting of glaciers, in Greenland, Antarctica, Iceland, and on mountaintops will not happen overnight, but will go on over a long time, at different rates of melting.

Because of the huge amount of ice that had accumulated, if the ice of the glaciers should fully melt, it would raise the sea level by hundreds of meters, reducing dramatically the available dry land. However, such melting is likely to proceed at too slow a pace to make such an increase in sea level a realistic prospect any time soon. Even at a slow pace, the melting of the ice, combined with the warming of the sea water, will contribute to *some* rising of the sea level. That rising would have serious consequences for coastal areas, and especially for the many cities located along those areas. The main question is: by how much will the sea rise? And how fast?

The melting of the ice on mountaintops that feeds important rivers, rivers that provide needed fresh water to millions of people in some areas, can create short-run problems because of the impact this can have on water availability, and on agricultural production, especially for heavily populated areas. This can promote droughts in some areas. Droughts could become more frequent and could lead to a sharp reduction in agricultural production and to food scarcity, creating famines and forcing millions of people to relocate. The occasional bursting of glaciers on top of mountains can also lead to other immediate, but less serious, disasters, as did the February 2021 breaking of a glacier in the Himalayas, which caused the collapse of a dam on the Ganges River, leading to the death of hundreds of people.

It is difficult to predict how much the sea level might rise by, say, the year 2100. However, the sea *will* rise and the rise *will* have implications for coastal areas and for some of the world's largest cities that are close to the sea and are at the current sea level. Netherlands-style adaptations have been mentioned as a possible way to adjust to the sea water rise. However, such adaptations are not likely to be of much help over the longer run, and for higher sea level rises. This would also be enormously costly. Migration out of the affected areas would be the main realistic alternative.

The warming of the sea, combined with a higher sea level, will continue to lead to increasingly powerful and more frequent storms, storm surges, and storm damage in some areas. The storms will hit coastal areas especially hard and will damage cities and surrounding areas in those locations. Category 5 hurricanes and typhoons, events that used to be very rare in the past, have become more frequent and unwelcome visitors. They are also occurring earlier in the season, and for longer periods after the hurricane season was supposed to have ended. The year 2020 was one of the worst cyclone seasons on record.

Given the higher sea level and water surges, typhoons and hurricanes have become more damaging to coastal cities. Insurance companies have reported increasing claims from storm damage, which, in turn, has led to higher premiums, and to pressure on local governments (as in Miami and New Orleans) to build infrastructure that can better protect cities from the major storm surges. When major natural events occur, it is often realized that the current infrastructure, which was built in the past, has become inadequate.

This inadequacy was discovered in February 2021, by Texans, when millions were left without electricity, water, and food supplies, after a record snowstorm had damaged the poorly regulated electrical power grid. Some citizens literally froze in their houses. The existing electrical grid, which had worked well in the past, in normal times, had become awfully inadequate for the new situation. Electrical wires that in many US areas hang under trees, instead of being buried underground, are often cut by major storms that damage the trees. These problems are becoming increasingly clear for other infrastructure as well, built for a less extreme reality.

Clearly, global warming is making it more expensive and more dangerous to live in particular areas. Some of the individuals living in those areas will conclude, sooner or later, that migration to safer areas may be a wise, if costly, and not always easy, option. Some such climate migration has been reported to be taking place already in the USA and other countries. Some economic activities are also likely to relocate to safer areas, starting a migration process that is likely to intensify in future years. The process of accommodating the climate change is likely to prove progressively more expensive and perhaps increasingly ineffective.

The larger storms, accompanied by much heavier rains, due to the increasing humidity that the warmer sea temperature creates, are leading to major floods that occasionally lead to many casualties and to large property losses. What used to be events that might take place every hundred or even thousand years have become frequent ones, some occurring within weeks of one another. Some of the recent floods have become more destructive and can be expected to become even more so.

At the same time, some areas have become much dryer and more subject to wildfires and heatwaves than they used to be, because of the higher temperature and the wind and sea current patterns. Some parts of Australia and the west coast of the United States have experienced these very dry conditions, and forest fires of historical dimensions have destroyed immense areas, including some with large populations, causing widespread property damage and loss of human lives. In other areas, the droughts have started leading to a process of desertification, with all its consequences. These dry spells, at times, are followed by huge rains that lead to landslides and other disasters.

The above description has provided some realistic idea of the short- and medium-run effects, mostly on human beings, of a temperature rise limited to, say, 2 degrees Celsius. Those effects are likely to become progressively more damaging, not only to humans but also, or especially, to other species that have less capacity of adaptation. The latter would be crowded out of their habitats by the actions of humans. Biological diversity would be progressively reduced, as it is being already reduced.

The two largest economies, those of the USA and China (and, increasingly, India), which account for a large part of global carbon emissions, because of their economic size and large populations would have to play the leading role in reducing the problem for the whole world. Without their full contribution, there would be little hope for significant progress. So far there has been more talk than concrete and sufficient action to deal with the developing problem (Galeotti and Lanza 2021). The commitments to zero net carbon emissions are still years in the future, at times for 2050 or even beyond.

In the next section, we briefly describe the scenario that would be created by a temperature increase of more than 2 degrees Celsius – a scenario that might approach that of the "uninhabitable earth" realistically described in a recent, informative book (Wallace-Wells 2019). While clearly uncertain, such a scenario is not an impossible one.

14.5 A Catastrophic Scenario

A catastrophic scenario could become a distinct possibility if the Earth's temperature should increase by more than 2 degrees Celsius, rising, by say, 3, 4, or even 5 degrees. The higher the rise, the sooner and the more disastrous the situation would become. Such increases would lead to a higher temperature of the oceans, causing them to expand more, to faster melting of the glaciers, which, together with the expansion of the seas, would lead to higher and faster-rising sea levels, and to more and more powerful storms and other serious weather events. These events would force the evacuation of most of the many large and small cities that are located at sea levels. The large cities include some of the largest metropolises in the world, such as New York, Miami, Rio de Janeiro, London, Tokyo, Manila, Mumbai, Dacha, Shanghai, and Naples. Some of these cities (as in Miami Dade County) have started to assign to "heat officers" the task of seeing what measures the cities can take to better protect themselves from the rising dangers.

The higher temperature would melt more rapidly the glaciers on top of mountains that feed many of the large rivers of the world. This would create enormous problems for the affected areas, leading to a large reduction in food production and to the forced migration of millions, or even billions, of people. The higher temperature would lead to dry land conditions and to the desertification of huge areas. It would also lead to heatwaves that would kill many people and to enormous wild-fires. Many humans, animals, and other species would find life very difficult, or even impossible. It would become increasingly difficult to feed the world population.

Whether the whole Earth or only major parts of it would become *uninhabitable* is difficult to tell. But, for sure, the Earth would no longer be the beautiful, blue, and hospitable planet that we have known. It is difficult to forecast this catastrophic scenario with any precision, but it is not unrealistic to predict that it is a possible one, if current trends do not change, and change soon and significantly. These changes are not likely to happen spontaneously, although the actions of many individual entre-preneurs and inventors may help to delay them.

The needed changes will require much governmental action and much intergovernment coordination, *and soon.* "Free-riding" actions by some governments will not help and will make a solution to the global warming problem difficult. Without global cooperation, followed by firm commitments, the chance of success will be much reduced. It must be realized that the world faces a potential existential threat, one that requires dramatic and not just cosmetic responses by governments. We are all in the same boat, and we had better learn to row in a coordinated fashion, to keep the boat afloat.

Part IV

Back to Some Theoretical Issues

15 HUMAN NEEDS AND ECONOMIC THEORY

In this chapter and the next, we return to some general economic considerations regarding the distinction between events that are *risky* and that can be dealt with more easily by market economies, and events that are highly *uncertain* (in the traditional Frank Knight definition discussed in Chapter 2), which are more difficult to forecast and deal with. We address the implications, for policy and for economic theory, of uncertain but still possible, future, disastrous events. We shall revisit some issues that were first raised in Chapter 4. The chapter will go beyond climate change and deal more broadly with public goods (or public "bads") and with problems that are, increasingly, crossing national frontiers and becoming global, such as pandemics and climate change.

We have observed that traditional economic thinking had focused on the provision of routine goods and services that individuals living in specific countries need and want. Adam Smith, and much economic theory after him, had made a strong case that the free market was the best way of delivering goods and services that people want, and also for creating incomes for market participants, so that people could buy the goods and services that they wanted. Smith had also warned that coordination on the part of those who provide the goods and services could easily lead to cartels. Thus *individual* action reigned sovereign in traditional economic thinking, and collective action received much less attention and support.

However, it was always recognized that some role had to be assigned to the government in a world that was structured around many countries and many national governments. Since the 1960s, and especially because of the work by James Buchanan, Nobel Prize in Economics, there has been a major School of Public Choice that wants little government, but is distinguished from Adam Smith's. Laissez-faire was assumed to be the preferred government role until the twentieth century, except by those who adhered to "socialist" thinking.

However, besides routine goods and services, individuals also have some collective needs. Some of these needs may be protection against some future, but *uncertain*, damaging events that would affect the whole community. These events may include epidemics, pandemics, major natural disasters, and others, in addition to foreign invasion that always attracted some attention. These needs, which are often less material, and at times less well-perceived, are more difficult to satisfy than normal routine needs, including those created by traditional *risky* events. For the latter, insurance companies can develop and offer individuals the possibility of protection, by paying premiums to them.

To satisfy the need for protection against *uncertain* events, the action of uncoordinated individuals is, generally, not efficient or useful. For these, actions coordinated on a larger scale become necessary. The more coordination among a large number of individuals that is needed, the greater becomes the *potential* role of the government to do the coordinating.

If the *uncertain*, disastrous events have a multi-country or global scope, as with pandemics and global warming, the needed coordination may have to be global, and not just national. Often, it will need to involve the governments of different, important countries, or even those of the whole world, which now number about 200. A national government that acts alone may not be able to do much about dealing with a pandemic, or to reduce global warming. For some events, all countries have to be made safer if everyone is to become safer. If a pandemic is raging in India or in Brazil, it is much more difficult for individuals in the USA or the UK to feel completely safe, and to continue with past activities, including global travel.

Collective action among many governments has a higher probability of making a difference in relation to some global emergencies. Once we recognize and accept the above, we must recognize the limitations of the classical role of *national* governments, and also that of classical economic theory, which gives a limited role to the action of the national governments and none to global government, and a much greater role to the actions of individuals.

The limitations of traditional thinking were due to the fact that the probability of disastrous, uncertain events could not be statistically estimated, as it could be for risky events. Therefore, they tended to be ignored, in spite of the historical evidence of their existence, and in spite of their relative frequency in the past. Once the possibility of the existence of *random or uncertain events* is recognized, the need to modify the traditional policy framework becomes evident. However, while the need may become clearer, it is not easy to determine how to do it, especially when the events have global scope.

The general, traditional, theoretical framework that guided market economies did recognize that national governments had some limited role to play in market economies, such as setting some rules and providing some *national* public goods. But policies and actions remained country-specific. Generally, economic theory largely ignored the existence and the consequences of difficult-to-predict events, and especially those that have multi-country, or even global, implications, such as pandemics and global warming. And, depending on the time horizon of different countries, which may be influenced by the average life expectancy of their populations, future events were given different weights or importance. Poorer countries had shorter time horizons, because of lower life expectancy, and worried less about possible, future disasters and more about immediate needs.

The paradigm that has broadly guided the behavior of markets has continued to be the one that students of economics learned from basic price theory. That paradigm was influenced by the writings of some of the great economists of the past, such as Walras, Marshall, Mises, Hayek, Friedman, and Stigler. It stressed that governments should promote well-behaved, competitive markets, and that competition would lead to market equilibriums that, in the long run, would promote and maximize welfare.

In that idealized, economic world, market forces tend to decrease higher profits toward a lower, competitive equilibrium, and deliver the lowest prices for what consumers bought, leading to what economists called a Pareto optimum. In this process, government would play a minimum role, apart from guaranteeing property rights, the sanctity of contracts, the promotion of law and order, and the protection of the nation itself. The action and power of a government would also be strictly limited to its own borders.

The equilibrium created by well-working markets would require flexible market prices, prices that reflected the full costs of the goods and services sold and some minimum profits. However, little attention was given to how market prices would be corrected for the possible existence of externalities, because the prices would not adjust automatically for them. If the production, or the consumption, of some goods – say, the consumption of fossil fuels, or of beef – created environmental costs, these costs must be reflected in the prices, and the corrected prices must be the right ones (Stern and Stiglitz 2021a, 2021b).

The above aspect had been stressed by Pigou (1920), who had proposed the use of regulations to deal with externalities. However, it was later qualified by Coase (1960), who had suggested negotiations between polluter and polluted, assuming that both are in the same country and both are guided by the same national laws. *Law and economics* are inevitably country-specific. The need to use carbon taxes has been recognized in recent years; however, those taxes have played a relatively limited role so far in determining market prices. Also, the difficulties of determining the correct carbon taxes have received less attention than they deserve.

The above issues raise fundamental questions as to how close the real markets have been to the idealized one. Most of the economists who had supported the theoretical thinking set out above, about the role of well-working markets, had also expressed deep skepticism about the wisdom of government intervention that would be required to make the needed corrections in the market prices. Once market equilibrium was achieved, with or without the above corrections, enterprises would be left with no buffer to deal with unexpected shocks.

The possibility of undesirable shocks was simply ignored. In that framework, enterprises would have a strong incentive to keep inventories low, and to keep their labor force at a minimum. They would hire as few workers as possible, pay them as little as possible, and would push for government policies that made the dismissal of workers easy, when the need for them fell. Enterprises would fight to reduce the power of labor unions, as was done in the USA, the UK, and elsewhere in the past four decades of market fundamentalism. Governments would focus their attention on short-run needs and, until more recent years, they had generally aimed at maintaining some equilibrium in the fiscal accounts, and stable general prices. Their long-run needs or policies would ignore possible pandemics, climate changes, and other "Acts of God."

The market fundamentalism that has prevailed since the 1980s stressed that government policies should not pose obstacles to the free market. In this world, companies would have little incentive to retain profits for "rainy days." They would not set aside resources to provide precautionary buffers to cope with unexpected future shocks. Both workers and enterprises would rely on debts when the shocks came.

Governments were expected to keep taxes low and public spending directed mainly toward satisfying the short-run needs of voting citizens.

Elections would have much influence on what public money was spent on, because the time horizons of the average voter and of governments are generally short. The interests of future generations would receive little attention. As a consequence, public spending would often be behind in meeting future infrastructural and other long-run needs, such as those in public health. There would be little spending directed specifically to the long run, or to difficult-to-forecast needs, including possible pandemics and other disasters.

Within the above framework, a government that decided to spend more money to better prepare for potential, but uncertain, future needs – for example, by building sufficient and long-lasting infrastructure to better protect people against some possible natural disasters; by accumulating enough assets for future pension payments; by creating some spare capacity in areas such as the health sector; and by simply setting aside some resources to be better prepared to meet possible future expenses due to unanticipated events – would be criticized and would risk losing the next election. Long-term problems, including the need to address climate change and to face future pandemics, would receive little, if any, attention. Short-termism and myopia would prevail, in both market behavior and government operations.

In recent years, governments have been encouraged by a few vocal and media-savvy economists, to cover some of their spending with public debt, rather than with taxes. This was an offer that many governments could not refuse, as David Hume (1970) told us three centuries ago. This new thinking has helped to push public debts to record levels in many countries, including the USA. In fact, the world has never been as indebted as it is today. At the end of 2020, global debt (both public and private) reached 355 percent of the world's GDP. As reported by the IMF (2021), the average fiscal deficits of advanced countries reached 11.7 percent of GDP; for emerging markets it reached 9.8 percent; and for low-income countries, 6.5 percent. These debts are likely to have made it even more difficult than in the past to deal with future uncertain, but damaging events. In 2021, public deficits will continue to be very high, and public debts even higher.

In recent years, governments have been advised by some economists to abandon traditional fiscal prudence and what had been considered fiscal prudence or orthodoxy, in favor of a "New Monetary Theory" that argues that significant government spending can and should be financed with public debt, supplied by central bank loans, in a world in which inflation has been seen as a problem of the past, and is no longer a current or future problem. It has been argued that the growth rates of economies would routinely exceed the costs of borrowing, making it easy for governments to deal with debt problems in future years.

Adherence to the above optimistic advice would make it unnecessary for countries to face unexpected spending needs with regular resources. It would require less need to keep some precautionary resources for future unexpected spending. When additional needs came, governments could just borrow more from central banks. The traditional, or orthodox, view, held in the past by major economists, including David Hume and Adam Smith, was abandoned. That view had been that the existence of a *sound* budgetary situation, to face possible future spending needs, was one of the good reasons to maintain some "fiscal space."

In a world in which major disasters and pandemics are realistic, though uncertain, future possibilities, and where they may have become more frequent because of climate change and factors that may lead to more frequent pandemics or cyclones, there may be a need for some new thinking. That new thinking might indicate novel and desirable ways to adapt the traditional, classical modus operandi that economists had supported and promoted until recently.

The new thinking should suggest ways to still promote economic efficiency and democratic objectives, but to do a better job in anticipating uncertain, but possible, future shocks. Perhaps, it should also do a better job in dealing with the growing income inequality observed in several important countries in recent decades, which has been raising questions about the ethics of the market economy. It should also recognize that an increasing number of issues have global dimensions and implications, and that they may require global and not just national solutions.

Because of cheaper, faster, and more comfortable means of travel in recent decades, and because of higher average incomes and easier means of transportation, there has been an explosion of global travel and global tourism, and of contacts among people from different areas and regions of the world. There have also been more and closer contacts between different animals, and between humans and diverse animals, than in the past. Tours to previously little-visited jungle and other isolated locations have increased.

These contacts inevitably expose people to more and, often, new, viruses and microbes, and increase the potential for epidemics and pandemics. Several potential epidemics in recent decades have started in these ways and the number of infectious diseases has grown, while there are concerns about the efficacy of existing antibiotics, due to their overuse in past years. We may be moving to a new era of more frequent epidemics and pandemics and need to be better prepared for them.

Viruses and bacteria can now travel much faster and further than they did in the past, from one place to another. They can emerge from isolated areas, where they might have existed harmlessly in the past, to places where they can spread rapidly and do much damage to people, if they are not quickly controlled, in spite of more advanced medical knowledge, especially in the generation of vaccines. More frequent epidemics are likely to result, as the current coronavirus pandemic did.

The above developments have implications for government roles. They require more investment in the health sector, and, especially, more spending directed at *basic* research on health, research especially dealing with pathogens. Such fundamental research is mostly financed by governments. They also require more collaboration among governments, for example in the availability of vaccines to countries that are too poor to buy them. In future years we may need a *vaccine passport* to travel, and to have universal value, such a passport must have global endorsement.

The most recent report on the environment by the United Nations, issued on December 9, 2020, concluded that climate change is changing the world that we have known, and that, if not controlled, it might make at least some areas of the Earth potentially difficult places to live in. Without major and relatively rapid changes, humanity might experience what may in time become the *mother of all catastrophes*. This threat is no longer a distant one, but has become a closer one. It may materialize within the time horizon of the lives of our children or grandchildren. It is also no longer a problem limited to just one area of the Earth, or to one group. It is one that will affect major areas or even the whole planet, and the whole human race and other species. If there ever was a true global emergency, this might be it.

The above observations inevitably invite some reflections on what should be the role of governments in a world where uncertain but damaging events (pandemics, natural disasters, climate change) are becoming, or may become, more likely, but are still events that are not statistically predictable before they come. They have gone from "if" to "when."

There may be two forces moving in opposite directions. Some forces may be leading to alleviation in the climate change problem, including, especially, the growing use of green energy. And other forces are continuing to contribute to climate change and to other problems, including pandemics. Which of these forces will prevail, and how soon, is an important question. It is always difficult to determine when an "uncertainty" comes close to becoming a "risk," and when it becomes a manageable or "insurable" risk. Even if the higher world average temperature should remain at the current level, and/or if its increase were contained within 2 degrees Celsius, the environmental costs would still be likely to increase. At this stage of the game, it may be more realistic to be pessimistic than optimistic.

Especially in the most advanced countries, today, when everything seems to fail, citizens turn to and expect their governments to intervene and help. This is a major departure from what often happened in the distant past, when governments had few financial means and almost no trained administrators who could play helpful roles. It should be recalled that an *administrative* or *bureaucratic* state is a relatively recent creation. One with more financial resources and competence is an even more recent one (Tanzi 2018b).

A first observation concerning government interventions in the modern world is that, when major catastrophes are realistic possibilities, even though they are difficult to forecast with any precision, as to timing and intensity, they should provide an additional reason for governments to be ready to intervene, *should the need become a reality*. This can be facilitated by pushing for efficient (and not smaller) government, and for keeping their fiscal balances and their public administration in good order. When "fiscal space" is not there, it is always more difficult for governments to intervene efficiently and quickly.

Available fiscal space always makes it easier for governments to step in more quickly, with additional spending, or with tax cuts on the citizens most affected, with available and trained personnel, and with fewer concerns about the sustainability of public finances. Governments that are already burdened by high debts and by running high fiscal deficits, and that already rely on distortive taxes, naturally have fewer degrees of freedom to act. Therefore, the *initial condition* of the fiscal accounts should always remain an important consideration, in spite of the new, mentioned unorthodox thinking on the sustainability of public debt.

Similar observations can be made concerning the behavior of private enterprises. In this context, a comparison between the behavior of American and Japanese enterprises may be instructive. In normal times, Japanese enterprises tend to hold larger shares of their profits as precautionary balances. They use these profits to retain their workers during recessions when sales and profits fall. American companies do not hold their profits and, when crises come, they simply lay off some of their workers, potentially shifting the problems of the unemployed workers to the government. The consequence is that the unemployment rate fluctuates much less in Japan than it does in the USA, which follows a view that was promoted by Milton Friedman, fifty years ago, that the only responsibility of private enterprises is to earn profits for their shareholders. American economists have considered Japanese behavior as less conducive to longer-term economic growth.

Most workers save little. They normally depend on their current wages to support them and their family's standard of living. Many of them do not keep precautionary balances. When they lose their jobs, they lose their incomes, and many of them face immediate economic difficulties, including, in some countries such as the USA, the loss of health insurance, or their home. These difficulties may be partly reduced, *in the short run*, by governments using temporary unemployment compensation programs, which, in turn, may be facilitated by the initial conditions of the governments' public finances and by the use of higher taxes on the rich.

Owners of corporate shares normally have some, or much, accumulated wealth. Wealth provides an important buffer against unanticipated, negative shocks. With the popularity of the corporate form of business organization that, over the years, has replaced what used to be enterprises owned by single, or by few, private owners, many richer individuals now allocate their total wealth in the shares of different corporations. They spread their proverbial eggs among many baskets, reducing their total risk. The poor performance of a single corporation, or even of a few, is likely to affect less the total purchasing power of many shareholders than does the loss of jobs for workers.

Because of the impact of "market fundamentalism" on policies since the 1980s, the tax treatment of capital income and of some sources of income that are especially important to high-income individuals became significantly lighter over past decades, compared with that for *dependent* workers. Some studies (such as that by Saez and Zucman 2019) have estimated that, in the USA, the *average* tax burden of normal workers is now similar to that of the richest individuals. Others have found that, after the 2017 US Tax Cuts and Jobs Act, in 2018 billionaires paid a lower effective tax rate, 23 percent, than workers, 24 percent. These important aspects are often ignored in discussions of the desirable tax burdens of workers and of owners of capital and high-level managers.

15.1 The Impact of the Current Pandemic

Let us now deal more directly with the current pandemic and with the use of taxes at this time (first half of 2021). The pandemic hardly has been neutral in its impact on different sectors of the economy and on the income distribution. During the ongoing pandemic, millions of workers lost their jobs and their incomes. Some of them lost their lives. Many did not have assets to fall back on, and some might remain unemployed for some time. Unemployment claims have been high (many millions) and are expected to remain relatively high (though falling) for an unknown period. Poverty rates have increased.

Political debates continue to rage as to how much and for how long to help, with government assistance, the unemployed workers and small enterprises (restaurants and bars, barbershops, beauty parlors, dental clinics, gyms, movie houses, etc.) that are facing economic difficulties caused directly by the pandemic. As is often the case in these situations, the information available to governments to assist the truly needy is not sufficiently good to avoid mistakes in policies.

The long-run impact of the pandemic on the real economy remains uncertain and worrisome, in spite of optimistic official forecasts. Forecasts made by official sources, such as the IMF's World Economic Outlook, traditionally, have had a high chance of being wrong, as Keynes argued in his book commenting on forecasts in general (Keynes 1921b). The longer the pandemic lasts, the greater will be its long-run consequences for the countries' economies and for many citizens.

The pandemic is likely to change permanently some economic arrangements, such as working, shopping, and learning from home, attending conferences and meetings, where to live, and so on. It may also change travel, vacation, and entertainment habits. It has influenced death and birth rates, retirement rates, and choices of jobs.

Consumer confidence has been low, and global trade has suffered. The debts of governments have exploded. Poverty levels have increased and life expectancy has fallen. The pandemic has affected the supply side of the economy and also the demand side, and it will continue to affect economic output until its health effects are significantly and permanently contained.

There has been a tendency by policymakers to deal with the pandemic mainly as if it were a normal recession, created by falling demand. This tendency has encouraged public spending and public borrowing. The US federal deficit reached a record high share of GDP in 2020, and it will continue to be very high in 2021, and probably in years to come. In several other countries, such as Italy and the UK, public debt and fiscal deficits have increased even more. Public debts had never been at current levels, especially in peacetime. Many American states may find it difficult to meet their constitutional, balanced-budget obligations, without sharply cutting spending, or without getting significant federal assistance. Many, especially small, enterprises will not recover, and their owners and employees will continue to face economic difficulties.

A remarkable aspect of the current crisis is that the US stock market, which should have fallen to accompany the sharp fall in output and the rise in unemployment in 2020, has been doing very well. Its current level (May 2021) is at a historical high, this at a time when the number of individuals infected by Covid 19 in the USA has exceeded 30 million and deaths are approaching 600,000. The real estate market has also been doing very well, because of low mortgage rates and the desire of many city-dwellers, who can afford it, to have more space during lockdowns, and to be able to work from home, while borrowing rates for mortgages remain low. However, many of the lower-income individuals who had rented their lodgings are having difficulties paying their rents, which have been increasing. Many risk becoming or have become homeless.

In sum, those who owned wealth, or had high and safe occupations, or good pensions, are doing well economically, in spite of the pandemic, while the rest are doing much less well. This disconnect between what is happening to those who own most wealth, and/or have permanent jobs and incomes, and to workers who receive low and minimum wages and are ironically called "essential workers" (those in health care, personal services, food supply, farms, and others) is nothing short of extraordinary. It seems that in today's economy, it helps if your occupation is *not* "essential."

The workers in "essential" activities are the ones who are paying a high price, in both personal health and income, for the pandemic. They are not only more exposed to the dangerous health effects of the pandemic, but many of them have lost both their jobs and their income (Torpey 2020). Individuals who do not need to work, because they have accumulated assets or have safe pensions, are doing really well.

The stock market is compensating many of them with its record rise, and managers of large enterprises have continued to receive multimillion compensation packages, even when their enterprises have lost money, as was the case with Boeing, Hilton, Norwegian Cruise Line, and several others (Gelles 2021).

These developments cannot be seen as a compliment to the ethic, the fairness, and the utilitarian performance of the market economy, as it is now structured, especially in the USA, or, perhaps, to that of the current government role in some countries. These developments are likely to have an impact on popular attitudes and on social relations in future years. Some economists continue to object to any increase in minimum wages and on higher tax rates, but do not object to absurd and, at times, clearly undeserved managers' compensations.

There may be several reasons for the above disconnect between the real economy and the stock market, but two seem particularly important. They are: (a) the tax and other policies adopted by the USA, and followed by several other countries, especially since the 1980s; and (b) the monetary policies that have been followed by the Federal Reserve System and by other central banks in recent years. These policies have combined with the process of globalization of trade and finances, and with the coming into existence of large, global, and technologically based monopolies, which now account for a significant share of the total value of the US stock market. These de facto monopolies have continued to make large profits and to pay few taxes on their profits during the pandemic, generating large incomes for those who own their shares and having long-run and uncertain effects on the economy and on society.

The current crisis has shown what may be considered a shortcoming of *market fundamentalism*, and the limitation of the *trickle-down* assumption that had been used to justify it by its advocates. The view that a free market is similar to a favorable tide, a tide that "lifts all boats," had been promoted, but it has been shown to be naive. The tide has been lifting some boats far more than others, and in a way that does not reflect popular or prevalent notions of economic justice or fairness. Luck, implicit monopolies, being in the right place and having the right connections, having attended the right schools, and other factors, seem to be playing larger roles than effort and true merit.

The shortcomings have made it more obvious than it had been in the past that the spontaneous trickle-down must be aided by adequate government tax, spending, and regulatory policies, policies that should not replace the fundamental allocation role of the market, but that must assist the market in promoting more equitable results and spending power. Significant trickle-down has failed to emerge *spontaneously* from the freer work of the market, which market fundamentalism tried to promote. The government must play a compassionate, complementary role, as it has done in some countries, and as it had tried to do in the decades after the war, until the 1980s.

It is not possible to discuss in detail past tax policies, and how policies may have played a role in the current dichotomy reported above. We shall limit our observations to a few, rather general, points, starting with the statement that, as several studies have shown (including some recent ones by the US Federal Reserve System and the Census Bureau: Semega et al. 2020; US Federal Reserve 2021), over the past four decades, the share of total income and total wealth received by a small share of the population (the top 1.0 or 0.1 percent) increased in a remarkable way. These individuals appropriated most of the economic growth in those years. Many of them have continued to benefit from the recent behavior of the stock market and of other assets, and, more recently, from the tax reform of 2017, which sharply reduced taxes on corporations.

There has been little trickle-down in recent decades; mostly, it has been "trickle-up," from average workers to wealth owners. Since the 1980s, government policies, and the manipulation of some of those policies by well-placed individuals, played a major role in this trend. These policies have included tax, regulatory, and, in more recent decades, monetary policies. We shall ignore the regulatory policies in the following discussion and limit our comments in this and the following chapter to tax and monetary policy.

15.2 Tax Policy

Many readers may not be fully aware of the major changes in tax policy that have taken place since World War II, and especially since the 1970s, in both the USA and in several other advanced countries. In 1944–45, the tax rate on the highest tax bracket, for US federal individual income tax, was 94 percent. The rate was reduced to 91 percent in 1950, to 70 percent in 1965, to 50 percent in 1982, and to 28 percent in 1988 (Pechman 1987). Because of concerns about rising fiscal deficits in the late 1980s, the rate was increased a little for later years. It is now

37 percent on the highest, *reported*, *taxable* income. Note, however, that the actual, properly measured income received by many taxpayers, the income that actually determines the potential spending power of a person, is generally much higher, as the Nobel Prize winner economist John Hicks (1939) wrote many years ago.

The reductions in tax rates over past years have meant that the tax landscape for very rich individuals (especially millionaires and billionaires) has changed considerably. They benefited enormously from reductions in the tax rates on their incomes, in addition to major economic change in regulations and some of the changes brought by market fundamentalism, which also benefited them. They experienced huge increases in their before-tax incomes, and large drops in their *average* tax burdens. Their shares of total national income and wealth increased significantly.

Individuals in the middle class and especially average workers, benefited far less, if at all. Furthermore, while in 1965, in the USA, the average compensation of the CEOs of the largest corporations had been about 20 times that of average workers, that compensation grew to 61 times in 1989, to 312 times in 2017, and probably to even higher levels in later years. "From 1978 to 2019, compensation grew 14 percent for typical workers [and] 1,167 percent for CEOs" (Gelles 2021, p. 24). Tax reductions on the high incomes of individuals were not limited to the USA, but were paralleled in other, especially Anglo-Saxon, countries. For data on OECD countries, see Messere 1993 and Tanzi 2011.

In conclusion, while the share of revenue from individual income taxes in GDP changed little over the decades after World War II, the share that richer individuals paid fell, while that paid by average workers rose, and pressures continued for further tax cuts.

Over the same decades, the main statutory tax rate on the profits of US corporations also fell significantly. Until 1969, it had been 52 percent. It was reduced to 46 percent in 1979–81, to 34 percent in 1988, and then to 21 percent in 2018. This was an enormous reduction. The share of corporate tax revenue in GDP over the decades fell from more than 5 percent to just 1 percent of GDP. In spite of this sharp fall, some US observers have continued to complain that the corporate tax rate of 21 percent of *taxed* profits is still too high; and President Trump suggested that it could be further reduced if he had remained in power. The Biden Administration is likely to call for an increase in that rate to finance infrastructure and other public expenses. There is also a current call to introduce minimum corporate income taxes globally to reduce tax competition and to stop the race to the bottom.

In addition to the fall in the main *statutory* tax rates on *reported* taxable income, the rates that are the visible tips of the icebergs, there were many other, less visible, structural changes in the tax treatment of income from capital and in that of the compensations of CEOs and other high-income individuals over the past four decades. These less visible changes would require much space to describe. They have included the favorable treatment of some incomes, such as long-term realized capital gains, of income from "carried trade," changes in depreciation rules, and a shift in the compensation of executives toward lower-taxed stock options.

These changes have further reduced the *effective* tax rates on high incomes. Furthermore, *unrealized* capital gains, which in the 1950s and 1960s had attracted much attention from tax experts, who thought that they should be taxed because they increased the wealth and spending power of those who received them, and were thus "income," have remained untaxed during a period that has seen great market capitalization, in part caused by lower corporate tax rates and by falling shares of labor income, by the buying of their own shares by corporations, using their own profits, or using cheap loans made possible by Federal Reserve policies. The above changes have been described by some observers as "corporate welfare," or "welfare for the rich" (Harvey and Conyers 2020).

The globalization of economic activities that took place, especially since the 1980s, and the deregulation of the financial and trade markets opened many new channels for "high net worth individuals" and for multinational or global corporations to reduce their effective tax payments through various forms of tax avoidance. They have done so by shifting (and often hiding) income and wealth in foreign jurisdictions (in "tax havens" and in low-tax countries) where they enjoy low-tax or even tax-free status, and where they can maintain anonymity. (See Zucman 2015 on the quantitative importance of this factor.) Revenues from taxes on corporations are now sharply down and some large global corporations have been paying no taxes.

The tax revenue that is lost every year by national governments, due to global abuses and tax avoidance, has been estimated (by the Tax Justice Network, the OECD, the IMF, and some other sources) to amount to hundreds of billions of US dollars. In the G7 countries, between 2011 and 2017, average wages grew by 3 percent, while dividends to the wealthy grew by 31 percent. They grew even more in later years. This was hardly a "friendly, *rising* tide that lifts all boats." The tide has helped especially rich individuals, and it was largely due to policy changes over recent decades.

Tax planning by enterprises and by rich individuals has become and is now a major *global* activity. It is operated by a growing supply of well-informed, clever, and well-paid tax advisors, who know all the tricks, have contributed to the creation of some, and who can design tax-avoiding strategies for wealthy individuals and for corporations, exploiting the many tax complexities and ambiguities that exist and that have grown in many countries' tax systems. Tax planning is aided by tax competition among countries and by lobbying activities. Tax competition has made it attractive, especially for small countries, to lower their official tax rates to attract economic activities and mobile profits from other countries. There is still no effective international supervision of this tax-avoiding activity, one that would be capable of monitoring and controlling questionable actions.

A large and growing literature has provided information on these tax-avoiding schemes, made possible by global economic activities, and facilitated by tax complexity and by anachronistic tax rules (see, for example, some papers in Pogge and Mehta 2016, and an earlier book by Tanzi 1995). National governments have been unable or, at times, unwilling to deal successfully with these schemes. Published estimates (or, at times, informed guesses) indicate that several trillions of US dollars are now hidden in foreign bank accounts, escaping national tax compliance. The tax gap for the USA had been estimated to be about $700 billion a year.

16 CONCLUDING THOUGHTS

16.1 Introduction

The architecture of the taxation of global corporations and of globally active rich individuals has become increasingly anachronistic and is in clear need of redesign. That architecture was largely created before: (a) the world became highly globalized; (b) much world production became *multi-country* production; (c) the activities of many individuals became increasingly global; and (d) many sales lost their physical content and became virtual. A current push, supported by the US Biden Administration, is to promote minimum taxes on corporations for all countries. Such a policy would help to reduce tax competition. It remains to be seen if it will be adopted globally.

There is still no *truly global* institution, one with the skills, the prestige, the resources, and the authority to try to do the job of redesigning and monitoring new tax rules (not rates) *for the whole world*, and selling those rules to all governments, as the World Trade Organization has tried to do, with mixed success, for trade relations. Such an authority, which seems much needed, would exercise a direct surveillance function on the tax behavior of each member country; however, it would still leave to individual countries some degree of freedom in the determination of tax rates and the use of some taxes. The membership would need to be global for the institution to be effective. Such an organization, or authority, has been suggested in several publications over three decades by Tanzi (1988, 1995, 2016b). The idea has attracted some attention, but, so far, no concrete action.

16.2 Monetary Policy

The monetary policies followed in recent years by the US Federal Reserve Bank, by the European Central Bank, and by some other major central banks have made large and increasing amounts of very cheap credit available, not to everyone, as would be the case with the classic "helicopter money," but mainly to governments and large economic actors, some operating in a *shadow banking* sector, a sector that, in recent decades, has significantly replaced traditional commercial banking.

Monetary policy has become increasingly complex because it does not follow specific monetary rules and it has also drifted, in its real effects, into fiscal policy. Some of its operations have become de facto fiscal operations. This has happened without the political controls that are supposed to exist for fiscal policy decisions. A consequence has been that its long-run effects, on prices and on economies, have become more uncertain and less predictable, compared with the more desirable, short-run economic effects. As such, those effects have been easier to ignore.

Large financial and economic actors and governments are better-placed and more able than average citizens and small enterprises to access the cheap credit that is made available by unorthodox monetary policies, such as *quantitative easing*. These actors have used the cheap credit to promote their own economic interests, which are not necessarily, or always, identical to the public interest.

In addition, the very low or, at times, negative interest rates have boosted the prices of assets, such as stocks, bonds, and real estate, helping the better-off, who own most of the wealth. They have also reduced the need of governments to raise taxes, encouraging them to rely on cheap debt and leading, progressively, to higher public debt, which will expose the countries to uncertain, but potentially serious, future consequences. Fiscal sustainability in the future will inevitably be compromised.

Recent data, on rates of saving by wealth classes, indicate that, in the USA, while those in the top 1 percent of wealth distribution save about 40 percent of their income, those in the bottom 90 percent save almost nothing. The 9 percent of people in between those two groups save about 10 percent. If correct, these data (Financial Samurai online) do not point toward a future with less inequality. These high savings will inevitably have major, future real effects on the economic activity and on its composition.

The central banks have largely ignored the possible and significant distributional or equity consequences of their monetary policies because they have considered them *outside the scope of their mandates* and, therefore, *not their concern*. The share of total profits and incomes that has been going to those who operate in the financial sector has also increased significantly over the years. For example, in the USA, finance now takes about one-third of all profits, up from 10 percent thirty-five years ago and even less before. This dramatic change has raised increasing questions about the impact of the financial sector on national welfare (Wolf 2008; Rajan 2010; Zingales 2015).

Most citizens and small enterprises do not have access to the cheap credit made available by central banks. They have continued to depend on commercial banks or, at times, on unofficial sources for their borrowing, and to pay high, and at times very high, interest rates on the money they borrow. Exceptions have been loans given by special institutions (mortgage banks and car dealers), to borrowers who post valuable collateral, such as houses and new cars, against the loans, and who borrow in transactions that have very low administrative costs.

There have been reports of refinancing of mortgage loans given to the owners of large and expensive houses and apartments. These owners have refinanced their properties mainly to get cheap credit that they could invest in the currently well-performing stock market, expecting that those assets will continue to increase in value, as they have in recent years. This was the behavior that helped to precipitate the 2007–08 financial crisis. Hopefully, history will not repeat itself, and this time will actually be different. However, bubbles are being created and they will make the future more uncertain.

The above dichotomy has created two monetary universes: an expensive one for normal, middle- and lower-income citizens, and for small enterprises, mostly involved in the production of goods and services; and another universe for large operators and major institutions, including governments, numerous corporations, and hedge funds, many of them involved in financial exchanges and other activities, and not in the direct production of traditional good and services. It has also created conditions for future asset bubbles. As in many areas, short-term benefits may have been acquired against longer-term uncertain dangers. The above policies may indicate that uncertain events, such as reductions in asset prices and their consequences, are being ignored because they are uncertain, as happened periodically in the past.

Million dollar compensations became common and more socially acceptable for well-placed, well-connected, or simply lucky individuals, in past decades. Extravagant salaries were paid even to individuals who were running enterprises that lost a lot of money. At times, neither merit nor performance could justify those inflated compensations. And at times, as in 2008, million dollar bonuses were paid just hours before the enterprises declared bankruptcy.

As mentioned earlier, in recent years, in the USA, cheap loans to the federal government replaced, in part, the taxes that higher-income individuals had been paying in the past. This change contributed to the large growth in public debt, and to the lower taxes on the rich than would have been imposed without the availability of cheap debt. Once again, uncertainty about future consequences of policies made governments ignore the dangers that, in the past, have often accompanied high public debts. The above important but likely aspects of monetary policy have been largely absent in recent discussions. They deserve more attention and more analysis.

16.3 A Greater Role for Taxes during Pandemics?

The role of taxes in normal times should differ, to some extent, from their role in exceptional times. Exceptional times require exceptional policies. In exceptional times, including major wars, pandemics, and other major emergencies, a main focus of taxation should be not only the traditional one of providing needed revenue to the government, but also to do so by ensuring fairness in the economic system. It should focus, in part, on what the tax system could do to alleviate the pain *and* to better spread the costs of crises.

This objective can be achieved by taxing more, during emergencies, those who have more taxable capacity, rather than to continue to pursue exclusively what might be longer-run objectives of taxation. These longer-run objectives might include: (a) a consistently fair and efficient tax regime; (b) the promotion of green policies to deal with the long-run issue of climate change; (c) some desirable long-term redistribution of income; (d) making tax systems more transparent; and (e) sustaining employment and economic growth.

While these and similar objectives are always important, changing tax systems to promote them, in the presence of other more immediate and more urgent needs, is likely to bring complexity and uncertainty in the policies, and to be counter-productive. For example, relying more on a value added tax, where this tax exists, simply to get more revenue, may not be desirable for equity reasons during major pandemics (Bird 2020).

Seven or eight decades ago, the first recipient of the Nobel Prize in Economics, Jan Tinbergen, argued that it is always better to direct the use of policy instruments toward well-specified, single objectives, whenever this is possible, rather than to pursue multiple objectives with single instruments. This focus helps keep policies simple and focused, and it improves the chance of achieving the main, desired objective, at a given time.

During a major crisis, which tends to affect different groups differently, as during a pandemic, a main objective of tax policy should be the promotion of short-run equity, while providing some needed revenue to the government. During these crises, lower-income individuals tend to suffer more than high-income individuals. Therefore, it would seem natural and desirable to ask how the tax system could make all citizens share in the costs of the crisis, in some relation to their ability to do so, while trying to keep the fiscal accounts in better shape, to reduce the need for excessive public borrowing. Those who have more taxpaying capacity, and who save more, should contribute more to those objectives than they might in normal times.

During past major wars, various countries introduced *excess profit taxes* on enterprises that, because of the war, were making high profits, and they raised the highest marginal tax rate of personal income tax. Some temporary taxes on wealth or on income were also imposed, as occurred in Ireland and Iceland after the financial crisis of 2008, and in Australia, Germany, Japan, and Italy after other emergencies. A pandemic should be treated as a war.

Given the dichotomous impact that the pandemic has been having on the economy and on people, it would seem fair to impose exceptional, but time-limited taxes on those individuals who have high incomes and wealth, and who are paying a low price for, or are even benefiting from, the pandemic. These exceptional taxes would remain in place while the pandemic continued to have its impact on the economy. The taxes would reduce government borrowing and would lead to lower future public debts, debts which will need to be serviced in future years. High public debt inevitably increases risk for the future, even when it may provide benefits in the present.

The simplest short-run options might be: (a) an increase in marginal income tax rates, the rates applicable to high personal taxable incomes and on corporate profits; (b) a tax on wealth ownership above some given high level; and (c) a financial transaction tax on the trading of corporate shares. The temporary nature of these taxes would reduce or minimize whatever disincentive effects they might be assumed to have when imposed in normal times. Especially for taxes on wealth, there may be technical issues that might arise and that must be dealt with (for examples, see Oh and Zolt 2021). A simple option might be the taxation of wealth held in corporate shares, for which information should be easily available.

As mentioned earlier, in the USA the value of financial wealth has grown significantly in recent years, in part due to the tax reduction of 2017 and earlier years. Financial wealth has continued to grow significantly during the Covid 19 pandemic. Therefore, the taxes paid might largely come out of higher market valuations (out of "excess profits"). The additional, higher personal income taxes would be paid largely out of the highest incomes of individuals, who have more ability to pay.

The financial transaction tax, also recommended in the past by Keynes and, in more recent years, by the late James Tobin, could be levied at a low rate on the value of stocks traded. Given the high trading volume, such a tax could raise significant revenue, even with a low rate. Being a *temporary* tax, it would not lead to maneuvers to avoid it, as it would if it were used over the long run. Should the stock market continue to boom, the tax would hardly be felt by those taxed.

The current pandemic has raised uncomfortable questions about the fairness of the market economy, when that economy works without some government correctives, and when it ignores social and global aspects. Those questions are especially pertinent in times of major global crises that disproportionally impact some groups. It must be recognized that the social correctives (progressive taxes on high incomes and public spending programs directed at those in need), can significantly reduce the Gini coefficients that the market, as it operates, tends to generate. Those correctives would also tend to increase, in the eyes of many citizens, the legitimacy of the market system and its fairness, especially in countries that are democratic.

These correctives could be accompanied by well-calibrated global policies to help poorer countries, and by the use of carbon taxes that would remove the subsidies that many, and especially individuals with high standards of living, have been receiving from their con-sumption of the use of fossil fuels and other polluting products. Only the existence of these correctives could justify Friedman's view that corporate leaders in market economies should focus exclusively on maximizing shareholders' returns, and should ignore all social responsibilities. Without those correctives, that view simply makes no sense, especially in the presence of many "termites," that distort the work of the market (Tanzi 2018a).

Popular attitudes about the fairness of the uncorrected, or little corrected, market economy have become less favorable over the years. Such attitudes are likely to continue to become more negative if current conditions and policies do not change. Growing populism could become a serious challenge for the future of market economies and for democratic systems, potentially leading to much less attractive alternatives.

Growing public and private debts and other developments are also making the economic and physical conditions of future years more uncertain. The warming of the planet and the Covid-19 pandemic have made the Earth a less hospitable place than it had been for humans in the past. Policies that are strictly national in scope, and that are focused exclusively on national interests, have become less effective in dealing with issues that are global in scope, such as the generation of *global* public goods and the prevention of various *global* public "bads."

We are now at a juncture in the history of mankind. Various uncertainties, some with dangerous or even existential implications (economic, technological, distributional, environmental, political, biological), have appeared. They have been raising growing doubts as to whether the idea of "progress," an idea that the Industrial Revolution had brought to the nineteenth century, still prevails today, and if it still points toward a better future for humanity, as it had in the nineteenth century.

That nineteenth-century idea of progress was poetically described in part of an Italian poem, composed in 1864. Freely translated from the Italian, the poem stated:

Go forward, go forward, divine stranger,
Explore the room that the Gods gave you.
If that room still hosts slaves and tears,
it is because of its still young age.

The original Italian version read:

T' avanza, t' avanza divino straniero,
conosci la stanza che i fati ti dieron,
se schiavi, se lacrime ancora rinserra,
e' giovin la Terra.

The poet was Giacomo Zanella (1820–88), and the poem clearly incorpor-
ated the then new, and strongly held, belief in *progress* as an inevitable
characteristic of a better future for mankind. The better future would be
generated by ongoing political and technological changes that, at that
time, were changing the old world. The belief that the future of mankind
would inevitably be better than the past is now no longer strongly and
widely held.

As we have stressed in previous chapters, many potential or even
existential dangers have appeared on the horizon, and they now worry
many experts and some ordinary citizens. These dangers are accompanied by uncertainty about future outcomes. However, they now challenge
the idea of the inevitability of progress, and that of a better future
for humankind.

Because of the uncertainty that accompanies them, the dangers continue to be ignored by many people and by many governments, as, for
example, with global warming and future pandemics. These dangers also
challenge the ability of strictly *national* policies to deal with some of them
that, increasingly, have become global in scope and that require solutions coordinated on a global scale. Pandemics and climate change are
clearly among them.

A book published by the OECD in 2021 has reminded us that the past
two centuries saw enormous progress for the human race. There is no
question that, today, humans are much better off than they ever were in
earlier centuries and millennia. According to the OECD study, since
1820, the world's per capita GDP has expanded thirteen times, the total
population has grown by seven times, and the world's GDP has increased
by ninety times. These results were achieved while the working week
contracted from between sixty and ninety hours to forty hours; and
children are no longer made to work in mines and other dangerous
activities. Life expectancy has also become much longer.

This was extraordinary progress and Mother Earth was capable of
carrying all that extra weight and made that progress possible. But there
were costs along the way. The costs have become visible in recent
decades. The key question now is: can such progress continue in the
future? Or have we overloaded the Earth to such an extent as to make
future progress much more difficult? Only time will tell, but the signs
are not as good as they could be.

By further pushing economic growth for the world population without making major corrections to the kind of growth that is possible,

humans may be making future progress more difficult or even impossible. Governments should no longer just push for economic growth. They should push for the right kind of growth. That kind of growth is not likely to be produced spontaneously, through uncoordinated individual and national government actions, as it has been in the past.

This book will conclude with an allegory.

There are two trains travelling on a single track of a railroad. They are running in opposite directions. One is operated by individuals who strongly believe in individual freedom and who give little weight to collective actions. They stress the importance of decisions made by individuals and by libertarian, laissez-faire national governments. Both the individuals and the policymakers in this train believe that the main goal of national policies and of individual actions should be to continue promoting economic growth and higher standards of living for the masses, without any impediments. The more freedom of action and the greater growth, the better.

The other train is operated by environmentalists who are worried about global warming and about other potential disasters, and by individuals who are altruistic, have a longer time horizon, and worry about the welfare of future generations. They are more internationalist in their thinking. They believe, as did some major thinkers of the 1950s (such as Einstein, Gandhi, and Churchill), that we need an effective, *global*, institutional umbrella to guide some important decisions that affect the whole globe. The umbrella could be a *world government*, or, more realistically, some *effective* and powerful international institutions (such as the UN, Bretton Woods' institutions, the World Trade Organization, and the World Health Organization).

These institutions could forcefully and efficiently act as *proxies* for a nonexistent global government. They would promote global interests. These institutions would aim at reducing rent-seeking by some governments and some groups, and would aim at promoting global, sustainable interests, while still stressing possible individual freedoms where that freedom could be maintained (Tanzi 2008).

The two trains are now running on the same track and in opposite directions. Will they collide? Or will one of them leave the track, avoiding a collision, allowing the other train to proceed? Which will do so? The future of the human race may depend on that answer, even though some are likely to see it as unrealistic and naive.

REFERENCES

Aggarwal-Schifellite, Manisha, 2021a, Study Aims to Quell Fears Over Falling Human Sperm Count, *Harvard Gazette* (May 11).

2021b, Understanding Connections between Literature and the Environment, *Harvard Gazette* (January 27).

Akerlof, George, 1970, The Market for Lemons: Quality, Uncertainty and the Market Mechanism, *Quarterly Journal of Economics*, 84(3), pp. 488–500.

Alfani, Guido, 2021, Economic Inequality in Preindustrial Times: Europe and Beyond, *Journal of Economic Literature*, LIX(1), pp. 4–44.

Arthur, W. Brian, 2015, *Complexity and the Economy* (Oxford University Press).

Barkley, Paul W. and David W. Seckler, 1972, *Economic Growth and Environmental Decay: The Solution Becomes the Problem* (New York: Harcourt Brace Jovanovich).

Barrett, Philip, Sophia Chen, and Nan Li, 2021, Covid's Long Shadow: Social Repercussions of Pandemics, IMFBlog, Insight and Analysis on Economics and Finance (February 3).

Barry, John M. 2004, *The Great Influenza* (New York: Viking Press).

Batini, Nicoletta and Miguel Segoviano, 2021, Denmark's Ambitious Green Vision, IMFBlog (January 11).

Bernstein, Peter L., 1996, *Against the Gods: The Remarkable Story of Risk* (New York: John Wiley).

Bevere, Lucia and Michel Gloor, 2020, Natural Catastrophes in Times of Economic Accumulation and Climate Change, *sigma* 2/2020 (Swiss Re Institute, April 8).

Bevere, Lucia and Rajeev Sharan, 2018, Natural Catastrophes and Man-Made Disasters in 2017, *sigma* 1/2018 (Swiss Re Institute, April 11).

Bird, Richard M., 2020, VAT During and After the Pandemic, *Tax Notes International* (September 28).

Birol, Faith, 2007, Energy Economics: A Place for Energy Poverty in the Agenda?, *The Energy Journal*, 28(3), pp. 1–6.

Blandford, Edward D. and Scott D. Sagan, 2016, eds., *Learning from a Disaster: Improving Nuclear Safety and Security after Fukushima* (Stanford University Press).

Blanning, T., 2008, *The Pursuit of Glory* (New York: Penguin).

Blume, Lesley M. M., 2020, *Fallout: The Hiroshima Cover-Up and the Reporter Who Revealed It to the World* (New York: Simon and Schuster).

Boccaccio, Giovanni, 2003 [c. 1351], *The Decameron*, 2nd ed. (New York: Penguin).

Bogmans, Christian and Claire Mengyi Li, 2020, A Greener Future Begins with a Shift to Coal Alternatives, IMFBlog (December 8).

Bollyky, Thomas, J., 2018, *Plagues and the Paradox of Progress* (Cambridge, MA: MIT Press).

Bostrom, Nick, 2014, *Super-Intelligence: Paths, Dangers, Strategies* (Oxford University Press).

Bostrom, Nick and Milan M. Circovic, eds., 2008, *Global Catastrophic Risks* (Oxford University Press).

Bullard, Nathaniel, 2020, Ten Charts that Tell the Weird Story of Oil and Energy in 2020, *Bloomberg Opinion* (December 30).

Burrows, Leah, 2021, 1 in 5 Deaths Caused by Fossil Fuel Emissions, *Harvard Gazette* (February 9).

Caesar, L., S. Rahmstorf, A. Robinson, G. Feulner, and V. Saba, 2018, Observed Fingerprint of a Weakening Atlantic Ocean Overturning Circulation, *Nature* 556, pp. 191–196.

Caldicott, Helen, ed., 2014, *Crisis Without End: The Medical and Ecological Consequences of the Fukushima Nuclear Catastrophe* (New York: New Press).

Cantor, N. F., 2001, *In the Wake of the Plague: The Black Plague and the World it Made* (New York: Free Press).

Chotiner, Isaac, 2021, How Pandemics Change History, *New Yorker* (March 3).

Cipolla, C. M., 1994, *Before the Industrial Revolution: European Society and Economy, 1000–1700* (New York and London: W. W. Norton).

Clements, Benedict J., David Coady, Stefania Fabrizio, Sanjeev Gupta, Trevor Serge Coleridge Alleyne, and Carlo A. Sdaralevich, 2013, *Energy Subsidy Reform: Lessons and Implications* (Washington, DC: International Monetary Fund).

Coase, R. H., 1960, The Problem of Social Cost, *Journal of Law and Economics*, 3, pp. 1–44.

CoreLogic (Hazard HQ Team), 2021, *2020 Climate Change Catastrophe Report* (CoreLogic Inc.), available online at www.corelogic.com/wp-content/uploads/sites/4/2021/05/report-2020-climate-change-catastrophe-report.pdf (accessed August 11, 2021).

Crauwshaw, J. L., 2012, *The Plague Hospitals: Public Health for the City in Early Modern Venice* (New York: Routledge).

Dasgupta, Partha, 2021, *Economics of Biodiversity: The Dasgupta Review* (London: HM Treasury).

Davis, Debra, 2002, *When Smoke Ran Like Water: Tales of Environmental Deception and the Battle Against Pollution* (New York: Basic Books).

Davis, Kenneth C., 2018, *More Deadly than War: The Hidden History of the Spanish Flu and the First World War* (New York: Henry Holt).

Deaton, Angus, 2013, *The Great Escape: Health, Wealth and the Origin of Inequality* (Princeton University Press).

Debenedetti, Franco, 2021, *Fare profitti: Etica dell'impresa* (Venice: Marsilio).

Dennis, Brody, Chris Moony, and Sara Kaplin, 2020, The World Rich Need to Cut their Carbon Footprint by a Factor of 30 to Slow Climate Change, UN Warns, *Washington Post* (December 10).

Di Bonifacio, Carlos and Carlo Stagnaro, 2021, The EU National Energy and Climate Plans: A Survey, IBL Special Report (2 February).

Diamond, Jared, 1999, *Guns, Germs, and Steel: The Fates of Human Societies* (New York and London: W. W. Norton).

Diaz del Castillo, Bernal, 1956 [1632 Spanish ed.], *The Discovery and Conquest of Mexico 1517–21* (New York: Farrar, Strauss and Cudahy).

The Economist, 2020, Making Coal History (December 3), pp. 25–28.

Editors of *Fortune*, 1970, *The Environment: A National Mission for the Seventies* (New York, Evanston, and London: Harper & Row).

Ehle, John, 1988, *Trails of Tears: The Rise and Fall of the Cherokee Nation* (New York: Doubleday).

Ehrlich, Paul R. and Anne H. Ehrlich, 1972, *Population, Resources and Environment: Issues in Human Ecology* (San Francisco: W. H. Freeman).

Fletcher, Catherine, 2020, *The Beauty and the Terror: The Italian Renaissance and the Rise of the West* (Oxford University Press).

Fogel, R. and B. Harris, 2011, *The Changing Body* (Cambridge University Press).

Folger, Tim and Keith Ladzinsli, 2020, So Great, So Fragile, *National Geographic* (December), pp. 40–61.

Friedman, Milton, 1970, The Social Responsibility of Business Is to Increase its Profits, *New York Times Magazine* (September 12).

Frydman, Roman and Michael D. Goldberg, 2007, *Imperfect Knowledge Economics* (Princeton University Press).

Galbraith, John Kenneth, 1977, *The Age of Uncertainty* (Boston: Houghton Mifflin).

Galeotti, Marzio and Alessandro Lanza, 2021, Como sará il 2021 del clima, lavoce.info (January 7).

Garrett, Laurie, 1994, *The Coming Plague: Newly Emerging Diseases in a World Out of Balance* (New York: Farrar, Straus and Giroux).

Gates, Bill, 2021a, *How to Avoid a Climate Disaster: The Solution We Have and the Breakthrough We Need* (New York: Alfred Knopf).

2021b, Losing Time Against Climate Disaster, *Harvard Gazette* (February 26).

Gelles, David, 2021, Despite Losses CEOs Prosper Amid Pandemic, *New York Times* (April 25), pp. 1, 24.

Getty, J. Arch and Oleg V. Naumov, 2010, *The Road to Terror: Stalin and the Self-Destruction of the Bolsheviks, 1932–1939*, enlarged ed. (Yale University Press).

Gladwell, Malcolm, 2008, *Outliers: The Story of Success* (New York, Boston, and London: Little, Brown).

Gleick, James, 1992, *Genius: The Life and Science of Richard Feynman* (New York: Pantheon Books).

Gray, Mike and Ira Rosen, 2003, *The Warning: Accident at Three Mile Island*, new ed. (New York and London: W. W. Norton).

Greenblatt, Stephen, 2011, *The Swerve: How the World Became Modern* (New York: W. W. Norton).

Greenspan, Alan, 2007, *The Age of Turbulence: Adventures in a New World* (New York: Penguin).

Guicciardini, Francesco, 1964 [1561 Italian ed.], *History of Italy; History of Florence*, trans. Cecil Greyson, ed. and abridged John R. Hale (New York: Washington Square Press).

Guo, Jessie, Daniel Kubli, and Patrick Saner, 2021, *The Economics of Climate Change: No Action Not an Option* (Zurich: Swiss Re Institute).

Gwynne, S. C., 2010, *Empire of the Summer Moon* (New York: Scribner).

Hackett Fischer, David, 1996, *The Great Wave: Price Revolutions and the Rhythm of History* (Oxford University Press).

Harvey, Phil and Lisa Conyers, 2020, *Welfare for the Rich: How Your Tax Dollars End Up in Millionaires' Pockets – And What You Can Do About It* (New York: Post Hill Press).

Hassey, Meg, Richard Liu, and Claire Auld-Brokish, 2021, Who Pays the Bill for Plastic Waste?, China Environment Forum (blog of the Wilson Center, January 7).

Hicks, John, 1939, *Value and Capital* (Oxford University Press).

Hobhouse, Henry, 2005, *Seeds of Change: Six Plants that Transformed Mankind* (Washington, DC: Shoemaker and Hoard).

Honigsbaum, Mark, 2020, *The Pandemic Century: A History of Global Contagion from the Spanish Flu to Covid 19* (London: Penguin).

Hooijer, A. and R. Vernimmen, 2021, Global LiDAR Land Elevation Data Reveal Greatest Sea-Level Rise Vulnerability in the Tropics, *Nature Communications* 12(3592).

Hosking, Geoffrey, 1992, *The First Socialist Society: A History of the Soviet Union from Within*, 2nd enlarged ed. (Harvard University Press).

Hume, David, 1970 [1752], *Writings on Economics*, ed. Eugene Rotwein (University of Wisconsin Press).

Hume, Neil, 2021, Miners Face Up to Climate Challenge, *Financial Times* (January 7).

IMF, 2021, *World Economic Outlook, April 2021: Managing Divergent Recoveries* (Washington, DC: International Monetary Fund).

Kahneman, Daniel, 2011, *Thinking, Fast and Slow* (New York: Farrar, Straus and Giroux).

Kay, John and Mervyn King, 2020, *Radical Uncertainty: Decision Making Beyond the Numbers* (New York: W. W. Norton).

Kelly, James, 1992, Scarcity and Poor Relief in Eighteenth-Century Ireland: The Subsistence Crisis of 1782–4, *Irish Historical Review*, 28(109), pp. 38–62.

Kelly, John, 2005, *The Great Mortality: An Intimate History of the Black Death, the Most Devastating Plague of All Times* (New York: Harper Collins).

Kenny, Charles, 2021, *The Plague Cycle: The Unending War Between Humanity and Infectious Diseases* (New York: Scribner).

Keynes, John Maynard, 1921a, *The Economic Consequences of the Peace* (New York: Macmillan).

1921b, *A Treatise on Probability* (London: Macmillan).

1930, Am I a Liberal?, in John Maynard Keynes, *Essays in Persuasion* (London: Macmillan).

1926, *The End of Laissez Faire* (London: Hogarth Press).

1936, *The General Theory of Employment, Interest, and Money* (New York: Harcourt, Brace).

Knight, Frank H., 1923, The Ethics of Competition, *Quarterly Journal of Economics*, 37, pp. 579–624.

1964 [1921], *Risk, Uncertainty and Profit* (New York: Century Press).

Kolata, Gina Bari, 2005, *Flu: The Story of the Great Influenza Pandemic of 1918 and the Search for the Virus that Caused It* (New York: Touchstone).

Kolbert, Elizabeth, 2014, *The Sixth Extinction* (New York: Henry Holt).

Kopits, George, ed., 2004, *Rules-Based Fiscal Policy in Emerging Markets: Background, Analysis, and Prospects* (New York: Palgrave Macmillan).

2013, *Restoring Public Debt Sustainability: The Role of Independent Fiscal Institutions* (Oxford University Press).

Kuznets, Simon, 1966, *Modern Economic Growth: Rate, Structure, and Spread* (Yale University Press).

Lane, Frederic C., 1973, *Venice: A Maritime Republic* (Johns Hopkins University Press).

Levi Montalcini, Rita, 1987, *Elogio dell'imperfezione* (Milan: Garzanti).

Lewis, Michael, 2010, *The Big Short: Inside the Doomsday Machine* (New York: W. W. Norton).

Liu, Xingrang and Ramesh Bansal, 2016, *Thermal Power Plants: Modeling, Control, and Efficient Improvement* (Boca Raton: CRC Press).

Lustgarten, Abrahm, 2020, Catastrophe's Harvest, *New York Times Magazine* (December 20), pp. 24–29, 51–53.

MacFarquhar, Roderick and Michael Schoenhals, 2006, *Mao's Last Revolution* (Belknap Press of Harvard University Press).

Malthus, Thomas, 1890, *An Essay on the Principle of Population* (University of Minnesota).

Mandelbrot, Benoit B. and Richard L. Hudson, 2004, *Mis(behavior) of Markets: A Fractal View of Risk, Ruin, and Reward* (New York: Basic Books).

Martin, W. R. and Robert Pindyck, 2019, Welfare Costs of Catastrophes: Lost Consumption and Lost Lives, NBER working paper 26068 (July).

McKibben, William, 1989, *The End of Nature* (New York: Random House).

Messere, K. C., 1993, *Tax Policy in OECD Countries: Choices and Conflicts* (Amsterdam: IBFD Publications BV).

Milanovic, Branko, 2005, *Worlds Apart: Measuring International and Global Income Inequality* (Princeton University Press).

Mises, Ludwig von, 2005, *The Quotable Mises*, ed. Mark Thornton (Auburn: Mises).

Morison, Samuel Eliot, 1971, *The European Discovery of America: The Northern Voyages* (Oxford University Press).

Moss, David A., 2002, *When All Else Fails: Government as the Ultimate Risk Manager* (Harvard University Press).

Musgrave, Richard, 1959, *The Theory of Public Finance* (New York: McGraw-Hill).

Nelson, Edward, 2020, *Milton Friedman and Economic Debates in the United States, 1932–1972*, Volume 2 (University of Chicago Press).

Nice, O. M., 2011, Piecing Together Fukushima: Nuclear Experts Hear New Details of the Fukushima Disaster, *The Economist* (May 5).

Nordhaus, William D, 2007, A Review of the *Stern Review* on the *Economics of Climate Change*, *Journal of Economic Literature*, 45(3), pp. 686–702.

　　2013, *The Climate Casino: Risk, Uncertainty, and Economics for a Warming World* (Yale University Press).

North, Douglass C., 1990, *Institutions, Institutional Change and Economic Performance* (Cambridge University Press).

OECD, 2021, *How Was Life? Volume II: New Perspectives on Well-Being and Global Inequality Since 1820* (Paris: OECD Publishing).

Oh, Jason and Eric M. Zolt, 2021, Wealth Tax Design: Lessons from Estate Tax Avoidance, *Tax Law Review*, 74.

Oldstone, Michael B. A., 1998, *Viruses, Plagues, and History: Past, Present and Future* (Oxford University Press).

Olson, Mancur and Hans H. Landsberg, eds., 1973, *The No-Growth Society* (New York: W. W. Norton).

Pechman, Joseph, 1987, *Federal Tax Policy*, 5th ed. (Washington, DC: Brookings Institution).

Petrucelli, Lyons, 1987, *Medicine: An Illustrated History* (New York: Abradale Press).

Pigou, A. C., 1920, *The Economics of Welfare* (London: Macmillan).

Pindyck, Robert S. and Neng Wang, 2009, The Economics and Policy Consequences of Catastrophes, NBER working paper 15373 (September).

Piotrowski, Matt, 2019, Nearing the Tipping Point: Drivers of Deforestation in the Amazon Region (Washington, DC: Inter-American Dialogue).

Plokhy, Serhii, 2018, *Chernobyl: History of a Tragedy* (London: Penguin).

Pogge, Thomas and Krishen Mehta, eds., 2016, *Global Tax Fairness* (Oxford University Press).

Pooley, Gale and Marian L. Tupy, 2021, *The Simon Abundance Index 2021*, Human Progress (April 22) (Washington, DC: Cato Institute).

Pope Francis, 2015, *Laudato Si': Encyclical Letter* (Vatican City: Libreria Editrice Vaticano).

Porter, D., 1999, *Health, Civilization and the State* (London: Routledge).

Posner, Richard A., 2009, *A Failure of Capitalism: The crisis of '08 and the Descent into Depression* (Harvard University Press).

Powell, Alvin, 2020, Six-Year Deluge Linked to Spanish Flu, World War I Deaths, *Harvard Gazette* (October 5).

Prescott, William Hickling, 1980, *History of the Conquest of Mexico and History of the Conquest of Peru* (New York: Modern Library).

Rahmstorf, Stefan, 2002, Ocean Circulation and Climate During the Past 120,000 Years, *Nature*, 419, pp. 207–214.

Rajan, Raghuran G., 2010, *Fault Lines: How Hidden Fractures Still Threaten the World Economy* (Princeton University Press).

Rhodes, Richard, 1997, *Deadly Feasts: Tracking the Secrets of a Terrifying New Plague* (New York: Simon and Schuster).

Rohatinski, Zeljko, 2017, *Time and Economics: The Concept of Functional Time* (Cham, Switzerland: Palgrave Macmillan).

Rosen, W., 2007, *Justinian Flea* (New York: Penguin).

Saez, E. and Zucman, G., 2019, *The Triumph of Injustice* (New York: W. W. Norton).

Samuelson, Paul, 1947, *Foundations of Economic Analysis* (Harvard University Press).

Sandel, Michael J., 2012, *What Money Can Buy* (New York: Farrar, Straus and Giroux).

Schlossberg, Tatiana, 2020, Seaweed: An Unusual Feed for Cows, A Powerful Fix for Greenhouse Gases, *Washington Post*, Health and Science (December 15), Section E.

Segrè, Gino and Bettina Hoerlin, 2016, *The Pope of Physics: Enrico Fermi and the Birth of the Atomic Age* (New York: Henry Holt).

Semega, Jessica, Melissa Kollar, Emily A. Shrider, and John F. Creamer, 2020, *Income and Poverty in the United States: 2019*, US Census Bureau, Current Population Reports, P60–270 (Washington, DC: US Government Publishing Office).

Sen, Amartya, 1981, *Poverty and Famines* (Oxford University Press).

   1999, *Development as Freedom* (New York: Alfred A. Knopf), Chapter 7.

Shafir, Minousche, 2021, *What We Owe Each Other: A New Social Contract* (London: Bodley Head).

Shiller, Robert J., 2000, *Irrational Exuberance* (New York: Broadway Books).

   2012, *Finance and the Good Society* (Princeton University Press).

Sierra Martín, César, 2021, The Plague of Athens, *National Geographic*, History (May–June), pp. 34–45.

Siliezar, Juan, 2021, Antarctic Ice Sheet Melting to Lift Sea Level Higher than Thought, Study Says, *Harvard Gazette* (April 30).

Small, Meredith F., 2021, *Inventing the World: Venice and the Transformation of Western Civilization* (New York and London: Pegasus Books).

Smil, Vaclav, 2021, *Grand Transitions: How the Modern World Was Made* (Oxford University Press).

Smith, Adam, 1937 [1776], *The Wealth of Nations* (New York: Modern Library).

Snowden, Frank M., 2002, *Naples in the Time of Cholera, 1884–1911* (Cambridge University Press).

   2019, *Epidemics and Society: From the Black Death to the Present* (Yale University Press).

Solimano, Andres, 2020, *A History of Big Recessions in the Long Twentieth Century* (Cambridge University Press).

Spohr, Kristina and Daniel S. Hamilton, eds., 2021, *The Arctic and World Order* (Washington, DC: Brookings Institution).

Stern, Nicholas, 2006, *The Stern Review: The Economics of Climate Change* (London: HM Treasury).

Stern, Nicholas and Joseph E. Stiglitz, 2021a, Getting the Social Cost of Carbon Right, *Project Syndicate* (February 15).

   2021b, The Social Cost of Carbon, Risk, Distribution, Market Failures: An Alternative Approach, NBER working paper 28472 (February).

Stirling, Stuart, 2005, *Pizarro: Conqueror of the Inca* (Stroud: Sutton).

Swan, Shanna H., with Stacey Colino, 2021, *Count Down: How Our Modern World Is Threatening Sperm Counts, Altering Male and Female Reproductive Development, and Imperiling the Future of the Human Race* (New York: Simon and Schuster).

Tainter, Joseph, 1988, *The Collapse of Complex Society* (Cambridge University Press).

Taleb, Nassim Nicholas, 2004, *Fooled by Randomness: The Hidden Role of Chance in Life and in the Market* (New York: Random House).

2007, *The Black Swan: The Impact of the Highly Improbable* (New York: Random House).

2012, *Antifragile: Things That Gain from Disorder* (New York: Random House).

Tanzi, Vito, 1988, Forces that Shape Tax Policy, in Herbert Stein, ed., *Tax Policy in the Twenty-First Century* (New York: John Wiley), pp. 266–277.

1995, *Taxation in an Integrating World* (Washington, DC: Brookings Institution).

2008, The Future of Fiscal Federalism, WZB discussion paper SP II2008–03 (Wissenschaftszentrum Berlin), also in *European Journal of Political Economy*, 24, pp. 705–712.

2011, *Government Versus Markets: The Changing Economic Role of the State* (Cambridge University Press).

2013, *Dollars, Euros and Debt* (London: Palgrave Macmillan).

2015, Hayek and the Economic Role of the State: Some Comparison with Keynes' Views, in Konrad Hummler and Alberto Mingardi, eds., *Europe, Switzerland and the Future of Freedom: Essays in Honour of Tito Tettamanti* (Torino: IBL Libri), pp. 465–482.

2016a, Pleasant Dreams and Nightmares in Public Debts Scenarios, *CESifo Forum*, 17, special issue, pp. 40–43 (Munich: ifo Institut/Leibniz-Institut für Wirtschaftsforschung an der Universität München).

2016b, Lakes, Oceans and Taxes: Why the World Needs a World Tax Authority, in Thomas Pogge and Krishen Mehta, eds., 2016, *Global Tax Fairness* (Oxford University Press), pp. 251–264.

2018a, *Termites of the State: Why Complexity Leads to Inequality* (Cambridge University Press).

2018b, *The Ecology of Tax Systems: Factors that Shape the Demand and Supply of Taxes* (Cheltenham: Edward Elgar).

2018c, *Italica: L'Unificazione difficile, tra ideali e realtà* (Fasano: Schena).

2020a, *Advanced Introduction to Public Finance* (Cheltenham: Edward Elgar).

2020b, Perfect Markets, Perfect Democracies and Pandemics (Ibero-American Association of Local Finance (AIFIL), in tribute to the late economist Luiz Villela).

2020c, *The Economics of Government: Complexity and the Practice of Public Finance* (Oxford University Press).

2021, Some Reflections on Transition: Its Roots, Complexity of the Process, and Role of the IMF and Other Organizations, in Eloise Douarin and Oleh Havrylshyn, eds., *The Palgrave Handbook of Comparative Economics* (London: Palgrave), pp. 369–388.

Torpey, Elka, 2020, Essential Work: Employment and Outlook in Occupations that Protect and Provide, *Career Outlook*, US Bureau of Labor Statistics (September).

Tuchman, Barbara W., 1978, *A Distant Mirror: The Calamitous Fourteenth Century* (New York: Alfred A. Knopf).

Turner, Adair, 2020, The Costs of Tackling Climate Change Keep on Falling, *Financial Times*, Opinion (December 11), p. 9.

US Federal Reserve, 2021, Distribution of Household Wealth in the US Since 1989, in *Survey of Consumer Finances and Financial Accounts of the United States* (US Federal Reserve), available online at www.federalreserve.gov/releases/z1/dataviz/dfa/distribute/chart/ (accessed August 14, 2021).

van Overtveldt, Johan, 2007, *The Chicago School: How the University of Chicago Assembled the Thinkers Who Revolutionized Economics and Business* (Chicago: Agate).

Vicarelli, Fausto, 1984, *Keynes: The Instability of Capitalism* (University of Pennsylvania Press).

Wallace, Chris, with Mutch Weiss, 2020, *Countdown 1945: The Extraordinary Story of the Atomic Bomb and the 116 Days that Changed the World* (New York: Avid Reader Press).

Wallace-Wells, David, 2019, *The Uninhabitable Earth: A Story of the Future* (New York: Penguin).

Washington Post, 2021, Air Pollution from Farms Leads to 17,900 US Deaths Per Year, Study Finds (May 12).

Weitzman, M. L., 2007, A Review of the *Stern Review on the Economics of Climate Change*, *Journal of Economic Literature* 45(3), pp. 703–724.

Wike, Richard, Katie Simmons, Bruce Stokes, and Janell Fetterolf, Many Unhappy with Current Political System, report, October 16 (Pew Research Center).

Winchester, Simon, 2005, *A Crack in the Edge of the World: America and the Great California Earthquake of 1906* (New York: HarperCollins).

Wolf, Martin, 2008, *Fixing Global Finance* (Johns Hopkins University Press).

Woodward, Sir Llewellyn, EBA, 1962 [1938], *The Age of Reform, 1815–1870*, 2nd ed. (Oxford: Clarendon Press).

World Meteorological Organization, 2021, *State of the Global Climate 2020* (Geneva: WMO).

Zingales, Luigi, 2015, Presidential Address: Does Finance Benefit Society?, *Journal of Finance*, 70(4), pp. 1327–1363.

Zucman, Gabriel, 2015, *The Hidden Wealth of Nations: The Scourge of Tax Havens* (University of Chicago Press).

INDEX